THE WINDING STAIR

From Morley Boy to Westminster Knight

Sir Rodney Brooke

Scratching Shed Publishing Ltd

SIR RODNEY BROOKE CBE DL was born in Morley, near Leeds. After leaving school, aged 15, he worked for the local newspaper before joining the Town Hall as the office boy. That began a career in the public sector. He became chief executive of West Yorkshire County Council and Westminster City Council. He chaired several national organisations, including the regulatory body for universities. He was appointed CBE in 1996 and knighted in 2007. He holds the Orders of Merit of France and Germany and is an Officer of the Order of the Aztec Eagle of Mexico.

Sir Rodney was present at the last ever reading of the Riot Act and in *The Winding Stair* reveals inside stories from some of the most notorious events of the late 20th century: the mysterious death of Helen Smith in Jeddah; how Home Secretary Willie Whitelaw defied the ministerial code to intervene in the Yorkshire Ripper murders; why the police authenticated the Wearside tape as the voice of the Yorkshire Ripper; how 56 fans died when Bradford City Football Club ignored his warning of fire risk; police and the miners' strike; espionage and sex scandals in Dolphin Square; the sale of three Westminster cemeteries for 15p; Westminster's homes for votes scandal; and the £42m penalty imposed on Tesco heiress Dame Shirley Porter.

He also shares other fascinating anecdotes such as the invention of the guillotine in Halifax; how in Huddersfield you had to tell the driver if you took a corpse on a bus; and Dame Shirley Porter's encounter with the pooper-scooter.

By the same author
Managing the Enabling Authority
The Environmental Role of Local Government
The Councillor: Victim or Vulgarian

'Few, if any, public servants can match Sir Rodney Brooke's 60-year record. Aged 75, he has just ended six decades of unbroken service across local government, the NHS, education, utilities and beyond, which gives him a surely unique perspective. It was in 1955 that he forsook a tentative start in newspapers and went to work at his local town hall as office boy and would-be articled clerk. Six decades later, his career has taken him around the world – he has been honoured in five other countries in addition to his UK knighthood – and occasionally landed him in the headlines. In 1989, he found the media camped outside his home when he finally quit as long-suffering chief executive to Westminster council leader Shirley Porter as the authority's homes-for-votes scandal was unfolding.'

The Guardian, 21 January 2015

'I had the pleasure of working with Rodney Brooke when we were both employed by West Yorkshire Met County Council in the 1970-80s, he in a very senior position, me in a quite junior one! He was held in the highest regard, has had a long and very distinguished record of public service and his wise judgement and keen sense of humour shine through in these memoirs.'

HM Lord-Lieutenant of West Yorkshire, Ed Anderson CBE

'*The Winding Stair* is a fascinating tale of how a Morley boy, who left school aged 15 to work on the local newspaper, rose to the top in public life and became a knight of the realm. Rodney shares the inside stories of well-known events of the last half-century.

They include private discussions with Home Secretary Willie Whitelaw on the hunt for the Yorkshire Ripper; policing the miners' strike; and Rodney's role as Civil Defence Controller for Yorkshire, when he was to retreat to an underground bunker in the Pennines and restore order after a nuclear holocaust.

The book is also extremely funny: he deals with shrimps in the drinking water; constipated dogs in Trafalgar Square and Christmas turkeys in the mortuary. And reveals why dogs could bark at night in Ossett, but not Otley.'

Baroness Blake of Leeds CBE

Cover photography: Simon Wilkinson at SWpix.com
Other photography: © Sir Rodney Brooke
– unless stated otherwise

A catalogue record for this book is available from the
British Library.

Typeset in Warnock Pro Semi Bold and Palatino
Printed and bound in the United Kingdom by

Bumpers Farm, Chippenham, Wiltshire SN14 6LH
T: +44 (0)1249 659705 www.cpi-print.co.uk
CPI ANTONY ROWE LIMITED
Registered Office: 110 Beddington Lane, Croydon, Surrey CR0 4TD

For Mariella, Freya, Alice and Theodore

And to Jeremy Beecham, whose mind illuminated
local government for more than five decades

The rising unto place is laborious; and by pains men come to greater pains; and it is sometimes base; and by indignities men come to dignities…All rising to great place is by a winding stair.

Francis Bacon, *Essay No XI,* the 1625 and final edition

Contents

Foreword
by Lord Beecham

Rodney Brooke's book is splendidly entertaining. It is also a threnody for local government. The four decades he spent working for local authorities coincided with their emasculation, most notably by the Thatcher government.

Rodney's career began in the great days of local government, when the London train would be held until the arrival of the Clerk of the West Riding County Council. On arrival in London, the Clerk would send his card to Whitehall, intimating that he would be pleased to receive the Permanent Secretary if he cared to call on him at Claridge's.

The arrogance of Sir Bernard Kenyon, the West Riding County Clerk, prompted Local Government Minister Dick Crossman, to write a *Times* article entitled The Divine Right of County Clerks. Major local authorities like the West Riding County Council did not hesitate to acquire great houses and estates, like Wentworth Woodhouse, Wentworth Castle, Bretton Hall and Fountains Abbey.

It was in that era that Rodney started, age 15, as the office boy in the Town Hall in Morley, Yorkshire. In those days even a tiny council like Morley provided a water supply for its residents. Rodney's first experience of litigation came when a prize boar escaped after the council's contractors demolished a wall by its reservoir up in the Pennines.

When he qualified as a solicitor, Rodney went to work as a

prosecutor for Rochdale Council. And back then, even small towns like Rochdale had their own police force – as well as their own burglars. Virtually all local government services were provided by the Council. His book is peppered with anecdotes about his work in Rochdale, Leicester, Stockport and the West Yorkshire County Council.

As you are about to read, Rodney was involved in some of the most dramatic episodes in local government – the last reading of the Riot Act, the inquest into the mysterious death of Helen Smith in Jeddah, the hunt for the Yorkshire Ripper and the Bradford City fire, when 56 spectators died in front of the TV cameras. He reveals some fascinating and hitherto unknown stories behind these events.

The book climaxes with his turbulent time as chief executive of Westminster Council, notorious for the scandals of its leader, Dame Shirley Porter. It ends with his resignation and the press camping on his lawn. A remarkable end to a remarkable book.

● *Jeremy Beecham – Baron Beecham DL – was a British Labour politician and a senior figure in English local government. He was leader of Newcastle City Council, the first Chairman of the Local Government Association and the elected Chairman of the National Executive Committee of the Labour Party.*

Preface – The Golden Jubilee

On 4th June 2002, eight proud horses drew the golden state coach, its four gilded tritons glittering in the sun, to St Paul's Cathedral. Inside the coach was HM the Queen, arriving to commemorate her Golden Jubilee. In the expectant congregation sat the Duke of Devonshire. He was not only a Duke but also a Knight and a Commander of the British Empire.

I sat next to the Duke. Like him, I was a Knight and a Commander of the British Empire. I also held the Orders of Merit of France, Germany, Senegal and Qatar and was an officer of the Order of the Aztec Eagle of Mexico. Seeing my medals, a casual observer might have thought that I outranked the Duke.

Forty-five years earlier such a thought would have been unimaginable. Then the Duke was at Eton. I was an office boy in Morley Town Hall. In the intervening years I became the last person to read the Riot Act, dealt with the collapse of system-built flats, reorganised the structure of local government in two counties, coped with the miners' strike, investigated the mysterious death in Jeddah of Helen Smith, anticipated the Bradford City fire which killed 56 spectators, dealt secretly with Home Secretary Willie Whitelaw over the Yorkshire Ripper murders and sold three Westminster cemeteries for 15p. The world's press camped on the lawn of my house in Yorkshire when I resigned from Westminster City Council and Dame Shirley Porter was surcharged £42.5m for rehousing homeless people in asbestos-ridden flats.

One Day at Butlins

By Rodney G. Brooke, Aged 7

＊

Written and composed at Morley Bridge
Street Infants School and reproduced
from his essay book by kind permission of
Miss H. Buttery (Head Mistress).

ON Friday I went to Butlins holiday camp at Filey. I went to
work once first, then I had lunch at dinnertime cafe. Then
daddy went to Butlins camp in car which shally was ours.
Daddy went on the Zechick bus. I and Mummy followed on
the country past two bus. Mummy had arranged with daddy to
meet her outside the gates. When we arrived Daddy was not
there. So we walked on towards the flower beds. Soon we
came to a flower bed that said Butlins on it. Soon Daddy came
back and stood on our shally. It was on the same row as the
minagage of Butlins shally. We were on A row and number
twelve shally. On every shally was the rumpets roam and
adraet tripacie so was a patting green. We walked down the
camp and saw many interesting things. When we past the
childrens play room I saw them having a competition. They
were throwing table tennis balls in a box and if the balls went
in the box it was a goal. A little further up we saw a Punch
and Judy show for the ones that were left out of the competition.

Then we had tea. There are three dining halls, the Glemsoe,
the kent, and the york. Our diningroom was the kent. When
we had finished tea we went back to our shally.   And had a
wash. When we came out I saw a little train affair, at once
I dashed off to get on. I got on a seat by myself. Just as we'd
past the york dining hall a, omnibussetir ran alongside the
train and jumped into my carriage. He asked me iff I was
enjoying myself at Butlins.   We went all round the camp.   I
did enjoy it.   When we came back I told Mummy and
Daddy all about it. It was grand.

There is a place called fairyland and we went to it. There
was the old fashioned a shoe and I imagined my head on the top
of the shoe. There was a house and you could go upstairs and
see out, there are three chairs and you could sit on them. One
chair had collapsed when somebody had sat on it.

When we came out I went in to a seaside-cars
house. There was a fire in both fire-places, and two chairs.
Then we went into a castle dangenes, then spin the tower. You
had a beautiful veiw of Butlins. When we went out of
fairyland, we went to a place where they let you go on four
wheel bicykdoloe, for twowheelitaps. I and Daddy went on one.
We went round where you put the handkbke, then on to the
peol to the beach. I ran on to the beach while Daddy sat on
the bicycle. Soon I came back and I and daddy
pedalled, up to where the road wideded out a bit then we
found round and did the same over and over again.

Soon I got tired of doing it over and over again
So I got off the bicyhcle and went to the cliff edge and looked
throu the field glasses on the field glasses is a wheel and if
I twisted the wheel in a diffent angle you only seemed a yard
or two away from the deck. You could see the sailors faces, and
you if they were smiling or frowning. Next off the sailors
were there in the cabin, and the captain was on the look-out.

After I'd been there for a while and spotted a few
younght and my steamer, I went back to daddy on the brickdvle.
We changed places I steered back. I leveel the ride. We went
at an alterway speed, as the road going slightly down and we
pedlled away as fast as we could and soon we got to the end
off the road. Then we went round the camp. I enjoyed it as
much as the beach ride. It was great fun. I did enjoy it.

After I had spent five minutes on the cliff edge
I went back to daddy. Then we pedelled back to the camp. I
enjoyed it very much but I don't think daddy did. Then went
back to the stand where they sold the bicykles, and got off it.
Mummy was waiting for us. I told her I had had a lovely time.
Then we went into the vieuwsoe ballroom and saw heat off
people dancing.   Soon a little girl and a boy were running
across the ballroom, floor, and fell, the girl kurt her nose and
the boy kurt his leg, his knee was bleeding. I suppose there
joareads took them to the first aid stachen. There are nurses
there and they will bindage the little girls nose up and the little
boys knee up.

After I had been in the vieuwsoe ballroom for
about twelve minuts we went iwo another ballroom. After we
had been in there about three minuts I saw a man with a table
sat infront off him.   Pinned in front off the table was a notice
that said Doctor Anthany Dare, on, I clamed mummmy and
Daddy it and we walked over to him to see what he was doing.
When we were two squaite I looked at a pile of papers on his
desk, on the bask off the papers it said iff you want your finger
print cive to Dokter anthany Dave.   Just then   somebody came up and asked for their finger print Mr. Dare put
some sort of blockiung on their hand and prssed it against the
paper of once the paper had a black kart on it. Athany looked
very closly at the paper and told the lady her fortune. Then
he diprod some cotton wool in something to kis desk. It looked
like water. But I knew it was nervelix. Mr. Dare rubbed the
nervellix on the lady's hand. After Mr. Dare had rubbed a
lot off nervelix on the lady hand, it soon became quite clean and
the lady looked very very pleased. She paid a shilling.

Very soon afterwards a girl about 17 or 18 came for her
finiger print. Mister anthany Dare did the same, reackily
like the lady hand only this time he wroat her fortchune down,
and Mister Anthany Dare was a very busy writer and the girl
could not read it so Tony had to ex-plain it. Soon he came to a
word he did not know himself, so he had to take another hand
print. Soon After that we went out off the ballroom.
At noon as we were set in the fresh air we went back to our
shally and had another wash. Turhed ourselves up and went to
Dinner, It was the best supper I had had for ages to comer,
and, ages, that were past. We hol some oxtail soup and afterwards steak and kidney pie, carrots, new potatotesto, rubbing
and twicseietmies to finish. It was great. After we had had our
dinner we went to a theate, there was two fimettres the old
vic and at the other theatere teatary. We went strate in as it
had all-ready started. After the Theatre was over I, summary and
Daddy went back to our shally at that time it was time for me
to go to bed. So I sunk into a cosy bed the softliest and the
best I ever got into in all my life.

After a good nights rest I got up early and I and Daddy
walked on the sesloes for a while then we came back and hol
breackfast it was a good Breakfast too. We had followkdoe and
Tomarto sauce. After Breakfast we sat in some seats which
were on the grass, as we were sitting there enjoying our-selves
we saw the train on his last round. It was fun watching all the
people coming and going to and from the camp carrying cases
and looking here and there a little while. Oh how I do wish I
lived at Butlins for ever and ever.

THE END

Sir Rodney's first attempt at creative writing, aged 7

1. 1939-1962: Life in a Yorkshire Mill Town: Mungoes and Shoddies

The world was created at teatime on Saturday, 22nd October 4004 BC, according to the Biblical chronology of Archbishop James Ussher. My own world began exactly 5,943 years later, at the same time on the same auspicious date, a few weeks after the beginning of the Second World War.

My birthplace was the grimy town of Morley, skulking on the outskirts of Leeds. The Leeds trams clanked to the edge of Morley but expired at the foot of Churwell Hill. The ascent had been abandoned after a runaway tram careened down the hill, killing six passengers. Churwell Hill had siblings: like Rome, Morley was built on seven hills. No other resemblance did it bear to the Eternal City. Its *raison d'être* was the textile industry. Not the high quality worsteds for which the Yorkshire mills were famous: Morley specialised in mungoes and shoddies, made from the greasy rags collected by the rag and bone men and the waste left over from the manufacture of superior worsteds in Huddersfield and Bradford. The rags were woven onto a cotton warp and the resulting fabric used for donkey-jackets and other rough cloth. Not for nothing was the area known as the Heavy Woollen District.

The Winding Stair

Standing in for St Peter's and St John Lateran during my youth were the Ebenezer and Zion Methodist chapels, later converted to a DIY store and a carpet warehouse. Thirty-five black, clanging mills took the place of the palazzi of the Colonna and Farnese. The reverberations of their looms kept the town awake, save on Sundays when the turmoil stopped, like the end of a headache. That silence is now eternal: looms in the scrapyard, stone floors torn up to serve as footpaths on the Pennine Way. The surviving mills now house offices and warehouses. Even in the later days of their functioning, the arrival of the motor car enabled the mill-owners to abandon their soot-encrusted mansions in Morley and to escape to the elegance of Harrogate or the rural greenery of the Wharfe Valley. Morley did not enjoy the cultural yeast of the Jewish families which leavened society in Leeds and Bradford. The town's main cultural product was the rugby club, where the mill-owners circumvented the Rugby Union's ban on remuneration by finding well-paid jobs for promising players.

As well as the syncopation of the looms, the town boasted some olfactory distinction. Alternating in the air were the smells from the gas works; the heavy aroma from Green's dripping works, as animal flesh was melted into fat; and, in the springtime, the stink from the midden sewage spread on the rhubarb fields: the legendary West Riding rhubarb triangle lay within the Morley boundaries. The heavy consumption of opiates by Queen Victoria and her subjects caused constipation. To relieve the symptom, Victorian bowels came to rely on rhubarb. In a curious reciprocity, sale of opium to the Chinese was required to provide the wherewithal to buy rhubarb, then mostly grown in China. Rhubarb was also believed to be a great prophylactic. The Opium Wars with China were as much about British access to rhubarb as about opium. But 'Opium Wars' sound better than 'Rhubarb Wars'.

The journey of Chinese rhubarb to England was arduous,

sledged across the snows and mud of Siberia. But – by happy chance – it was discovered that rhubarb thrived in the soot-laden atmosphere produced by the Morley mill chimneys: Morley was able to supplant the Chinese supply. Pink Express rhubarb was forced by candle-light in the rhubarb sheds, emerging audibly from the earth with a popping sound. Every midnight I was awakened by the Pink Express special train, which whisked the rhubarb to London to arrive at dawn at Covent Garden. To attract advertising, the local paper, the *Morley Observer*, despatched rhubarb to capture the attention of likely London advertisers. One bunch ended on the desk of Giles, the famous *Sunday Express* cartoonist. He responded with a cartoon and the caption 'Blimey: bloodshot celery'.

The rhubarb train disappeared in 1950 but the rhubarb growing survives. In the annual rhubarb festival, the biggest rhubarb pie in the world occupies the dish manufactured for the legendary Denby Dale pie.[1]

On the Morley Quirinale looms the Victorian Town Hall, a memorial to civic pride, designed to contend with its great

---

[1] The Denby Dale Pie tradition started in 1788 and has a chequered history. The 1846 pie slipped off its stand and was trampled to death by hungry onlookers. The 1887 pie was put together by a fancy London chef and contained game. It stank when opened. Remembered as the High Pie, it was hastily interred, the resulting mound now known as Pie Hill. In the crust of the 1928 pie a fissure opened as it descended into Pie Field and the gravy escaped: that was the Dry Pie. The last pie was made to celebrate the 2000 millennium. That pie weighed 12 tons, contained three tonnes of beef and a tonne of potatoes, lubricated by 22 gallons of John Smith's Best Yorkshire Bitter. The pie dish sailed up the Calder and Hebble Canal with a drinking party on board. The pie itself was transported to Pie Field by a 70-foot wagon. It fed 100,000 people including our children and us.

counterpart in Leeds. The Morley edifice is only slightly less pretentious than its more famous Leeds sibling. In my youth the Town Hall was flanked by the Jacobean Manor House, birthplace of Sir Titus Salt, philanthropic builder of the model village of Saltaire. It had also been the home of Captain Thomas Oates. He was the leading conspirator in the Farnley Wood Plot, Morley's unsuccessful attempt to assassinate King Charles II. The Manor House became the surgery of our family doctor, Dr Wigoder. His partner, Dr Geoffrey de Keyser, was famous for his involvement in the Piano Competition founded in Leeds by his wife, Dame Fanny Waterman. The site of the Manor House, itself long demolished, is now occupied by the Co-op store.

Below the Town Hall still stands Morley Hall, built in 1683 and the grandest house in the town. In that house I was born, just as the Second World War broke out. My imposing birthplace was not an indicator of the wealth of my family: the house had been presented to Morley Council for use as the municipal maternity hospital. In a fit of patriotic fervour, I was named after HMS Rodney, a battleship of which much was vainly expected in the gathering conflict.

From the world of war my earliest memory is the suffocating, clammy rubber of my child's gas mask as we took refuge in the air raid shelter. Though Morley's mungo and shoddy industry was not exactly a key target of the Luftwaffe, the night would occasionally be interrupted by the noise of exploding bombs when a stray Heinkel bomber mistook its target. The damage could be seen the following morning. The day always began with the jingle of the harness of the milkman's horse and float: my earliest job was to go out with a tin jug and receive a decantation from the milk churn. Food was scarce, limited both in variety and volume. Even potatoes could be unobtainable. Sweets and chocolates were unknown. My first experience of chocolate, two years after the end of the War, was chocolate-covered Ryvita. It was disgusting.

Like everyone, our family life was governed by coupons, points and ration books. After the war even bread was rationed. Meat rationing continued until 1954. Portion sizes were dictated by the Ministry of Food – 2oz cheese, one egg per person per week. Acquisition of luxuries like oranges depended on the family relationship with the shopkeeper. Queueing for food was a way of life. Supermarkets did not exist, nor were there any national grocery chains in Morley. Small shopkeepers, reserving food for their favoured customers, held a commanding position in society. Those raised in the abundance and variety of the 21st century can scarcely imagine life in the 1940s.

Our family was not one of those with influence among the shopkeepers. My mother was unequivocally working class. One of seven children, as a child she shared a bedroom with her six siblings in a two-bedroomed back-to-back house, whence precipitous stone steps led down to a freezing external lavatory below the house. To avoid the descent a bucket under the kitchen sink was kept for urination, its aroma enriching the fetid fug of the tiny house. Only for defecation was the journey to the frigid lavatory obligatory. Its incidence was postponed for as long as possible. Ablutions took place in cold water, except on Sunday when a fire was lit and a tin bath filled with hot water from the boiler by the grate. The urine bucket and the tin bath survived until my Grandmother was rehoused to a council bungalow soon after her eightieth birthday.

Morley was a place of great hardship in the slump between the two World Wars. Jobs were scarce. My uncle Fred would bitterly recount how he unsuccessfully sought relief from the Public Assistance Committee, chaired by a member of the same Ebenezer Chapel which Fred attended. Refusing Fred money, his fellow chapel-attender told him to 'wear out more shoe leather' in search of a job. Fred was eventually taken on as yardman by a local Tory magnate, County Councillor Sir Harry Hardy. Sir Harry made Natural Organic Manure, abbreviated to

NOM. NOM was made from *devil's dust*, material spewed from the machine called a devil, which shredded the rags to make the mungoes and shoddies which were Morley's life blood. During the week Uncle Fred wore an overall infused with grease from the NOM. At weekends, when the middle classes don comfortable old sweaters, he, like other working class men, sported a three-piece suit and a stiff-collared shirt. Thanks to his job with Sir Harry, Uncle Fred and Auntie Mary graduated from a back-to-back terrace house to the respectability of a modern semi, elegantly christened 'Ersanmyne'. Fred stayed in the same job for a half century until his eventual retirement and, in gratitude for his rescue by Sir Harry, became a dogged and lifelong Conservative.

Because my maternal grandfather was usually unemployed, my grandmother was the bread-winner, taking up cleaning jobs and laying out corpses. A dominant personality, her image was identical to Giles's cartoon grandmother in the *Sunday Express*. She used a vocabulary incomprehensible in the present day, even in Yorkshire. It was populated by Norse words like *'laike'* (play) and *'clois'* (grass). *'Put t'wood in t'oil'* meant 'close the door'. *'Tin tin tin'* meant 'it is not in the tin'. In regular family usage was the word *'thoil'*. The word still survives in the Yorkshire *argot*, since it has no English equivalent. It denotes an ability to pay the advertised price but an inability to steel oneself to do so. So, when Harvey Nichols opened its Leeds branch, Yorkshire matrons would commend the merchandise but declared that they could not *thoil* the price.

Her children inherited my grandmother's thrusting personality. The squalor of their upbringing gave them a powerful motivation to leave the slums. Through their own exertions or by marriage, my mother and her siblings moved into respectable but small semi-detached homes and saw themselves as part of the lower middle classes. After a fist-fight with my grandfather, Uncle Harry, then aged 18, took the passage to Australia under the notorious child migration scheme where (after suffering some of the abuse endemic in the scheme) he became a prosperous tradesman. My Uncle Alfred did even better: he married the daughter and sole heiress of a fish-and-chip shop proprietor. Other suitors had been deterred by her deafness. Buoyed by the profits from the fish-and-chip shop, Uncle Alfred became the first member of the family to own a car. He resolutely refused to offer lifts to his brothers and sisters.

Though none went to university, the children of my mother and her six siblings – my generation – threw off their working class background and entered the middle class proper as solicitors, accountants, and teachers, or as the wives of those professionals. Such professions are now open only to graduates, closing an escape route for members of the working class with an aversion to debt. Cousin Margaret married an Army officer. Barry and Susan became teachers, Ronnie an accountant, Edwin a prosperous builder, myself a solicitor. The ascent through two generations from the bottom of the pile to seriously respectable middle class was far from typical, as I realised when I later encountered my Morley contemporaries, still unaspiring members of the working class.

Most eminent of my cousins was the eldest grandchild, my cousin Merle, daughter of Uncle Fred, the manure yardman. She married the son of a local magnate, a man of some prominence and wealth, accrued from egg-packing. Merle's husband's own services to egg-packing were rewarded with an OBE and a Jaguar. In later years cousin Merle maintained that her husband's OBE was superior in rank to the CBE conferred upon me. Though half-convinced, my mother vigorously disputed precedence, stoutly maintaining the superiority of my own rank – from which she drew her vicarious status in the Morley Townswomen's Guild. (Sadly she died before my knighthood, which would have settled the argument.) On one occasion my mother invigorated a funeral by hissing 'you bitch' at Merle when the latter assumed a more prominent seat than my mother. Merle and her husband were anathematised by my mother. Unlike the rest of the family, they did not attend the ritual Christmas family gatherings. The family believed that this was because her husband was too snooty to come. The real reason, I now suspect, was that Merle was embarrassed by her working class relatives and did not wish to expose her Jaguar-driving husband to them. At an Athenaeum dinner many years later I found Merle's husband to be a charming and urbane fellow diner.

But I leap ahead. Like her siblings and cousins, my mother left school at 13 and joined the mill as a weaver. Casting round for a suitable husband who might deliver social advancement, she hit upon the most eligible male of her acquaintance, my father. Though he had also left school at 13 to work in the mill, he was the son of the mill overlooker. My father might reasonably be described as fallen middle class. However, he managed to leave the mill and get a job as a sales representative, a job which he kept until his death, aged 65.

Sir Max Hastings described the origins of his family in *Did You Really Shoot the Television?* (Harper Press, 2010). To epitomise the humble background of his family and speaking of 1877, he described how the 'family's income never much exceeded £400...the family inhabited the genteel lower-middle-class world familiar to us from *The Diary of a Nobody.*'

Ninety years later my father's annual income never exceeded £500. He worked until he died in 1967. His ambition was that his commission might one day take his weekly earnings over £10 (the lower classes computed their wages weekly, not annually). It never did. Recourse was regularly needed to the pawnbroker's shop and the bailiffs were never far away. In winter my regular duty was to dredge coal from the local slag heap. Despite poverty, my Father was possessed of immense chutzpah. On one occasion, armed only with the name of a

Life in a Yorkshire Mill Town

Leeds official – and to my intense embarrassment – he blagged himself and me into the 1961 Rugby League Championship Final at Odsal Stadium in Bradford, where the great Lewis Jones led Leeds to victory over Barrow.

I possess only one relic of my father, a copy of *Nicholas Nickleby*, the volume emblazoned with the inscription 'presented to George Brooke, second in attendance at the Wesleyan (Ebenezer) Sunday School 1912'. It is unlikely that my father ever read his prize. To the best of my knowledge he never read a book. He was, however, a prominent Thespian in the Amateur Dramatic Society of the Ebenezer Primitive Methodist Chapel, the social hub around which revolved the social life of the family. In that capacity he took the role of the Oxford undergraduate Lord Fancourt Babbarley in *Charley's Aunt*. The Methodist Minister gave him voice coaching so that he might plausibly ape the accent of an Oxford undergraduate.

Notwithstanding the improvement in his accent and his promotion from the mill to his job as a sales representative, my father failed to deliver the social status which my mother coveted. He was quite happy to combine his job with snooker at the Morley Liberal Club. Harassed at home, he sublimated his talents in the Morley pubs. There he had an enviable reputation as a raconteur. When the male members of the family returned from their Christmas trips to the pub, there would be a cry 'George was in good form tonight'.

My father's failure to deliver the requisite social advancement had been a severe disappointment to my mother. In substitution she pinned her hopes on me. She determined to promote my education. Until that reached fruition, she promoted her social status by trumpeting my superiority. Thus, in 1947, the *Yorkshire Post* carried the following story:

The Winding Stair

REQUEST TO MORLEY BOY

A seven-year-old Morley boy, Rodney G. Brooke had a surprise to-day when he received a request from holiday camp chief Mr. W. E. Butlin, for his autographed photograph. Rodney wrote a school essay while at a Butlin camp, which was highly commended by the Education authorities.

I assume that it was the essay which was highly commended, not the Butlin camp. Interestingly the story also included my address, something which would certainly not happen today. Sixty-four years later my cousin in Australia sent me a copy of the essay: in 1947 it had been forwarded by my proud mother to his father, who had emigrated on the assisted passage at the age of 18. Until his death he had kept the essay as a memory of his origins in Yorkshire.

School in Wakefield

In the days before comprehensive schools there was a stark division between secondary modern schools and grammar schools, delineated by performance in the 11-plus exam. As well as secondary modern schools, Morley possessed its own grammar school. But the elite school was acknowledged to be the Queen Elizabeth's Grammar School at Wakefield, its charter granted by the eponymous monarch in 1591. It was a direct grant school, where the West Riding County Council had reserved one of the four forms of entry for boys excelling in the 11-plus examination. Fee paying pupils occupied the other three forms of entry.

Impelled by my mother, I passed the examination and secured entry to the Wakefield Grammar School – the only boy from Morley to do so that year. But upon my being offered a place my mother developed Doubts. Was this a step too far? Was it sensible to sever me both geographically and socially from my working class roots? To resolve her mind she consulted the usual source for advice to the working classes – the family doctor. Dr Wigoder had officiated at my birth and presided over my childhood illnesses. My mother therefore attributed to him a continuing interest in my welfare. Dr Wigoder opined that my attendance at Wakefield Grammar School would be a good thing. And so I came to take the green West Riding bus on the daily ten-mile journey to the historic grammar school in the cathedral city of Wakefield. At each stop in the coal-mining villages through which we journeyed the bus collected squatting queues of miners, their faces black from coal-dust.

Today Wakefield seems a shadow of its former self, rescued from terminal decline by the superb Hepworth Gallery, opened in 2011. But in 1951, when I joined the school, it was the county town, with handsome Georgian terraces around the church and the attractive old school building. Compared to Morley, it seemed to me a Yorkshire Venice, a repository of history, culture, wealth and gentility. The schoolteachers seemed very different to those in my elementary school: Oxbridge graduates, they seemed to me the epitome of sophistication. The Headmaster, Dr Grace, was of a distinguished appearance and spoke in an accent foreign to me, clearly superior to that spoken by the Morley mill-owners. His distinction was sealed by the Bentley in which he arrived at the school. The form teacher in my first class was Miss Fanny Dadswell. At the end of my first year in the school, Miss Dadswell migrated to the United States, whence she sent a package of boiled sweets to her former pupils, then unfamiliar with sugar-based luxuries.

Ten years after I left school Tony Crosland became the Secretary of State for Education. He expressed his determination 'to close every f***ing grammar school in England'. His quest remains unrequited. Back in the 1950s debate on education was still polarised between the comparative virtues of comprehensive and selective schools. Comprehensive schools, it was argued, raised the general level of achievement. Selective schools enabled working class children to escape from the narrow expectations of their parental background. In the educational jargon, they provided doors not floors: the clever working class boy could open a door to avoid mines, mills and factories and escape to join the middle classes. The West Riding County Council 11-plus examination ensured that only the most able boys entered the Wakefield Grammar School by way of the West Riding scholarship. It clearly favoured middle class children, though, as Lord (Edward) Boyle pointed out, 'the proportion of Tory voters in the electorate is more than double the proportion of grammar school places'.

The grammar school opened the eyes of the scholarship boy who did gain admission. Mixing with the sons of doctors and solicitors revealed a middle class world of which I had no knowledge. They took for granted aspirations which I scarcely knew existed. The immediate consequence was to reinforce my acute sense of social inferiority. Interestingly this was ameliorated when I noticed that one of my contemporaries, the son of a pharmacist, had a patina of grime behind his ears. Clearly the middle classes had feet (or ears) of clay.

In my first week at school I was sent out of the room for causing a disturbance.

I had been stung by a bee and shrieked in response. My explanation was disbelieved. I supposed that the explanation of a middle-class boy would have been accepted. The class distinction seemed institutionalised. The middle-class pupils enjoyed each other's society outside school. They attended each other's birthday parties in their parents' comfortable detached houses. The scholarship boys were not invited. In any case I would never have expected these products of the middle classes to enter my parents' shabby home. Moreover I lived ten miles away. Unlike the middle class parents, my parents had no car. I was separated from my fellow pupils not only socially but also geographically.

Unsurprisingly the scholarship boys enjoyed greater academic success than most of the paying pupils. Perhaps, like me, they had a motivation to work harder. Nevertheless my perception was that the positions of authority in the school eluded the working class boys. Those places always seemed to go to the middle class boys. Curiously the honours achieved in the school were no passport to success in later life. In my own generation were a number of boys who achieved some distinction, like David Hope, future Archbishop of York, member of the House of Lords and, after retirement from his archiepiscopal see, vicar of our parish church, St Margaret's Ilkley. Others I encountered in later life included Brian Willott and Chris Nuttall, both of whom rose (almost) to the top of the Civil Service and were appointed CBs.

Fifty-five years after I had left the school, the local press announced my appointment as chairman of the regulatory body for higher education. As a result, the headteacher of Wakefield Grammar School invited me to tour the school, where I studied the honours boards. The names of Lord Hope, Brian Willott and Chris Nuttall were conspicuously absent. The honours boards contained no names which would echo in posterity. The school had failed to identify the real achievers.

Despite my social unease, school was a glorious escape from working class life in Morley. I dreaded the summer holidays, a week of which was spent in the depressed coastal town of Saltburn, where the days dragged on interminably. Every dreary day was spent on the beach, guarded by the squat wartime pillboxes, built to repel German invaders. We stayed in a boarding house, where the curious arrangement, then not uncommon, was that we rented a sitting room and two bedrooms. My mother bought our food and handed it over to the landlady, Miss Chapman, who would cook it for our breakfast and dinner. Miss Chapman's younger sister, Irene, was 'in business' – working as a secretary in Middlesbrough. I was given her bedroom, while she presumably slept with her elder sister. The bedroom contained Irene's memorabilia, which included nostalgic volumes in which young men had penned their admiration twenty-five years previously. Somehow their esteem had evaporated, leaving her to share what remained of her life with her sour spinster sister in the rundown seaside resort.

School was infinitely preferable to Saltburn. But because of my social diffidence and the need to catch the bus back to Morley, I took part in no out-of-school activities. Across the road from Queen Elizabeth's Grammar School was the Wakefield Girls' High School, whence mysterious creatures emerged to share the bus back home. They maintained a presence which I found intimidating but which brightened the journey.

I did have one out-of-school activity: being moderately proficient in French, I was chosen to play Monsieur Jourdain in *Le Bourgeois Gentilhomme*, developing an histrionic ability which stood me in good stead in greater life. The production taught me one other great lesson. In the middle of the second act I inadvertently skipped to dialogue in the third act. Some of the cast followed me; others did not. After a few minutes I realised my mistake and reverted to the second act. Those who had stayed with the second act had by then given up and had moved on to the third act. Those who had quickly moved with me to the third act stayed there. As a result most of the cast gave an impression of complete incompetence. I, on the other hand, remained supremely confident throughout, being the only person who knew what I was doing. At the final curtain I gained the applause of the audience. Lesson: applause goes to the confident, not the correct.

Together with a dedication to rugby football, the school had a relentless commitment to academic success. Brighter pupils had an accelerated progression through the school. I was one of two pupils (Brian Willott being the other) who skipped not just one but two forms. While most pupils staidly took their GCE O levels aged 16, I took mine aged 14. Despite this double elevation I continued to do well in examinations, at the cost of some social deprivation. In the annual class tests, results in the arts subjects would be published earliest. I was invariably top of the aggregated marks in these subjects. Then the sciences and maths results appeared, reducing my lead. Finally there appeared the art and woodwork results. More often than not these administered the *coup de grâce* and placed Brian Willott in the top spot.

In those days you either passed or failed the GCE O level: there was no grading. In the elitist view of my teachers, its only function was to sort out the mentally deficient from the rest. Having taken the GCE O level, I entered the Sixth Form aged 14. The idyll did not last long.

My parents had the clear assumption that I should start earning money when I reached the school-leaving age of fifteen, like all the other Morley lads whose parents they knew. I postponed telling the school for as long as possible. But four weeks before the end of term, the time came for the distribution of books to be read in the vacation. I then had to confess. For me, it was a humiliating experience. My teachers were clearly disappointed. The Deputy Headmaster summoned my parents to a conference.

For my parents, this was the most arresting experience of their lives. Flattered by the interest of an Oxford graduate, they discussed the interview at length for several years. Three weeks after the interview, I overheard one of their discussions. The Deputy Headmaster had assured them that he had contacted an old college friend, the admissions tutor at Brasenose, his former college. He told my parents that it was almost certain (subject only to reasonably plausible A-level results, which should be easily attainable) that I would be offered a place to read history at Brasenose College, Oxford.

The interview prompted my parents to consult my mother's cousin, Arthur Hall. Arthur's mother was a mill worker, like my own mother and her siblings. Ill health prevented Arthur's father from working. As a result Arthur had an upbringing of acute privation. Like me, he secured entry to grammar school. Like me he joined Morley Town Hall as the office boy when he left school. The War gave him an escape route: he volunteered for the Royal Air Force. A sight defect ruled him out as a pilot, but as the navigator of a Bristol Beaufighter, a two-seater fighter plane, he developed an instinctive rapport with his pilot. He was the Hon Michael Benn, eldest son of Viscount Stansgate, brother of Cabinet Minister Tony Benn and uncle of Leeds MP Hilary Benn.

The understanding between Arthur and his aristocratic pilot was the key to their tally of ten combat victories (plus a V1 flying bomb), gained in North Africa and northwest Europe. One of the outstanding night-fighter crews of the war, they were each twice awarded the DFC. Arthur took pleasure in telling the story of being shot down by friendly fire near the Firth of Forth. He parachuted safely into the grounds of Yester House, the 18th century stately home of the Marquess of Tweeddale. There he was entertained to an excellent dinner of game from the estate. Though puzzled by the profusion of cutlery, he solved the conundrum by copying the choice of his neighbour at the table. Meanwhile his patrician pilot had landed near a farm labourer's cottage, where he was frugally fed on porridge, both at dinner and breakfast. The story was repeated in cousin Arthur's obituary in *The Times*.

After the War Arthur rejoined Morley Town Hall. There he used his termination payment from the RAF to pay the required premium to the Town Clerk so that he could be articled and become a solicitor. Having qualified, he had become Deputy

Clerk to the Shipley Urban District Council (and later Clerk of the Bromsgrove District Council and, after the 1974 local government reorganisation, Town Clerk of Bromsgrove Council). Arthur assured my parents that attendance at Brasenose College, Oxford would be supererogatory, citing his own career as evidence. His advice fortified my parents in their resolution to defy the School's advice. The Brasenose offer did not outbalance the prospect of a steady income. 'What', they speculated, 'was the good of a history degree? What jobs led from that?' Frustratingly, at the end of one of their discussions of the question, I heard my mother say,' Well, it's not as if Brasenose College was Oxford University'. The conference with the Deputy Headmaster produced no change to their views. I was still to leave school when I was fifteen.

Would they have come to a different decision had they understood the Oxford collegiate structure? At the time their decision devastated me. Leaving school severed me from all my known friends and acquaintances. All my visions had crystallised round the images imposed on me by the school, with Oxbridge as the immediate goal. My academic success had laid this prospect at my feet. Its disappearance seemed to remove all purpose to life. I fell down a cliff of despair.

Hoping to retain my attendance, the school had insisted on giving me books required for study in the second year of the sixth form. Their return required one final forlorn voyage to the school. I handed them in at the school office. No-one marked my arrival or departure.

2. The *Morley Observer*, Bernard Ingham and the Talking Dog

My immediate posting restored my will to live. My destined employment was at the *Morley Observer*. A family business, its proprietor, George Stead, was the grandson of the paper's Victorian founder.

In Morley, no more stimulating opening could have been found. The attenuated state of today's local press gives no clue to the buzz and excitement generated in the newsrooms of local newspapers in the 1950s: they were microcosms of their national counterparts. In those days Bradford alone generated three local daily newspapers as well as several weeklies. To me, the *Morley Observer* reporters seemed Olympian figures, giants among the pygmies of the town.

My post was distinguished with the title of junior reporter. The title gilded reality: my real job was to do errands for the reporters and the printers. Invigilated by the Father of the Chapel, the printers still used hot metal in the presses. A typical errand was to take a photograph to Leeds, where it would be transmuted into metal for the printing press. The job launched my passion for the theatre: the newspaper received free tickets for the Leeds shows and these were often passed to me. Usually they were for the first house on Monday evening at the Leeds Empire music hall, fabled as the graveyard for comedians. Eric Morecambe, half of the comedy duo Morecambe and Wise, quoted a member of the Leeds audience as saying 'Ee lad: tha were so funny last night I almost 'ad to laugh'.

The vanished era of the music hall was nostalgically recalled by J B Priestley in *Lost Empires* and by John Major (whose father was a music hall comedian) in *My Old Man*. At the Leeds Empire the show was accompanied by the resident eleven-man band, conducted by the ever-present Ronnie Roberts. There I saw declining American stars like Laurel and Hardy and Frankie Lane; comedians like Morecambe and Wise, the Crazy Gang, Ken Dodd, Frankie Howard, Benny Hill and Max Wall; the latest British heartthrobs, like Dickie Valentine and Frankie Vaughan; ventriloquists, magicians, and, of course, the Tiller Girls, whose precision high-kick dancing began in 1889. Bill Haley came with his Comets twenty years after they first rocked around the clock: middle-aged matrons harked back to their teens, abandoned their seats and jived in the aisles. A perennial act was Wilson, Keppel and Betty, faintly lubricious 'Egyptian' sand dancers, whose career spanned the war and ended with the end of the music hall. Jack Wilson and Joe Keppel were constants, but Betty went through a dozen mutations. In 1936 they performed in Berlin and were condemned as immoral by Dr Goebbels, a pronouncement which must have boosted ticket sales.

The advent of radio damaged but did not destroy the attraction of the music hall. The audience came to see the flesh of the disembodied voices they had heard on the airwaves. Television administered the *coup de grâce*.

The Leeds Empire, a splendid theatre designed by the famous theatre architect Frank Matcham, was demolished in 1961 to make way for a shopping centre. But the tympanum which surmounted its stage door still crowns the rear portico of Harvey Nichols. Matcham's superb Baroque shopping arcade also survives, a theatrical confection of wrought iron, Siena marble, mosaics, and faience from the Burmantofts pottery in Leeds.

The downmarket theatre in Leeds was the City Varieties, one of the original 'music halls', created in 1865 in a hall above the White Swan pub. In its Victorian heyday it had featured Charlie Chaplin (one of the 'Eight Lancashire Lads'), Lily Langtry and Houdini. It had long suffered a decline and in my youth offered its audience a staple diet of strip-tease artistes and tableaux of nude women: the edict of the Lord Chamberlain condemned naked models to immobility. Armed with peashooters, the younger generation would try to induce a quiver in the living flesh. In its later manifestation, the City Varieties, now the oldest music hall in continuous use (thanks to the incineration of its nearest rival), became famous as the home of the *Good Old Days* on television.

The upmarket theatre in Leeds was the Grand. The free press tickets for the Grand were usually snaffled by the Observer's proprietor, Mr Stead. Occasionally they would drift down the ranks to me. At the Grand I saw my first opera when I was 15, sitting in the stalls with my free press ticket. Watching the same opera, up in the gods, the young Alan Bennett clutched the gold safety rail so hard (he wrote) that he had gilt over his hands. Like Alan Bennett I was completely wowed. The opera was *Turandot*, starring the Australian soprano Sylvia Fisher as the eponymous princess. While blessed with a superb voice, the diva was of minute height but substantial weight. It was difficult to imagine a succession of handsome princes going to their doom because of her physical attraction. And, of course, it could not have been her conversation which attracted them, since they saw her only from afar and could exchange no words. I learnt early to suspend disbelief.

Occasionally I was let loose to do some reporting: usually no more than collecting the names of the prizewinners at the Flower Show. Morley travel agents were regular advertisers and had to be humoured. I was sent to ask them where Morley holidaymakers were bound on their vacations. I filed the story *'Most Morley holidaymakers are off to the Costa Brava, with Spain a close second'*. Fortunately it was spiked, as was *'Passengers hit by cancelled train.'* I relished the letter about our recipe for Scotch Eggs: *'A good recipe, but you did not say 'shell the egg''*. Another favourite was *'Police found safe under blanket'*.

My most rewarding assignment was to interview a talking dog at the Spotted Cow in Drighlington. Also sent to interview the dog was a young reporter from the Hebden Bridge Times, Bernard Ingham. When scratched vigorously on the chest the dog would (unsurprisingly) growl. The growl was implausibly interpreted by the entrepreneurial landlord as speech. It was clear both to Bernard and myself that there was no story in a dog which could not talk. But, after a few pints, we found that the dog was talking quite fluently. We sought its views on foreign policy and the economic situation and filed our stories. Bernard (aged 88 as I write) and I still remain in touch, though the relationship became temporarily strained when, as her long-serving Press Secretary, he adopted and disseminated Mrs Thatcher's scathing view of local government. Nevertheless he took our teenage children on a memorable guided tour of Number Ten.

My daily duty as a junior reporter included going to the Town Hall. There I would enter the anteroom of the Town Clerk's Department and ring the bell. After an interval, up would shoot a glass panel. Through the hatch would jut the face of a lumpish lad. 'Anything for the *Morley Observer*?' I would ask. Without response, the panel would slam down. After an interminable wait, up would shoot the panel once more and the acned face reappear. 'Nowt for t'*Observer*', it would grunt and the panel was slammed down. Occasionally another face would be introduced to brief me on some municipal matter or to place a statutory advertisement in the *Morley Observer*. The dwellers beyond the hatch combined stupidity with spite and lack of charm.

With this contrast in my mind, the residents of the *Morley Observer* newsroom seemed to me even more god-like as the weeks passed. Their names are engraved on my memory, from which more recent and more eminent names have faded. The News Editor was Arthur Wilkinson ('Wilkie'), the charismatic heart of the paper. His compelling personality and dedication held the news room together. An Oxford graduate, he was an unusual presence in such a provincial setting. The reason for his presence, as I now conjecture, was that he was gay. At a time when homosexuality was a criminal offence Morley must have seemed a safe bolt-hole. The idea of homosexuality was too avant-garde to occur to the Morley *gendarmerie*.

Wilkie's most famous *protégé* was Vincent Mulchrone, a man of immense charm, great talent and a quenchless capacity for alcohol. Working in his shadow were Leslie Bielby and Derek Hudson. They also appeared to me as immensely able and committed reporters. Under the stimulus of Wilkinson, the team of reporters was as dedicated to producing a gripping paper as the reporters on any national newspaper. They seemed absolutely committed to the *Morley Observer*. Though they discussed seeking jobs on regional or national newspapers, none seemed to make any serious attempt to leave: Wilkie's charisma gripped them.

Chief among the *Observer*'s targets was the council and those who served on it. Unlike its modern council counterparts, anxious to present their works to the voters, the ambition of the Conservative councillors who controlled the council was to prevent any part of its activities from being glimpsed by the townsfolk. This, of course, further stimulated the natural instincts of an aggressive newsroom. Reciprocally the council closed down its already narrow avenues for feeding information to the *Observer*.

The *Morley Observer*, Bernard Ingham and the Talking Dog

Even to my fifteen-year-old self the situation was quite clear. The council was jamming its thumb into a hole in the dyke to stop a leak which could never be staunched. The reporters would always have the upper hand. They were regularly fed by the opposition: the Labour councillors had a natural desire to push stories into the press, choosing, of course, those which favoured their own construction. As a result the (completely erroneous) impression gained by the Conservative councillors was that the paper was a Labour puppet. The council redoubled its attempts to stem the flood of stories, achieving, of course, entirely the opposite.

At the age of 15 and brooding deeply on my own future, I came to two conclusions. The *Morley Observer* was not exactly the *Times* or the *Manchester Guardian*. If such apparently excellent reporters finished up in the Morley newsroom then competition in the newspaper business must be pretty hot. And, given the stupidity I encountered in the Morley Town Hall, promotion in local government should be a piece of cake. Stimulating though was the atmosphere in the *Morley Observer* newsroom, I decided that I should look elsewhere for my career. I might well have persevered with a career as a journalist had I known that the *Morley Observer* reporters were as exceptional as I thought and that all were destined for national eminence. In particular, Vincent Mulchrone became the highest paid reporter in Fleet Street: a collection of his *Daily Mail* articles (*The Best of Vincent Mulchrone*) was republished 25 years after his untimely death from leukaemia. His portrait is in the National Portrait Gallery. As chief reporter of the *Yorkshire Post*, Derek Hudson became famous as the first journalist to wade ashore with British troops on their invasion of the Falklands Islands in April 1982. Leslie Bielby became the Washington correspondent of *The Times*.

My career thoughts crystallised when the ugglesome lad behind the glass panel left the Morley Town Clerk's Department. His post of office boy was advertised. Dazzled by the success of cousin Arthur Hall, Deputy Clerk of Shipley Urban District Council, my parents urged my application. I succumbed to their pressure. Invited for interview, my fifteen year-old self sidled through the Doric portals of the Town Hall, rehearsing long vowels as I went. Learning vicariously from my father's elocution lessons for *Charley's Aunt*, I had begun to acquire a moderately plausible middle class accent. (Had I known that Harold Wilson and successors would make a Northern accent fashionable, I would have stuck to my native Yorkshire.)

I quivered into the Town Clerk's office to face the interviewing panel. Its chair was Councillor Miss Clara Hepworth, a benign elderly spinster, offshoot (like most of the Morley Conservative councillors) of a Morley mill-owning family. Her kindness mitigated my nerves. The interview went well: I was appointed, thus forsaking the stimulating and subversive atmosphere of the *Morley Observer* for the stifling atmosphere of the Town Hall. My appointment was subject to the condition that I acquired certified proficiency in shorthand and typing within one year of appointment. My salary was £13.18s.5d per month.

During my seven years in the Town Clerk's department Miss Hepworth took a benevolent interest in my progress. [Thirty-five years later her nephew John Holroyd, then Patronage Secretary in No 10, took a similar interest in me.] I started in the job the following week.

3. Local Government and the Drunken Helot

The local government which I joined in 1955 presented a disorderly clutter of local authorities. At the bottom of the pile were parish councils whose powers were limited to local functions like the provision of allotments, public lavatories, bus shelters and village halls. Above them lurked urban and rural district councils, too small to aspire to the dignity of a borough and sometimes with a population of only a few hundreds. Above them in the municipal pecking order were borough councils like Morley, which provided local services to 35,000 souls. Their responsibilities included local roads, housing, local planning, slum clearance and public parks.

Superior yet again were the county borough councils, which governed the larger urban agglomerations. Unlike the smaller borough councils, they provided all local government services in their areas. They included great cities like Leeds, Bradford and Manchester as well as smaller authorities like Dewsbury, which attained county borough status when the qualification was a population of 50,000 and thereafter had clung precariously to their independence. Though ancient cities like London and York had their civic origins in the Middle Ages, the main industrial city councils emerged in the nineteenth century. The second generation industrialists felt responsible for the cities their fathers had created. 'There is no nobler sphere for those who have not the opportunity of engaging in imperial politics than to take part in municipal work', wrote Joseph Chamberlain, Lord Mayor of Birmingham and later a dominant figure at Westminster. In the late Victorian era the municipalities mopped up the functions of a congeries of ad hoc bodies - 'juntas' (as the *Birmingham Journal* described them) – a process reversed a century later as local government powers were fragmented and distributed to Government-appointed quangos and private companies.

Before the second world war the typical leaders of the great city councils were successful businessmen. After the war the city councils were often led by men from the working class, able men who reached eminence through local government. The leaders of the great cities might enjoy national prominence. In the 1970s the Leeds City Council was led by Sir Albert King, a figure of commanding presence. Nor might the leader be the only councillor to achieve importance. Another prominent Leeds City councillor was Sir Karl Cohen, whose name is still remembered in sheltered housing schemes in the city. Nationally famous in the world of housing, he knocked down the slums and built council housing at a time when both political parties shared the objective of providing public housing. On one occasion Sir Albert, a man of strict probity, charged Sir Karl with accepting undue hospitality. Sir Karl responded with Biblical authority: 'Thou shall not muzzle the ox that treadeth out the corn.' Sir Albert snarled back: 'Don't thee give me thy bloody Jewish Bible.'

Membership of the city or town council conferred status. In J B Priestley's 1938 farce *When We Are Married*, 'Councillor' Albert Parker and 'Alderman' Joseph Helliwell gloried in their municipal appellations. County councillors affected no such titles. Retired army officers often became county council members and retained the title of their rank, being addressed as 'General' or 'Colonel'. The patrician superiority of county councillors to their urban counterparts stemmed from the British social hierarchy, not from local government. It was often regarded as obligatory for the local gentry to take part in county government. Robert Carne, the doomed hero of *South Riding*, Winifred Holtby's 1936 novel of Yorkshire local government, was a member of the fictional South Riding County Council 'because Carnes had always been members'. Occasionally a peer would stoop to run the district council in which lay his seat: the Earl of Gainsborough was the chairman of Oakham District Council

Though noble membership of the county councils was usually confined to those younger sons who had not entered the armed forces, even the occasional peer would submit himself to the ballot box. In the 1970s the chairman of the Leicestershire County Council was the Duke of Rutland. His Grace supervised the business of the county council over a monthly lunch with the clerk. Aristocratic county councillors did not trespass on the preserves of the clerk. They did not expect to be troubled by administration but enjoyed meeting their contemporaries in county hall. They were often a gerontocracy. In the 1960s the chairman of the Leicestershire County Council was aged 91. He was eventually prevailed upon to retire. On the momentous day when he announced that he was making way for a younger man, he named his successor, who was aged 89.

Except in the cities and county boroughs, the county councils provided the main and most expensive local government services – police, fire, education, social services, strategic planning, libraries and main highways. They also ran the Quarter Sessions, the criminal courts. That was a function inherited from the old county magistracy, responsible until the Victorian era for local government services outside the towns and cities. Buttressing the county councils' patrician status was the lieutenancy. The lord-lieutenant of the county, the Queen's representative, usually saw himself (there were no women lords-lieutenant in those days) as linked to the county council whose area he represented.

Town clerks were creatures of the city or borough council and owed their appointments to the aldermen and councillors. But the clerks of county councils had an entirely different pedigree: their origin lay with the Quarter Sessions, whose responsibilities had been conferred in 1388. The national association of the clerks of county councils was the Clerks of the Peace Society. The duties of Quarter Sessions used to extend beyond crime, and included responsibility for roads, bridges, prisons, lunatic asylums, licensing, police, the militia and the poor law. They set the county rates. Until 1888, the clerks of the peace, the predecessors of the county clerks, were appointed by the *Custos Rotulorum*, himself appointed by the Crown. The office of *Custos Rotulorum* merged with the Lord-Lieutenancy in 1836.

When county councils were created in 1888 they took over the responsibilities of Quarter Sessions. They enjoyed the prestige of the county aristocracy. When the West Riding County Council was established, its first chairman was the Liberal Marquess of Ripon, former Viceroy of India, seigneur of Fountains Abbey and the Studley Royal estate. He was celebrated for having shot 556,813 head of game, an average of 67 creatures every day of his life, not counting the beaters whom he wounded. At the election of the chairman the Marquess voted for his Conservative counterpart, who reciprocated by voting for the Marquess. (A devout Catholic, Lord Ripon had been appalled to see the Baptistery at Assisi used for the manufacture of salami. He immediately bought it and transferred it to the keeping of the Church. As a result the main street in Assisi is named the Via Ripon.) In London the new County Council included as members the Duke of Norfolk, the Earl of Rosebery, the Earl of Dudley, Earl Cadogan, the Earl of Onslow and Viscount Mountmorres. Despite this noble membership the Prime Minister, Lord Salisbury, likened the county council to 'a drunken helot'.

The clerks of the peace became clerks of the new county councils. They continued to sit as clerks of the peace, responsible for administering the Quarter Sessions criminal courts, until 1972. They would usually also be clerks to the Lieutenancy and therefore exercised considerable influence over patronage and honours, including appointments to the magistracy. As a result the great county clerks enjoyed great prestige and self-conceit, conscious of a history of power independent of the county councils which appointed them. They enjoyed grandeur difficult for their present-day successors to imagine.

One distinguished county clerk was Sir Harcourt Clare, Clerk of Lancashire County Council until his death in 1922. When King George V and Queen Mary visited Lancashire in 1913, they stopped at the Lodge gates of Sir Harcourt's mansion and enquired upon the health of Sir Harcourt, who had recently fallen ill. Sir Harcourt had accumulated a bevy of other posts, such as clerk of the asylums board. The total annual remuneration, £14,000, amassed by Sir Harcourt for his various roles in the years before the First World War, exceeded the combined wages of every employee in his department.

Many county clerks followed the example of Sir Harcourt and collected lucrative multiple appointments. They would appoint a deputy to do the work but retain the emoluments. One famous clerk of Kent County Council named Flatts was particularly successful in accumulating remunerations. Within county hall the county council employed a hairdresser to encourage neatness among employees and, no doubt, to avoid the need for them to leave county hall to have their hair cut in town. The hairdresser was referred to as the Deputy County Barber, imputing to Flatts the retention of the salary of the substantive post. Flatts was Clerk of Cornwall County Council when he was appointed at Kent. For some time he retained both posts, collecting their respective salaries. Only when Cornwall and Kent councillors met in London did they discover that they shared the same Clerk. Given an ultimatum to choose between the jobs, Flatts protested that he was quite able to undertake both duties from his flat in London. Only with reluctance did he relinquish his Cornwall job. Later in his reign he complained to the county council that the management of his personal affairs distracted his attention from county council concerns. The county council appointed a senior clerk to handle Flatts's private business.

Clerk of the Warwickshire County Council for almost fifty years was Sir Edgar Stephens. When interviewed for the post, the 24-year-old Stephens was asked whether he was not too young for such a responsible job. He responded magisterially that William Pitt the younger was Prime Minister of England at the age of 24. When negotiating his salary Sir Edgar accepted a lower wage, provided that he could keep the fees imposed for searches of the local land charges register. He retained those fees until he retired at the age of 70 in 1967. By then they amounted to over £100,000 annually – equal to about £1.5m in 2022 money.

The exalted position of county clerks exempted them from challenge: they could get away with a great deal. The Clerk of Devon County Council in the 1960s, Vivian Lucas, was an alcoholic. The attendants on the express train from Exeter to London were primed to furnish a continuous supply of gin and tonics from breakfast onwards. From time to time Lucas would honour district councils with his presence, after taking a bibulous lunch in a local hostelry. His articled clerks would accompany him to carry his bag. Lacking Lucas's capacity, one of them was overcome at the afternoon council meeting and vomited over the municipal table.

County clerks considered themselves above the constraints

imposed on lesser mortals. One of my predecessors in the Wakefield county hall was Sir Charles McGrath. The office boy would carry his bag to Wakefield station when Sir Charles travelled to London. The stationmaster would hold the London train until the arrival of Sir Charles. In London he would send his card to the Permanent Secretary of the Local Government Board, informing him that Sir Charles was in residence at Claridge's and would be pleased to receive the Permanent Secretary if he cared to call.

Sir Charles finally overreached himself during the Second World War. He lived at Bolton Abbey, some thirty-five miles from the county hall in Wakefield. During the days of petrol rationing, Sir Charles used his 30 hp county council car, registration number DWT 1, to be driven to and from county hall. In 1942 an MP tabled a Parliamentary question to ask the Minister of Fuel and Power 'whether he is aware that Sir Charles McGrath, Clerk to the West Riding County Council, who had a motor car at his disposal for his official duties, took without authorisation in a period of 261 days 295 gallons of petrol from the county council's pumps and used them to run for private and pleasure purposes his private car, for which he had an allowance of about five gallons per month; and why there is such a delay in prosecuting this case?' Though no criminal proceedings were taken, Sir Charles was constrained to resign.

Sir Charles's successor as Clerk of the West Riding County Council in 1943 was his deputy, the gigantic Sir Bernard Kenyon. He held the post for 26 years. Sir Bernard employed an imposing butler. Legend had it that on arrival at Sir Bernard's house a visiting Permanent Secretary warmly shook the hand of the butler, mistaking him for the great man himself. One year Sir Bernard was chairman of the Society of the Clerks of the Peace. A metaphorical three line whip compelled the Secretary of State for Housing and Local Government to attend the Society's annual dinner. In his after dinner speech Sir Bernard was conspicuously offensive to the Labour Secretary of State, Richard Crossman. In his response Crossman politely ignored Sir Bernard's boorishness – but three days later published in *The Times* a coruscating article, headed *The Divine Right of County Clerks*. After the reorganisation of local government in 1974, Sir John Boynton, Clerk of Cheshire County Council became the first President of the Society of Local Authority Chief Executives. The press asked him why the Society was holding its first annual dinner at the Savoy during a time of austerity. 'Because', responded Sir John with appropriate chutzpah, 'we can't afford Claridge's.'

The clerks of the county councils regarded their counterparts in the great cities with unaffected condescension. In compensation, the town clerks of the county borough councils affected florid names – R. de la Zouche Hall (Halifax), R. Horsfall Turner (Scarborough), Julius Caesar (Keighley), R. Ribblesdale Thornton (Salford). Even the service directors of large cities followed the trend: from his schooldays in Leeds, Alan Bennett chronicles W. Vane Morland, Director of Transport. Engraved on his memory and on that of his Leeds contemporary, Keith Waterhouse, were the names of other municipal czars: George Guest, Director of Education and R.A.H. Livett, Director of Housing.

The clerks of the larger county councils expected to be knighted. Knighthoods were not uncommon among the town clerks of the bigger county boroughs. Even the town clerk of a small county borough like Rotherham (Sir Charles des Forges) could be knighted if he were felt to be particularly meritorious. Indeed in my own career I held three chief executive jobs in local government (West Yorkshire County Council, Westminster City Council and the Association of Metropolitan Authorities) where every incumbent had been knighted until the time of my immediate predecessor. Compare the honours lists during Mrs Thatcher's reign: not one single local government officer in

England received a knighthood during that time (and only one in Scotland, Bob Calderwood, chief executive of Strathclyde). No current local government officer is a Knight or a Dame. The rare knighthoods now occasionally awarded to local government officers are bestowed for other services, like organising the Commonwealth Games.

4. 1956-62: Morley Town Hall and the Queen's Lavatory

The town clerks and clerks of non-county boroughs and urban districts were of a lower order: professional inferiors to the county borough town clerks and social inferiors to the great county clerks. When the Deputy Clerk of the West Riding County Council telephoned, the Town Clerk of Morley, Edward Finnigan, would stand up to show appropriate respect, even though his posture would be invisible to the caller. Finnigan was an alumnus of the county borough of Barnsley. Though Barnsley was hardly a great metropolis, he correctly identified the town clerkship of a non-county borough like Morley as a demotion. He would reminisce nostalgically about his great days in Barnsley.

Though beyond the pale of the great county and city councils, even small local authorities like Morley then enjoyed substantial powers and considerable independence. They issued their own bonds for capital funding – Morley bonds paid half a point more than Leeds bonds and a whole point more than West Riding bonds. The Morley Council offered its own mortgages for house purchase by local residents. During my time in Morley, the Town Hall interest rates on the mortgages rose to five per cent. At the time the rate was dismissed as extortionate – only to peak at 15 per cent a few years later. The council's major preoccupation was its slum clearance programme, instigated by Dr Alan Withnell, its Medical Officer of Health, who enjoyed a joint appointment with the West Riding County Council.

Compared with the hamstrung local authorities of today, the council's powers were virtually unfettered. While it could not parade the grandeur of cities like Leeds and Bradford, Morley enjoyed great municipal pride. The Morley Town Hall was an epitome of the pomp and wealth of the mill-owners who created the town and whose money had financed the municipality.

Their names were incised on the 1892 foundation stone at the entrance to the Town Hall: Asquith, Bradley, Schofield, Rhodes, Hepworth, Marshall, Glover, Jackson. Sixty years later, when I joined the Town Hall, their namesakes held patrician sway over the council; they were the grandchildren and great-grandchildren of the founders of the town.

Their influence on the council had been diluted by extensions of the borough boundaries. During the thirty years before I joined the Town Hall in 1955 Morley Council had swallowed the Urban Districts of Churwell and Gildersome, buffers between Morley and Leeds; Drighlington, on the edge of Bradford; and the mining communities of East and West Ardsley. West Ardsley bordered Dewsbury; and East Ardsley adjoined Wakefield. As a result the Borough of Morley occupied the space between the four county boroughs of Leeds, Bradford, Wakefield and Dewsbury. The rhubarb fields separating Morley from Leeds dwindled as the towns encroached. The Morley municipality lived in constant fear of annexation by the City of Leeds. Its frontiers were defended vigorously by the West Riding County Council, itself seeing its area constantly diminished by piecemeal absorption into the big cities of Leeds, Bradford, Sheffield and the other adjoining county boroughs.

Until the Second World War Morley Council was controlled

by Conservative councillors. Its motto was *Labor Omnia Vincit*. In the 1945 local election the motto became literal as the Labour party swept to power. Morley followed the national pattern by installing a Labour administration in the Town Hall. Power passed from the mill magnates to union officials, miners and teachers. But, following the national trend, by the time I joined the council in 1955 its control had reverted to the hereditary proprietors, the mill-owners.

In those days local industries were owned and run by people who lived and worked in the town. They had a commitment to their local community. Even in the great cities employers were locally based. Patronage was expected. At the end of the nineteenth century Sir Joseph Beecham, proprietor of Beecham's famous little liver pills, was Mayor of St Helens. In November 1899 the Hallé Orchestra was due to visit, under its eminent conductor Hans Richter. When told that Hans Richter was ill Sir Joseph had no compunction in demanding the substitution of his twenty-year-old son to replace the great conductor. Thus began the professional conducting career of Sir Thomas Beecham.

As Sir Joseph belonged to St Helens, Morley employers belonged to Morley and Morley belonged to them. As Sir Joseph ran the St Helens Council, so the local mill-owners ran the Morley Council. They were Morley through-and-through: born and educated there. Their grandfathers had built the mills. The grandsons were a part of the working community. They lived in the borough. They had attended the same primary schools as the weavers. Years later, when the mills had been taken over by international conglomerates (and before they closed for ever), an old weaver reminisced to me about the changes in the bosses he had known. Talking about the former mill-owner, said Bert, 'you could set your watch by 'im. Ivery morning 'e'd be at t'end of loom at ten to eight. 'How art thou, Bert?', 'e'd say. 'Nobbut middling', ah'd say. 'Gerron wi' it then', 'e'd say'. The mill-owners sold out to the conglomerates. 'Now', said Bert, 'we've got six bosses and tha doesn't see 'em from one Preston Guild till t'next. They're all off doing courses on 'uman relations.'

The old mill-owners ran the council hands-on, as they ran their mills. Morley was their town. Their grandparents had built the mills. Their money had built the Town Hall. Their descendants believed that they owned it. They regarded it with a great deal of pride, a symbol of the prosperity which their ancestors had created. They also perceived the council as serving their interests. When the Borough Surveyor condemned part of Bradley's mill as structurally unsafe, Cllr Humphrey Bradley instructed the Town Clerk to rescind the notice. It was withdrawn immediately.

The town received its ultimate accolade on 28 October 1954, the year before my arrival in the Town Hall: a royal visit from the young Queen Elizabeth II. In anticipation of the distinction, £1,200 had been spent on making the Town Hall ladies' lavatory fit for a Queen. Disaster! When the Queen came, she evinced no desire to visit the gilded latrine. The Mayor, Alderman Joseph Rhodes, tried his best. Taps were put on. The Queen was led past tinkling fountains. They were of no avail: she declined the opportunity. It was later learnt that she had visited the lavatory in Dewsbury, a great coup for the rival town.

An even more ignominious fate had been dealt to the Town Clerk of the great City of Leeds. When the Queen's Grandmother, Queen Mary, came to open Leeds Civic Hall in 1933, Her Majesty suffered a fly in the eye. Because the staff of the Leeds General Infirmary were watching the opening ceremony from the Hospital balcony, the efforts of the Town Clerk, Tom Thornton, to secure First Aid met with substantial delay. Like her grandmother-in-law, the Queen was not amused. The King, a short-tempered man, was vitriolic. As a result Tom Thornton never received the knighthood to which his office would normally have entitled him and which was conferred on his counterparts in the other cities which received a royal visit.

The Winding Stair

Never unduly royalist, the Morley Observer had panned the municipal profligacy of the expense of catering for the Queen's bladder. It duly gloated at her continence. The council needed a scapegoat to shoulder the blame for the abortive expenditure. As usual, an officer filled the bill – the Town Clerk, Edward Finnigan, castigated for failure to curb the expenditure. I once asked a senior councillor why he and his colleagues treated officers so badly. 'Well', he said, 'politics is like a game of football. And in a game of football – you have to have a football'.

In those days the Town Clerk of a local authority enjoyed no right to command other chief officers. He was regarded only as *primus inter pares*, the first among equals. Often a Town Clerk with commanding presence would function as a chief executive. Such was not the case in Morley. The Borough Treasurer, Stanley Ineson, did not have a high opinion of the Town Clerk; and strongly disputed the territory. Finnigan, the Town Clerk, would not demean himself by descending to the Treasurer's office. Nor would the latter obey a summons to the Town Clerk's office. As a result there was no communication between the council's two senior officials.

The polarisation of the two senior officers had become part of the political scene. The Town Clerk occupied some ascendancy among the town's Conservative councillors. Politicians assume that all share their commitment to politics and are committed to one party or another. To protest neutrality or indifference to them seems an insult, demeaning their own *raison d'être*. In Morley the councillors believed the Town Clerk to be a Conservative. This precipitated the Labour Party into the hands of the Treasurer, fortifying the two rival camps. Each would brief against the other.

Those believing Finnigan to be a Conservative had some justice: when he retired, he was elected as a West Riding County Councillor, representing the Conservative interest. His immortality is assured. On the walls beside the stairs to the lavatories in the Gamecock Inn at Austwick in North Yorkshire are displayed historic public notices from Morley Corporation. They forbid urination, spitting and the like. Each has the suffix 'Edward Finnigan, Town Clerk'.

Given his presumed political sympathies, the Town Clerk did not have an easy relationship with the controlling group when the Labour Party regained power in the council. But in those days it was unheard of to sack an officer. Instead the Town Clerk and Labour leadership lived with their hostilities. 'I should have put some cardboard down my trousers – just been caned', he once told me, figuratively rubbing his behind after a visit from the Labour leader. The latter was the formidable Alderman John Dews, a charismatic head teacher (and father of the BBC producer John Dews, famous for his *Age of Kings* series on BBC TV and winner of a Tony Award. As a trainee teacher he had briefly taught me at Wakefield Grammar School).

When Alderman Dews and his fellow councillors wished to interview the Town Clerk, they would knock peremptorily on the door to his private office and demand entry. That was not the official route. Outside the Town Clerk's personal office was the outer office, which contained the staff of the Town Clerk's Department. In the corridor outside that office was an external bell. When it tolled, my duty, like my pimply predecessor, was to lift the glass panel which hid the office from the external world and demand the errand of the bellringer. If the visitor wished to see the Town Clerk, the office boy – me – would submit that request to higher authority. Contemptuous of such hierarchy, the Labour councillors declined to subject themselves to my interrogation and stalked across the corridor to rap on the door of the Town Clerk's office.

This unfettered access disconcerted the Town Clerk. But his office window overlooked the bus stop outside the Town Hall. Alive to the bus timetable, he could spot the arrival of unwelcome visitors: in those days Labour councillors did not have cars. So it was that one day I was sticking stamps on envelopes, when out of his inner sanctum erupted the Town Clerk, clutching his overcoat. 'Come with me', he commanded. Reaching the end of the building, he furtively peered round the corner. Having seen that the coast was clear, we left the town hall by a postern gate and made for his car. 'Rodney', he said, 'I want to show you the council's housing estates. I think you should see them'. The Town Clerk drove me aimlessly round several estates. Then he entered a telephone box and phoned the town hall. 'The coast is clear', he said. Reassured by the phone call we returned to the Town Hall. His early warning system had successfully avoided a visit from the Labour leader, Alderman Dews.

In the general office, where the Town Clerk's staff worked, hung a bell. Its peal was activated by the Town Clerk. Silence descended when it clanged, work suspended. One ring would summon me; two the Chief Clerk, Mr Percy Lumb; three Miss Effie Sykes, his personal secretary (who enjoyed some prestige from being the mistress of the Borough Surveyor, Mr Donald Bradley); and so on. The usual reason for a summons to me was a request for the provision of a cup of tea, the making of which was an important part of my duties. I had the responsibility for concocting and distributing tea to all the staff in the office. Except for myself, all my colleagues took milk in their tea, I devised the labour-saving idea of adding milk directly to the teapot. I was severely reprimanded when the practice was detected. My protestations that the taste was exactly the same were rejected.

Disaster struck at the end of my first week. After tea-making, the most important part of my duties was to stamp envelopes and maintain the post book. I introduced new technology: a damp sponge to moisten postage stamps. Although the staff (including me) all worked on Saturday mornings, each Friday afternoon the balance of money and stamps was reconciled with the total postages inserted in the post book. The Chief Clerk's audit revealed that I was short by 2s.3½d. With relish, he summoned me to the Town Clerk to face disciplinary action. 'The money has to be made good', the Town Clerk insisted. My weekly wage was then less than £4. I was pledged to hand it over to my mother, who in return gave me five shillings as pocket-money. A loss of 2s.3½d was ruinous. Tears started to my eyes. The Town Clerk cleared his throat. Laboriously groping in his back trouser pocket, he excavated the appropriate coins and handed them to me. 'Once only do I provide the cash', he told me. 'From now onwards it is your responsibility'. The following week the post book showed a surplus of 3s.5d. From it the Town Clerk retrieved his 2s.3½d, the remaining 1s.1½d being confiscated. The following week showed a deficit which I had to make good.

It was very unusual for the post book to balance. However, every week several envelopes were addressed to the Ministry of Housing and Local Government. They were usually bulky and required more than the standard postage. No-one could check how many had actually been despatched or the cost of their stamps. So in future weeks I calculated any deficit and in the post book inserted a figure for postage to the Ministry of Housing and Local Government in the amount required to make up the deficit. Scrupulously honest, I always deducted any surpluses from previous weeks before inserting the spurious entries.

One of my main duties was to type copies or précis of documents. It is impossible for those brought up in the days of photocopying to appreciate the situation before photocopiers were invented. Rather than type out a copy of a multi-page circular giving necessary guidance to a chief officer, I developed the skill of writing a précis, a rare benefit from my bondage.

My serfdom as office boy was the low spot of my life. In the exciting environment of the *Morley Observer* I had enjoyed the stimulation of clever and committed people in a companionable atmosphere. There were no such people in the Morley Town Clerk's General Office. The office was mired in sloth and dreariness and ran without regard to innovation or efficiency. One of the clerks in the office had left the Gas Company in 1917, believing that the advent of electricity meant that there was no future in gas. Forty years later saw him still at the bottom of the local government ladder. Percy Lumb, the Chief Clerk, bullied the rest of the staff. Casual conversations between the staff (which might have created a spirit of joint-enterprise) were strictly forbidden. Almost every afternoon during pub closing time Alderman Malcolm Smith, a brewery representative and great friend of Percy Lumb, would turn up for tea. With giggles they would nibble 'chockie-wokkies', while the rest of the staff carried on with their work. The atmosphere was one of deep unpleasantness.

My unhappiness was deepened by the complete absence of friends. I lost contact with my schoolmates when I left Wakefield Grammar School. They looked forward to university: I was part of their past. Without friends I felt utterly isolated. Worse: I discovered that my assumption that industry and merit would procure advancement in local government was unfounded. Preferment depended on qualification as a solicitor, then absolutely necessary for a reasonable career in local government administration. The Act for the Better Regulation of Attorneys and Solicitors, enacted in 1729, was still in force. It required five years' service in articles before it was possible to practice as a solicitor. The Town Clerk, Mr Finnigan, demanded a premium of 350 guineas (£367.50) before he would give me articles. Such a sum was then more than the annual wage of a working man. Its procurement presented an impenetrable barrier. Despair set in.

My depression was occasionally cheered by a visit to my former colleagues at the offices of the *Morley Observer*, a delightfully anarchic contrast to the stifling atmosphere of the Town Hall. The scintillating staff of the newspaper had a decidedly iconoclastic bent. Since the local authority, under Conservative control, was a natural target, the local Conservative party was infuriated by the *Observer*'s jibes. The Town Hall reverberated with the spleen of the Conservative councillors.

But local newspapers were already in decline. The *Observer*'s profits were no longer able to sustain the lifestyle of its proprietor, Mr George Stead. However, he discovered an alternative source of funds. When he needed money (which was often), he would 'borrow' it from County Councillor Harry Hardy, the Conservative Morley manure magnate, in exchange for an IOU. The loans mounted up, but the councillor's generosity seemed boundless.

Councillor Hardy's agenda was not to finance Mr Stead's lifestyle. Disaster struck the *Observer* a year after my arrival in the Town Hall. Hardy's accountants announced that his loans to Mr Stead exceeded the value of the newspaper. Councillor Hardy now owned the *Morley Observer*. His first and only act as proprietor was to close it down. (Its title is now owned by a conglomerate.) No longer were the local Conservative councillors troubled by the incisive judgements of the local newspaper.

Shortly afterwards, a grateful country ennobled him as Sir Harry Hardy.

5. The Pig and I
Escape

At birth everyone is dealt a hand of cards. Now and then you have a chance to draw another card and it's the card which you draw which makes all the difference. Closure of the *Morley Observer* gave me the chance to draw that card. Suddenly a source of income opened up. Reporters on local newspapers provided the national and regional papers with much of their copy on regional issues. The papers paid for stories by 'lineage' – a payment of a fixed amount for every line of copy supplied and used. My continuing connection with the *Morley Observer* newsroom proved invaluable. When the paper closed down and my former colleagues left the town, they passed to me the agency for the national and regional papers. Thus I acquired a substantial additional income. The *Daily Express* actually paid an annual retainer of £50. While the income from local stories of national interest was unreliable, reporting sport, especially Morley rugby, provided steady and predictable earnings. It became possible to acquire the premium required to pay the Town Clerk for articles. Qualification as a solicitor became an option.

The wealthy Morley millowners took considerable pride in

their rugby team. As were the Olympics, in the 1950s and 1960s rugby union was professed to be an amateur sport. Payment was anathema. The millowners bypassed the restrictions. They sought out good players from the working class. To them, the millowners offered jobs in their mills, with suitably enhanced wages – provided that the players donned the Morley Rugby Union Club shirt. As a result, the Morley rugby team was then one of the leading clubs in the North of England. Its ground, improved by contributions from the millowners, had excellent facilities, so that county rugby matches were often played there.

In those days the West Riding had three evening papers. On a Saturday evening each published a special sports edition on coloured paper – in Leeds were the 'Yellow' (*Evening News*) and the 'Green' (*Evening Post*); and in Bradford the 'Pink' (*Telegraph & Argus*). I would phone through with a bulletin from the rugby match at half time. At the end of the game a quick phone call would give them the result, so that the paper could be on sale in the early evening. Visiting teams often had sports evening papers, which also required a bulletin at half time, followed by the result at the end of the game. The prose for the three Yorkshire papers had to be differentiated. An entirely different account was required by the papers from the area of the visiting teams. Naturally they expected the names of the visiting players to be featured, not those of the Morley players. By the time I had finished phoning through the half time reports the second half of the game would be well under way. I would ask friendly spectators to brief me on the scorers. My imagination supplied the missing details.

The evening papers had morning siblings, whose Monday editions called for longer and more reflective pieces. Their supply was simple: I had the whole of Sunday to write the copy. But between the Saturday evening sports editions and the Monday morning papers came the Sunday journals. Their demands varied from 50 words for the *Sunday Pictorial* (later renamed the *Sunday Mirror*) to 200 words for the *Sunday Times*. The deadline for the Sundays was 6pm on Saturday, not long after the end of the match.

The requirements could be substantial. In 75 minutes, I had to send the results and late scorers to the three West Yorkshire evening papers (and to any evening papers of the visiting team). Then I might have to write up to six stories for the Sundays. 200 elegant words for the *Sunday Times* were not too difficult. But creating 50 words for the *Sunday Pictorial* was always a challenge. In 50 words it might be barely possible even to list the names of the scorers. Rarely did I have time to write the copy: a few jotted notes enabled me to dictate the story at the required length to the copy-takers at the end of the line. The discipline gave me a continuing and uncanny ability to write or dictate to any given length.

When there was no home rugby game I was occasionally commissioned to report the Leeds United home game – and for a Yorkshire local paper, a Leeds United away game. While not particularly lucrative because of the travel costs, there were other benefits. In the press box at Manchester United's Old Trafford ground, I encountered for the first time champagne and smoked salmon, a luxury in the days before farmed salmon.

My time as a local correspondent coincided with the reign of Morley's most famous alumna and England's most successful sportswoman, the cyclist Beryl Burton. Five times world champion and thirteen times national champion, Beryl remained an amateur, and financed her cycling by working in the Morley rhubarb fields. One of her records still stands, over fifty years after she set it. At one stage Beryl's female record time was faster than the men's record: when she overtook the leading man she slipped him a liquorice allsort. Unfortunately her record-breaking rides all took place elsewhere so that, despite my efforts to devise an income-yielding story, I shared her inability to gain financially from them.

Beryl Burton did, however, gather posthumous fame: in June 2014 Leeds enjoyed the prestige of staging the start of the *Tour de France*. To chime with the event the Leeds Playhouse staged the play *Beryl* by Maxine Peake. A backcloth of 1960 grainy video showed Beryl Burton triumphing in the World Championship in Leipzig, then in East Germany. As the excited voice of the commentator screamed '*Jetzt kommen Beryl Burton, die Yorkshire Hausfrau...*' the exhilarated theatre audience, tears in their eyes, spontaneously rose to cheer her on. She is commemorated by the Beryl Burton gardens in Morley and the Beryl Burton Cycle Way between Harrogate and Knaresborough.

Though unable to profit financially from Beryl Burton's successes, I did gain an income in summer from cricket, though less lucrative than rugby in the winter. No Sunday papers demanded instant reports, but cricket reporting presented a different challenge. Morley was a straggling borough. It accommodated eleven cricket teams, playing variously in the Leeds League, the Bradford League and the Yorkshire Council. The three Yorkshire evening sports papers required the scores of each of the eleven teams in time for their Saturday evening edition. They paid 50d (about 20p) for each scorecard. Travel between the grounds required a journey of twenty miles. On hire-purchase, I acquired a motor bike so that I could cover the games.

On some of the grounds, the scoreboard was visible from outside the ground, so that I could jot down the score without dismounting. Starting my journey in Drighlington, the far north-west of the borough, the game would barely have begun before I had to leave on my rounds. In the middle of my journey was the cricket ground of J&S Rhodes, whose team played in the Leeds League. Their mill produced typical Morley donkey jackets from the mungoes and shoddies. The managing director was father to Helen Fielding, creator of Bridget Jones. When her father was batting the three-year old Helen was wont to wander onto the field at some personal hazard. When I reached the *ultima thule* of East Ardsley, I would press into a telephone box with the eleven scores, varying typically from 23 runs for 0 wickets in Drighlington to 234 all out in East Ardsley.

The sacrifice of my Saturday afternoons left me with a permanent aversion to spectator sport. I find it difficult to imagine why anyone would watch sport on a Saturday afternoon without being paid for it. But, crucially, sport provided me with a reliable source of income, boosted every so often with the 'lineage' for a news story, the fee paid per line. *Pools of blood* from a murder at the bottom of the road where we lived yielded a rich dividend. I was always attentive to the possibility of news stories – partly because of the immediate fee, but also because the newspapers which paid me might search for an alternative correspondent if I missed stories in my patch.

Promised a share of the money I earned from journalism, Town Clerk Finnigan agreed to take me as his articled clerk. While not reducing his demand for a premium of 350 guineas, he agreed to accept it at the rate of £73 10 shillings per year. There were two immediate obstacles: I had first to accumulate £73 10 shillings for the initial year's fee. Equally fundamentally, I had to acquire two A-levels, then an obligatory requirement for those undertaking the Law Society's solicitors' examinations. Moreover, though I had reached the required standard in typing, the Town Clerk refused to relax the requirement to attain the requisite standard in shorthand, despite its complete irrelevance to my duties. This required attendance at evening class, which limited my ability to take tuition for A-levels. Allowed only one half day a week off for study, I could attend half the relevant classes in French but for A-level German I was on my own. Somehow or other I managed to scrape the necessary passes, though I still wonder how I convinced the examiners of my comprehension of French symbolist poetry.

The interlude while I studied for the A-levels enabled me to accumulate the first year's premium. I became the articled pupil to the Town Clerk. My position and status changed from office boy to apprentice professional. It was no longer seemly for me to stick on the stamps and make the tea. Instead I was sent to work on electoral registration in an office across the road from the Town Hall. The Town Clerk was responsible to the Law Society for ensuring that his articled clerks were given suitable experience in the law. He had no hesitation in certifying that my training was appropriate. When I timidly enquired how electoral registration could constitute suitable legal training for my future life as a solicitor, the Town Clerk explained that the electoral register was compiled under the provisions of various statutes, all of which were undoubtedly laws and therefore relevant.

Bill Varley, the genial man responsible for electoral registration and for whom I now worked, enjoyed a comprehensive contempt for Town Clerk Finnigan. He also had a proper sense of his own importance. When Bill's office walls were due for repainting, he rejected the officially-selected colour and insisted on a shade of *eau-de-nil*. Despite three attempts at mixing the paints, the decorator was unable to match Bill's choice of shade on the colour chart. The painter's fourth attempt was remarkably successful. I asked him privately how such a close match had been achieved. 'Simple', he said. 'I painted the f***ing colour chart.'

Bill enjoyed a highly relaxed attitude to work. For three weeks during the compilation of the electoral register and during an election the two of us were extremely busy, working on occasions until midnight. But for the remaining weeks of the year there was little to do. The Town Hall had a table tennis table in the cellar, where my freedom to take two hours for lunch enabled me to develop a certain skill at the game. During the rest of the day Bill and I would play chess, poker or bridge, joined by the legal clerks upstairs. Scholarship was devoted to horse-racing and modest bets were made. A horse called Fernet Branca proved a reliable source of revenue when it ran at long odds. My duties included taking the bets to the bookie's runner, who would lurk on the street corner and disappear when a policeman came by: gambling outside the racecourse was then illegal. Twice a year the Town Clerk would cross the road from the Town Hall to visit us, his secretary prudently warning us in advance so that playing cards, chess sets and racing newspapers could be secreted.

During my time in Morley Town Hall the Cold War was at its height. The country aimed at preparedness for nuclear war. As well as electoral registration, Bill Varley was responsible for the council's contribution to civil defence. Different responsibilities were allocated to the different tiers of local authorities. At the bottom of the pile were the urban district councils and non-county boroughs like Morley. That responsibility included identifying local volunteers, including despatch riders who would carry messages by motor bicycle. In Morley the riders had been recruited and issued with bicycle clips so that they would be ready when the occasion demanded. One optimistic despatch rider, trousers bicycle-clipped at the ready, regularly visited the office, plaintively enquiring when his motor bike would arrive. The cold war ended long before his services were required – though not before 1980 when I was appointed county controller, responsible for organising Yorkshire's survival after the nuclear holocaust.

During the war a store of food had been accumulated for emergency feeding. Immured in the bowels of the Town Hall, it had long been forgotten by the authorities and was regarded as a perquisite of office by the Chief Clerk, the odious Percy Lumb. Despite its dubious provenance, he would complain bitterly when he discovered that the occasional tin was blown.

My income from journalism enjoyed a useful augmentation from canvassing for the electoral register – chasing electors who had failed to return their registration forms. Among others, my research uncovered the whereabouts of a charming old lady named Dracula Bland. Presumably her parents had stumbled on the name and bestowed it on their unfortunate daughter. Earnings also came from election fees, where I would act as poll clerk or (after a year or two) as presiding officer in local, county council and parliamentary elections. I also drew fees from ad hoc polls, including one eccentric survival. In the 1950s England was a very different country: consumerism had not taken root. Shopping hours corresponded to working hours: it was actively difficult for working people to shop. However, in those days relatively few married women had jobs. Sunday was still a day ostensibly reserved for religion. No shops were open save for off-licences. Their opening was allowed only for the sale of alcohol, without which the tedium of Sunday would have been unbearable.

Cinemas were also closed – but, as the permissive society made a cautious entrance, their opening could be triggered after endorsement in a poll following a people's petition. At one such ballot I was the Presiding Officer at a polling station in a Sunday School in East Ardsley, a township on the edge of the borough which did not have the benefit of a cinema. Unsurprisingly the issue did not attract great interest among the locals. During the fourteen hours during which the polling station was open only six voters troubled my four poll clerks and myself. Four of the five of us took it in turns to retire to the table tennis room.

On the floor above the Electoral Registration Office was the council's legal department, headed by Leonard Witchell. He was the former Clerk to one of the urban district councils compulsorily absorbed by Morley Borough Council. His subordinate status in Morley rankled and he made no attempt to conceal his scorn for Town Clerk Finnigan. Responsible to him were three legal clerks, Alec Clayton, Clifford Ward and Peter Saville, the three doing a job which could easily have been done by one industrious worker.

The Winding Stair

Alec was the only member of staff to own a motor car – a three wheeler Bond. Unable to wheeze from a standing start up the hill at the side of the Town Hall, Alec was obliged to start his journey home down the hill. Clifford Ward, the Land Charges Clerk, spluttered explosively to work on a tandem bike with an auxiliary motor. One old lady protested at the series of bangs which it emitted: 'The things some people do to call attention to themselves', she jeered.

A vastly different visiting vehicle was the Allard, a conspicuous two-seater sports car, most of whose dramatic size was expended on a bonnet of startling length. Its owner was Randal Herley, a BBC actor, famous for his participation in *The Goon Show* and *Coronation Street*. He was the elder brother of my senior articled clerk, Bill Herley, a handsome and charismatic cavalier and son of a Dewsbury doctor. Observing in the grocer's shop a sign reading *'Try our Penguin biscuits'*, Bill reached across and munched one, arguing to the irate shopkeeper that the notice constituted an invitation to sample the biscuit rather than to buy it. Sadly Bill's visits to the Town Hall became more and more infrequent and it became clear that he had no intention of tackling the Law Society examinations to which his articles entitled him. As Bill's desk in the legal department became unused, I was moved to occupy the vacancy.

Slum clearance was the council's major task at that time. For doctrinal reasons, the council proceeded not by compulsory purchase order but by clearance order. This removed the buildings but left ownership untouched. Since the houses were often in individual ownership, redevelopment was difficult. As a result the derelict sites survived until, decades later, the demand for housing in the Leeds metropolitan area justified the effort required to assemble ownerships and rebuild. When the mills closed Morley became a dormitory town.

The tragic death of Deanwood Pennine Ranger VIII

interrupted my monotonous diet of slum clearance orders. Deanwood Pennine Ranger was thrice a gold medal champion boar, whose prodigious fecundity had made him the beau of every sow in Calderdale. In Brontë country, high in the Pennines above Halifax, Morley Corporation's Withens Clough reservoir had been built by the council in 1891 to provide water for the growing town. Leading from the reservoir to Morley was a Victorian water main which required renewal. In reconstructing it, the contractors deviated slightly from the authorised route. The water main was near to the corner of a field owned by Deanwood Pennine Ranger's owner, pig farmer Jackson. In digging the trench for the new water main, the contractors demolished the wall bordering Jackson's land. Seizing the opportunity, Deanwood Pennine Ranger VIII bounded through the gap and made for Halifax and freedom, hotly pursued by Farmer Jackson.

Years of indulgence had unfitted Deanwood Pennine Ranger VIII for the chase and it was not long before Farmer Jackson caught up. Redirecting the boar towards his sty, the exasperated Jackson administered a vigorous thwack upon its rump. Startled, the disorientated animal took to flight and blundered straight into the pig farm's midden, where it plunged to a ghastly death.

Infuriated by the loss of his star performer, Farmer Jackson started legal proceedings against Morley Council. His claim for trespass was undeniable, as was the damage to the wall. Compensation was paid, the council indemnified by the contractors. But the main claim of Farmer Jackson was not for such trivia, but for the loss of his star boar, whose fertility had commanded substantial fees. The court upheld the Morley Corporation defence of *novus actus interveniens*: Farmer Jackson's thwack had broken the chain of causation between the original trespass and the death of the boar.

The farmer did not take his defeat lying down. After his

appeal from the judgment of the Court was dismissed, I received a telephone call from Inspector Smith of the Halifax Police. His enquiry was simple: 'We've just had a request for a licence to store explosives from a Mr Jackson. He wants it to blow up your water main on his land. Is that all right?' I explained that Halifax town centre might well be flooded if the application were granted.

Foiled by the consequent refusal, Jackson placed an advertisement with the *Halifax Courier*: 'Tenders solicited for the fracture and removal of Morley Corporation trunk water main where trespassing locally.' Prudently, like Inspector Smith, the *Courier* phoned to check before publication. I was called upon to chaperone the Chief Legal Clerk in his abortive attempts to placate the wronged pig farmer, my first visits to the bleak vastness of the South Pennines. In one of the sties I discovered a complete (though out-of-date) edition of Halsbury's Laws of England, bought by Farmer Jackson to provide a legal buttress to his arguments. The dispute was still in play when my articles ended and I was released from the shackles of Morley Town Hall.

Though it was difficult to identify any useful legal learning, life in the Legal Department was infinitely more agreeable than the Dickensian general office. It was enlivened by offbeat incidents. One of our female colleagues was embellished by a copious bosom. One day a little clerk, Maurice Hancock, felt threatened by the approach of these titanic mammary glands. Defensively he reached out to fend them off, prompting their owner to empty over Maurice the teapot which she was carrying (fortunately its contents were only cold tea dregs). 'I don't know what came over me', said the dazed Maurice. 'I were just transfixed by them.'

My income from journalism enabled me to pay the annual instalments of premium to my principal, though it was hard to see for what benefit, other than the formality of his certifying my attendance at the office. Mr Finnigan certainly felt no obligation to instruct me in the ways of the law, though, to be fair, it is unlikely that he retained any knowledge which might have been useful to me. A previous articled clerk, John Parsons, had threatened to sue for the return of his premium on the grounds that he had received no benefit from it.

Over the years, the Town Clerk had enjoyed an income from the premiums of several articled clerks. He always professed diffidence in accepting the money while counting out the cash. Only one of his several articled clerks had ever qualified as a solicitor – my cousin Arthur Hall. When Arthur rejoined Morley Town Hall after his distinguished service in the War he had used his service gratuity to pay the premium required by the Town Clerk. He told me of his nightmares about being trapped in the burning cockpit of his warplane. But, he said, his worst nightmare was always imagining himself back in the Town Clerk's Office in Morley.

I saw the Town Clerk only occasionally. On one rare occasion he sent for me. He had stumbled across a Court decision on the damage caused to adjoining properties by Lombardy poplars. He felt that I should type out three copies in order to further my legal education. Using two carbon papers and two fingers, I laboriously transcribed the judgment. It took a long time. I eventually sought an appointment with the Town Clerk and took him the transcript of the judgement with two carbon copies. He consulted his notes. 'Oh dear', he said. 'I actually need a top and *three* carbons…' I retreated and laboriously typed out a further copy, by which stage I knew the judgement by heart. I did not hurry. On my taking the further copy to the Town Clerk he again consulted his notes. 'Oh yes', he said. 'This last copy is for you'.

The Winding Stair

The Law

As well as remunerating the Town Clerk, the income from my journalism lubricated my private life. But my only human contacts remained my colleagues in the office and my parents. Feeling decidedly more cheerful, I decided that I had to do something about it. To articled clerks the Law Society circulated a bulletin which listed law students' societies. There was one in Wakefield. Groping for an avenue of escape I gathered my courage and applied to join. Though Morley was clearly outside the Wakefield catchment area, no-one objected.

Being the county town, Wakefield was full of firms of solicitors, In order to ensure a supply of articled clerks, they provided generous finance for the local Law Students' Society. The money was spent exclusively on food and copious supplies of alcohol until the local solicitors suggested that perhaps the Society's meetings should be preceded by an improving lecture.

In the Law Students' Society I had expected a body of people already bound together, but in fact many of the members were newly arrived from University. They included Michael Holdsworth and Martin White, both articled to the gigantic Clerk of the West Riding County Council, Sir Bernard Kenyon. They had come to Wakefield from Oxford and Cambridge Universities respectively. Both were destined to become lifelong friends and to have distinguished careers in local government.

Another member of the Wakefield Law Students' Society was Tony McVicar, son of the Deputy Clerk of the West Riding County Council. Together with a partner, I was invited to his 21st birthday party, by far the grandest event I had ever attended. I hired a dinner jacket and selected as my escort Jacqueline Carr, daughter of a friend of my mother. I collected her on my motor bike.

I had not anticipated that long dresses might present problems on a motor bike. Understandably, though to my

The Pig and I Escape

dismay, Jacqueline turned up wearing skin-tight gold lamé trousers. In those days female trousers were unusual, certainly on formal occasions. Every other girl at the ball wore a long dress. But Jacqueline's costume undoubtedly made her the most striking girl there. She was immediately surrounded by amorous swains and had no shortage of dancing partners. But I had other fish to fry: among the guests was Tony McVicar's father's boss, the ferocious Sir Bernard Kenyon. His presence seemed to me an opportunity to advance my career in local government. I engaged him in conversation, hoping that Sir Bernard would immediately grasp my intrinsic merit and promote my career. Such was not the case. It was clear that Sir Bernard was not captivated by my prepared aperçus. His eyes wandered around the room as I spoke, until they settled on Jacqueline's golden pants. 'Good God!' he ejaculated. 'Who brought *that*?'

Among the members of the Law Students' Society was another future lifelong friend, a natural eccentric, John Turner. He told me that he had read Old Norse at Cambridge. When I suggested that Old Norse might not be a very useful discipline, he assured me that only the previous week he had met an old Norseman by the Hardangerfjord when the language had proved invaluable. Uniquely among the articled clerks, John Turner owned motorised transport – a small Ford, presented to him on his 21st birthday by his wealthy parents. In it we adventured to the Yorkshire Dales, a landscape startlingly different to the grimy Heavy Woollen District in which my life had been largely confined. I was enchanted by this first encounter with the beauty of the Dales, later to form such an important part of my life.

John and I decided to extend our adventure in the Dales by climbing Ingleborough, one of Yorkshire's Three Peaks. In his autobiography Roy Hattersley chronicled his own unsuccessful attempt to reach the summit. Our own effort was equally unsuccessful: barely half way up we abandoned the ascent,

57

gasping for breath as we collapsed on the heather. The difficulty of the climb was an unexpected humiliation: I had no understanding that physical fitness would be required to reach the summit. My youthful self would have found it difficult to credit that later in life and for fifty consecutive years I would tackle Yorkshire's Three Peaks, ascending Ingleborough after first climbing Pen-y-Ghent and Whernside.

Weekend excursions with John were rare: qualification as a solicitor required me to pass examinations. For those without a degree, articled clerks were required to go to a Law School. A cheaper alternative was to attend a so-called 'statutory year' at a local University, in my case Leeds University. In those days there were no student fees. The 'statutory year' was simply the first year of the Law Degree course. The examination required was the normal first-year examination. Lectures occupied only two half-days per week, the remainder of my time being back in the Morley office. Despite being a part-time student only because of my Town Hall work (and my continued requirement to obtain qualifications in shorthand and typing), at the end of the year I received a gratifyingly high mark, attracting pressure from the University to stay on for the full degree – of course financially impossible for me.

After the statutory year at the University, the articled clerk without a degree was required to pass the Law Society's Intermediate Examination. Those tackling it normally attended a residential course either at the Law Society's own Law School in London or Gibson & Weldon's Law School in Guildford (the two merged in 1962 and are now the University of Law). The fees and boarding costs were, of course, beyond my financial reach. In those days local authorities had responsibility for financing students undertaking higher education. Working class boys like Alan Bennett and Richard Hoggart chronicled the paternal support they received from the Leeds Council and its Director of Education. Hoping for similar support, I applied to the West Riding County Council for a grant to enable me to attend the Law School.

Sir Bernard Kenyon himself attended the Education Grants Committee and bullied the committee into refusing my application. As a result I had to negotiate the Law Society's examinations without tuition. Officers of the Education Department clearly disliked Sir Bernard's intervention in their territory. They telephoned me to offer to fund a correspondence course and the purchase of books. The latter offered an unexpected and unorthodox source of income: they could be sold at half the list price to the Law Library of the Law School. There was thus a financial incentive to buy as many law books as possible – the risk being that the book might go to a new edition, when the old edition became unsaleable. I still retain one or two of the books which were marooned in my custody after their replacements had arrived on the scene.

Since I lacked a place to study at home, I took to going after work to the reference library in Leeds and worked there. In the library I met a similar coterie of law students. All save me had been to law school. They had failed the Law Society examination but hoped to succeed at a further attempt. A *camaraderie* developed which led to longer and longer coffee breaks.

Fortunately the Law Society's intermediate examination arrived before these siren voices completely seduced me. The examination was held in Bloomsbury. I had never previously been to London and set off nervously, the trip financed by the enlightened county council. Their generous overnight expense allowance allowed me to stay in the Bonnington Hotel, near the Bloomsbury examination hall. This was by far the most luxurious establishment I had ever visited. Intimidated by atmosphere and waiters, at dinner on the eve of the examination I ordered sweetbreads, believing these to be a rare Southern delicacy. It was several years before I discovered that I had eaten a cow's pancreas.

The Winding Stair

The intermediate examination successfully negotiated, after six months I faced the next hurdle set by the Law Society – a rather curious examination – in trust accounts and bookkeeping. On receiving the examination paper, the first task was to rule blank pages in simulation of an accounts register. I managed to learn enough by rote to enable me to pass the examination, though it is fair to say that I never had more than the dimmest understanding of its requirements. Of course, nothing in the exam ever had the slightest relevance to my professional career.

The trips to London were most agreeable and brought me into contact with fellow law students. It was not uncommon for unsuccessful students to take the Law Society's examinations on repeated occasions. As I progressed through the succession of examinations, I met again those who were still marooned in the earlier stages. The same faces re-appeared without necessarily making progress. After one examination, I met a familiar face. 'How did you get on?' I asked. 'I failed', he replied. 'Oh, hope for the best', I encouraged. 'No', he said, 'I failed'. I persisted. 'How can you be so sure?' 'Because I didn't turn up', he said. 'I went down to Soho and had a look round there instead'. [He did eventually succeed – after six attempts.] Taking in hand another part of my education, he took me down to Soho, where he and other comrades bantered with the ladies of the night. I doubt whether any were bold enough to enjoy their favours.

A devastating blow came at the end of 1961, with just three months to go before my final examinations. A member of the National Union of Journalists arrived in Morley and wanted to take over my lineage business. At that time journalism was a closed shop. With a Union member prepared to take on the job, I was automatically blacked by the NUJ. My source of income dried up overnight. I had no option but to pass the final examination at the first attempt. Failure would be fatal: the county council funded only one attempt at the examination. I had no source of funding to allow a second attempt.

Grimly determined, I prepared for the solicitors' final examination in London. The examination lasted for four days. In the following week it was succeeded by an honours examination, for those who wished to add this distinction to their qualification. I had no ambition to attain honours, but I did like the idea of a few more days in London at the expense of the county council. I told my principal, Mr Finnigan, of my intention to stay for a further week in London to take honours and that the county council would foot the bill. He told me that his son John had failed the final examination twice. To consider taking honours was ostentatious hubris. He clearly felt that such an aspiration was an aspersion on his son. I persisted in my intention.

Incensed by my obduracy, the Town Clerk contacted the county council to urge them to withdraw funding for my honours attempt. It was, he asserted, a conceit on my part. I had the clear impression that the staff of the county council education department took a proprietory interest in my future, frustrated by the intervention of Sir Bernard in their territory. In their book I was a very unusual bird. They told me with some satisfaction that they sent the Town Clerk away with a flea in his ear. Foiled in that attempt, Mr Finnigan visited my parents, sending a shiver of fear down their spines as he warned of my folly in diverting myself with an honours examination when I should be concentrating my mind on passing the basic examination – so challenging in itself that his own son had failed it twice. He talked of the abuse of public funds, by my taking the county council's money in what was obviously a hopeless quest. He reminded them of his kindness in agreeing to accept my premium in five yearly instalments rather than insisting on payment of the whole 350 guineas at the inception of my articles.

I was determined to enjoy an extra few days in London. I ignored the Town Clerk and carried on. After a gruelling four days of the Final Examination and a relaxing weekend, the

The Winding Stair

Honours paper seemed surprisingly straightforward. It included an optional paper on local government. Top marks here brought the local government prize. In the examination room I identified remarkably few articled clerks from local government. I doubted that I would gain Honours but thought I might win the local government prize. When the results came out I was surprised to find that out of a thousand candidates I was one of the eleven to obtain honours. [The ratio of one per cent success in honours has, I see, now increased to 10 per cent.] I was almost equally surprised to find that I had not won the local government prize, given what looked like the paucity of competition in the examination hall. I had not realised that the prize was awarded annually: those who had taken the paper earlier in the year were also considered for the prize. The winner was my Yorkshire friend Michael Holdsworth, who had taken the examination in February.

After the final examination there was a gap before the results were published. John Turner's Ford car gave me the first opportunity for overseas travel. With John and Martin White I made my first adventure abroad, with Greece our destination. We encountered a baffling cultural phenomenon in Salzburg, where we stayed in the Höllbräu Hotel in the Judengasse. Shown to our sleeping apartments, we found that the beds were not made up: only an eiderdown reclined on the mattress, without either sheet or blankets. As we left for a tour of the city we drew the attention of the management to the oversight. Annoyingly we found the beds in the same condition on our return. To our scepticism the management explained that that was how they were supposed to be, introducing us for the first time to the *duvet*.

We left Austria and crossed Tito's Yugoslavia. At the Greek frontier the officials refused us entry: as we departed from Austria we had noticed that our passport details were carefully recorded. At that time a junta of colonels had taken over the

Greek government and we were suspected of going to Greece to foment disorder. We had planned to return on the ferry from Patras to Brindisi, so had only one-way visas through Yugoslavia. As a result we found ourselves marooned in no man's land between the two frontiers and without the necessary visa. Since, *ex hypothesi*, we were anti-Fascists, Tito's Yugoslav police were sympathetic and allowed us to go to Skopje, where we could obtain new entry visas. When we arrived at Skopje we found that on the day before our arrival the town had been destroyed by a major earthquake which had killed over 1,000 people. We carried on travelling and eventually found a police post which granted formal permission for our re-entry. On return to Britain I procured a certificate signed by D J Nicolareisis, the Greek Ambassador, which read that '*Mr Rodney Brooke is by profession a solicitor, acting also as prosecutor on behalf of the British Police* (as I was by that time) *and is hereby recommended to the Greek Immigration Authorities and the Greek Police as a respectable person*' – an essential *laissez-passer* for the return to Greece which we planned for the following year.

Back in Yorkshire, my articles expired: the day came when I was to leave Morley forever. By a remarkable coincidence, this was the day when the Town Hall caught fire. Dramatic flames shot through the roof. As I admired the conflagration I suddenly remembered that my motor bike was in the Town Hall's central courtyard. I sped through the smoke and rescued it in the nick of time. Queen Street, the main road in front of the Town Hall, remained open as the fire fighters tackled the blaze. Below the flames, the number 52 double decker buses continued their sedate journey onwards to Leeds – until one of the giant granite globes which adorned the Town Hall parapet crashed down within yards of one of the buses. The bus showed a startling turn of speed as it zoomed down the hill to Leeds. The road was hurriedly closed. My last view of the Town Hall was gratifyingly apocalyptic. Surprisingly the conflagration was not blamed on me. Culpability was fixed on sparks which had spread from a blaze in the nearby Albert Mills.

The Town Hall was once the place where the millowners and the miners came together to run the town. Much though I hated my time there, I have a wistful feeling when I see the Town Hall reincarnated as a Leeds City Council Area Office, ending the proud traditions of the independent municipality. Though the roots of their democracy have withered, something of the old spirit lives on. Leeds City Council's members include the usual quotas of Conservative, Labour and Liberal Democrat councillors – plus five Morley Independents.

6. 1962-63: Rochdale, Sir Cyril Smith and Shrimps in the Water

It was 1962. Though unknown to me, the Beatles began their ascent to fame. Debts forced Accrington Stanley to resign from the Football League. A London smog caused many deaths. The first female judge was appointed. The USA began the Cuban embargo. Kim Philby defected to the USSR. The Christine Keeler scandal hastened the resignation of Prime Minister Macmillan.

Other than sympathy for Accrington Stanley, I took little notice of these events. Together with my friends Michael Holdsworth and Martin White I had to embark on the first serious stage of my local government career. In future I had to compete with them – Oxford and Cambridge graduates with the pedigree of the West Riding County Council behind them. Michael's wife Merle expressed sympathy at my lack of prospects: 'What a pity', she said, 'that Rodney can't get the top jobs because he hasn't a degree'.

The Law Society sent me a pamphlet entitled 'Practical points for solicitors entering the local government service', by Sir Howard Roberts, Clerk of the London County Council. He agreed with Merle: 'The man who has the university degree undoubtedly has the pull', he wrote. Despite this disadvantage,

The Winding Stair

I had to shake the dust of Morley off my feet and consider my future. Following the Town Clerk's dictum that County Boroughs were the real powerhouse, I applied for the Junior Assistant Solicitor's job in Rochdale. At that time local authorities had great difficulty in recruiting solicitors: pay in local government was substantially below what they would receive in private practice. I was invited for interview.

Sir Howard Roberts had strong views on preparations for the interview by the local authority committee: 'Some men appear before the committee without the slightest regard to the respect due to them as prospective employers. It is important that a man should dress as if he really respected the position of those before whom he is appearing and, equally, as if he expected them to respect him. A black coat, striped trousers and dark tie are most appropriate or, failing them, a dark suit.' The Morley outfitters disclaimed all knowledge of black coat and striped trousers, so I had to content myself with a dark suit.

On arrival in Rochdale I found only one competitor, a charming fellow from Wales. He hastened to assure me that as far as he was concerned, the job was mine. He had no wish whatsoever to take the job. 'I only come for the expenses', he said. 'What I do, you see', he said, 'is I put in for lots of these jobs. They pay first class train fare and I go on my motor scooter. I get a good profit from the expenses. And I see a lot of the country'. He succeeded in persuading the interview panel not to appoint him. The Town Clerk came out to offer the post to me. Having done this, he turned to the Welsh candidate and offered a taxi to take him to the station. I sympathised with the latter's embarrassment as he declined the offer.

My salary as a solicitor in Rochdale was £1,140, almost £100 per month before tax. My wealth seemed enormous, though my mother expected to receive a substantial part of my wages. Buttressed by such riches, I set about arranging my life in Rochdale. Coincidentally, Allan Withnell, the Medical Officer of

Health for Morley, a West Riding County Council employee, originated in Milnrow, then an Urban District bordering Rochdale. The next door neighbours of Dr Withnell's mother, Walter and Irene Bailey, were happy to accept me as a lodger at a weekly rent of £5, including my meals. Even after paying them £5 I still felt that I had joined the affluent society. Walter Bailey was a gentle giant. A retired lorry driver he had once played in the Rugby League for Rochdale Hornets. Like most of her generation, his wife Irene had not worked since their marriage. They had no children and treated me like an adopted son. It would be impossible to find two more kindly, good-hearted and generous people.

Dr Withnell's mother and the Baileys lived on a council estate. In those days one in three people lived in council houses (the figure is now one in ten). Intermixed in the council estate was a generous selection of the lower middle classes, who played a major part in organising the community: communal social occasions abounded. A sprinkling of cars dotted the estate roads. The occasional unkempt garden was the subject of popular obloquy and appropriate pressure from neighbours, who would tend the gardens of those too decrepit to attend to them.

The great program of social housing began after the First World War with 'homes for heroes'. The housing programme had been enthusiastically pursued by Conservative Governments. Harold Macmillan, then Housing Minister, made his name when he engineered the annual building of 300,000 council houses. Margaret Thatcher's Right to Buy scheme ended all this. The sale of council houses to their occupiers had a predictable result. The better estates were sold to their occupiers. The housing estates remaining in council ownership often became sinks of poverty and neglect. The financial consequence was to divert nearly £10bn annually to private landlords. Half the council housing sold to occupiers is now owned by private landlords. Instead of creating a property-owning democracy, council estate sales have created insecurity.

But in 1962 council housing estates were pleasant places to live. I was to board weekly with the Baileys, returning to Yorkshire at weekends. Three possible roads snaked over the South Pennines from Yorkshire to Rochdale. It was an arduous journey before the construction of the M62. Even outside winter there were difficulties. There were frequent pea-soup fogs in the years before the Clean Air Act 1956 eventually cleared the atmosphere. From time to time I had to dismount from my motor bike and scout on foot to identify the correct road forward.

In winter, crossing the Pennines was treacherous and could be unmanageable. The shortest feasible route was the A640, popularly known as Nont Sarah's after a remote Scammonden pub (now a party venue with hot tub, sauna and pole dancing). In winter the Nont Sarah's road was often closed because of snow. Thomas Telford's Snake Pass by Ladybower Reservoir was equally unreliable. The old turnpike road over Blackstone Edge offered a more straightforward alternative, but was also prone to closure in winter.

The trans-Pennine journey presented me with a major challenge: 1962-63 brought the coldest winter since 1814. Icebergs entered the Mersey at Liverpool. The coal shortage required power cuts of up to nine hours, which heightened the national misery. To save power the Government introduced a three-day working week. The snow was nine inches deep in the centre of Manchester. In January snowdrifts piled up and reached to the window of my Rochdale bedroom: I could walk out of the bedroom window and sink in the snow. In February more snow came, with gale force winds. A 36-hour blizzard created 20-feet drifts. A 200 feet snow overhang on the Snake Pass was detonated by gelignite. Each morning the radio news advised which (if any) trans-Pennine roads were open. It was often necessary to divert along the valleys through Holmfirth, where later the television series *Last of the Summer Wine* was filmed. Even that route was often hazardous in the snow. The thaw did not arrive until early March 1963.

In such conditions, my motor bike was not the ideal transport. Somehow both it and I survived the winter, but nemesis came in the Spring, when it skidded on a surviving patch of ice. A Milnrow Urban District Council dustcart scooped up the motor bike and me and deposited us at the local hospital. Both the motor bike and I were repaired, but the motor bike never smelled the same again.

I replaced the motorbike with a second-hand car, a box-like Ford Anglia. This had three gears only. The Pennine gradients were too much for second gear but not steep enough for first, so the journey was spent changing the gears up and down. The lack of synchromesh on first gear required mastery of the art of double de-clutching. With foot flat down on the accelerator, as it usually was when going uphill, the vacuum-operated windscreen wipers stopped. In rain the accelerator had to be released to maintain visibility, forcing a downwards gear change. But at least I was dry and frost-free on arrival at Rochdale Town Hall.

To Rochdalians of 1962, Manchester seemed almost as remote as London. But by comparison with Morley, Rochdale seemed metropolitan. The town was famous as the home of Gracie Fields and was the natural centre of its sub-region. The Rochdale Pioneers had formed the country's first Co-operative movement. Their first shop, in Toad Lane, is now a museum. Prominent among the Rochdale shops and restaurants were the outlets of the United Cattle Products company, abbreviated to UCP, whose windows were crammed with tripes, cow heel and other bovine extremities. Neighbouring Bury was famous for its black puddings. Its market boasted a stall with the banner 'The only skinful you can get for 4d' (four pence).

The Winding Stair

In the centre of Rochdale, the Esplanade outside the Town Hall maintained a claim to be the widest bridge in the world. It replaced seven former bridges which spanned the River Roch, a tributary of the River Irwell and Rochdale's eponymous river. The claim depended on which way you used the road. The sceptics argued that the river simply entered a culvert. Waterhouse's Gothic Revival Town Hall was on the edge of the underground river. Its tower was attached to the Town Hall proper by a bridge, under which the traffic could pass. My draughty office was on top of the bridge.

Work in the Rochdale Town Hall was completely different to anything I had encountered in Morley. I had elevated myself in the local government hierarchy – from the relative insignificance of Morley, where the main services were provided by the West Riding County Council, to work in a county borough, independently exercising all local government powers. My Morley legal experience was almost completely irrelevant. I was acutely aware that I had secured the Rochdale job only because of the absence of competition. I felt like an impostor whose bluff might be called at any moment.

Rochdale was one of the smaller county boroughs, with a population of only 80,000 – tiny compared with behemoths like Leeds and Birmingham – let alone the great county councils like the West Riding, with its population of two million. Though responsibility for national assistance had been removed from local government in the 1930s and hospitals in 1948, much remained. For only one local government service did Rochdale Council depend on outside help: sewage was channelled to Manchester for disposal. The council provided almost every other local service: it had its own water undertaking, police force, fire brigade, further education college and transport – all services now removed from local government. And, of course, it was responsible for services which still remain (if only partly) in local government – schools, highways, refuse collection and disposal, public health, housing, recreation and social services. It had a substantial programme to clear the slums by compulsory purchase. In the 1960s, like other urban authorities, slum clearance and house building were major preoccupations in Rochdale. Condemning unfit housing was a duty of the Medical Officer of Health, Dr Moir, a pawky Scot with an impenetrable Scots accent. The Lancastrian councillors usually failed to gather the import of his utterances and felt constrained to agree to whatever it was that he had proposed. After the meeting the committee clerk would ask the Doctor's secretary for a translation of his enigmatic pronouncements so that the minutes could be drafted accordingly.

On arrival in the office I was allocated a young and smartly dressed female secretary. These were the days before personal computers and dictating machines. Notebook in hand, the secretary sat next to my desk waiting for my dictation. Intimidated by her presence and fearing to dry up, my letters were always twice as long as they should have been. I completely failed to realise that the arrival of a young single male solicitor was a talking point in the typing room. The girls clearly liked teasing a naïve young man. So, on 1st April 1963, I responded to a telephone message from a Mr C Lion. The Belle Vue Zoo had anticipated the call and met my request with a recorded message.

My boss and the head of the Town Hall Legal Department was the Senior Assistant Solicitor, Gordon Campbell, a dashing lawyer in his early 30s. To me he seemed the last word in urbanity. Moreover, he had a local government pedigree: his uncle was Sir Colin Campbell, sometime Town Clerk of Plymouth, who is still commemorated by having a square and car park named after him. Shortly after my arrival, Gordon invited me to dinner. His wife, Elizabeth, a teacher of German, tried hard to overcome my painful shyness. After dinner she played German records, introducing me to *Muss I Denn*, the charming German folk tune mutilated by Elvis Presley. This was for me a deeply memorable occasion: other than the family Christmas teas, it was the first time I had eaten a meal in someone else's home. The conversation and the German music gave me a glimpse of a cosmopolitan world which extended far beyond that which I knew. Sixty years later, when I hear *Muss I Denn*, I am taken back sixty years to a modest semi-detached house in Rochdale.

Gordon Campbell was a commanding presence in the office. He would surely have risen to the top in local government – but sadly was diagnosed with cancer in his early thirties and died within a year. The other solicitor in the department was Bob Hinton, a Methodist local preacher and later Town Clerk of Hove. The articled clerk, Peter Welsh, was a charming and garrulous Irishman, subsequently to become Town Clerk of Windsor. Our immediate superior was Deputy Town Clerk, George Shaw, a sound if unexciting lawyer, later clerk of the Mersey Docks and Harbour Board, then still in public ownership. The Town Clerk, Kenneth Moore, was a gentle Quaker. He inspired in me great admiration, affection and loyalty. As Town Clerk, he held the post of emergency controller. If nuclear war broke out, he was charged with migrating to an underground bunker in order to re-establish government after the holocaust. He seemed to have no difficulty in reconciling his pacifist views with that role, probably because of the implausibility of the whole plan.

I found that I had no experience whatsoever of the legal tasks entrusted to me. Even my experience in the conveyancing of land was mostly irrelevant: Rochdale property was largely leasehold, with which I was completely unfamiliar. My senior solicitor colleagues would certainly have helped me in my lack of knowledge – but I dare not confess my ignorance, lest my imposture be discovered. Determined to conceal my ignorance by hard work, I took nothing for granted but researched everything. Slogging away at a lengthy abstract of the title to slum property which the council was to acquire, I discovered a fatal flaw. I raised a requisition on the title. The vendor's solicitor phoned me. 'New to Rochdale, are you, lad?' he said. I said that I was. 'I see you've discovered the flaw in the title', he said. Gratified by his perception of my perspicacity I admitted that I had. 'Well', said my interlocutor, 'what are you going to do about it?' This was a question which I had not considered. He persisted: 'We can't put it right now, can we? Does the council want the land or not?' he enquired, before taking pity on my bewilderment: 'Of course', he said, 'we all know about the title problem. We just ignore it. If we didn't there'd be no selling property in the town at all.' I carried on with the purchase.

One of the council solicitors was expected to be present at and advise the council committees. The town clerk, of course, would attend the Policy Committee. His deputy, George Shaw, would take the big-spending committees, Water and Transport. As the junior assistant solicitor, I was given the Entertainments Committee, perceived as least important. Its remit was, in fact quite wide. It ran not only the parks in Rochdale, but also the extensive Hollingworth Lake in the neighbouring district of Littleborough. The Lake had been created in the nineteenth century as the source of water for the Rochdale Canal. Here the council leased out pleasure boats in the summer. Every year the councillors on the Entertainments Committee made a pilgrimage to the Boat Show in London, where they posed as buyers, toured the booths and sampled the whisky offered by the vendors. Every fifth year or so they did actually buy a small boat.

The council made a modest annual contribution to the Hallé Orchestra. In reciprocation the Hallé would once a year give a concert in Rochdale's Champness Hall. In default of any other officer, I was responsible for liaison with the Orchestra and the choice of the programme. The Hallé would send me a series of musical menus, typically requiring me to combine an overture with a concerto and a symphony. After some brooding, I presented to the Entertainments Committee a programme which included Sibelius's Fifth Symphony. My recommendation did not go down well: 'Nay lad', the Committee expostulated: 'Tha'll never fill Champness Hall with Sigh-beelious. Only thing that fills Champness Hall is Gilbert and Sullivan'. The work of the great Finnish Master was discarded. A Gilbert and Sullivan selection had to satisfy the musical cravings of cultured Rochdalians.

Just as the Entertainment Committee attracted the attention of only the lowliest solicitor, so its members were the least important on the council. Although the council was Labour-controlled, in the bipartisan spirit of the day the Chair of the Entertainments Committee was given to a Conservative. The council's leading members were impressive. Labour chairman of the Finance Committee was the 27-year-old Michael English, later MP and chairman of Select Committees in the House of Commons. Towering above other councillors, literally and figuratively, was the giant figure of Cyril Smith who, at his peak, weighed over 30 stones. He was Mr Rochdale. He came from the most humble background, describing himself as 'illegitimate, deprived and poor'. He dominated the town as he flitted between the Labour and Liberal parties: the Rochdale electors voted for him, whichever party he belonged to. During my time in Rochdale time he had left the Liberal party (which he later rejoined and became the Party's Chief Whip in the House of Commons) and occupied the Labour benches. I would attend the Council meeting for the pleasure of hearing Cyril's speeches. Commanding the council, he spoke in sentences of elaborate construction: just when it seemed that he had irretrievably lost the thread, he would wend his way through a thicket of subordinate clauses to a grammatically correct peroration.

Cyril Smith's titanic bulk matched his forceful personality.

Rochdale, Sir Cyril Smith and Shrimps in the Water

The Committees which conducted the council business started at 6pm. Before the meeting it was the Rochdale custom to enjoy what was euphemistically called a 'committee tea'. This was, in fact, a full-blown dinner. The amplitude of the provision did not prevent Cyril from sending out for sandwiches in the middle of the Committee. Despite his vast size, he was a remarkably good table-tennis player.

Until 1974 councils like Rochdale included Aldermen – senior councillors who were elected to the aldermanic bench by their fellow councillors. They held office for six years and during that time did not have to face the electorate. Embarrassingly, Rochdale Council had one black sheep. Previously a teetotal councillor of eminent respectability, he was made an alderman. He was then advised that total abstinence was not good for his health and that he should take a drop of rum for medicinal purposes. Unfortunately he took to it like a duck to water. On the first occasion when he was before the court for being drunk and incapable, the *Rochdale Observer* made it a front-page story. As it became a weekly occurrence, the headline 'Alderman found drunk in gutter again' barely merited a paragraph on one of the middle pages. But he could not be removed from the council until his six-year term expired.

A key function of the council was the supply of water. As one of the more important committees, the Water Committee was attended by the Deputy Town Clerk, George Shaw. The more routine work was devolved to me. As a result I accompanied the Water Committee on its annual pilgrimage to the council's reservoirs. After an appropriately lubricated lunch, Committee members demonstrated their faith in the filtration plant by urinating in the reservoir.

The filtration plant was not always successful. It was responsible for teaching me a lesson which stood me in good stead in later life. The town's water supply became infested with small crustaceans, minute shrimp-like creatures which for some time defied attempts to eradicate them. The story reached the *Daily Express*. Its Manchester reporter took me out for a pub lunch. I diligently explained the steps taken by the council to address the problem. We established a most friendly relationship. Flattered by his attention and after two pints, I ventured a joke, saying 'I don't know why they are complaining. Why don't they put a lettuce leaf under the tap and make a prawn cocktail?' It seemed witty at the time, but did not look good in the columns of the *Daily Express* next morning. My local government career nearly came to a premature end. But at least it taught me a simple lesson which even Cabinet Secretaries have sometimes forgotten: if you don't want something to appear in the newspaper, don't say it.

Education, transport and water bulked large in the activities of the office, together with the slum clearance programme. There were prosecutions for the Rochdale Police and a mixed bag of local authority prosecutions. Breaches of the Clean Air Act were common. The test of contravention was the Ringelmann smoke chart, which measured the blackness of the emission. One day I answered the office telephone. On the line was a resident complaining of a smoke emission. I could see it from the office window. Taking out my Ringelmann chart, I confirmed that it was in breach of the law. 'Do you know where that smoke is coming from?' asked the complainant. 'No', I said, 'but, rest assured that action will follow whomsoever that person might be'. 'I'll tell you where it's coming from' was the response. 'It's coming from thy council's refuse incinerator'.

One regular piece of advocacy was to secure increases in bus fares. They required the approval of the Traffic Commissioners – as did any change in the route of the buses. A clutch of shops in Rochdale were halfway up a steep hill. Yet the buses stopped not by the shops in the middle of the hill, but at the top and the bottom. I delved into the history: research showed that the bus stops were unchanged from the days of horse-drawn buses.

With the advantage of continual motion, the horses could haul the bus up the incline. But they could not shift the bus from a standing start in the middle of the hill. The stops had to be at top and bottom and remained there even after the introduction of motor buses in 1926. I negotiated the re-siting of the bus stops.

Criminals and the Court

Advocacy in the informal atmosphere of the Traffic Commissioners was one thing, but speaking in court was more challenging. I had never previously entered a Magistrates' Court. On my first appearance a silence descended on the court. I looked round nervously to see what would happen next. Nothing happened. The Magistrates' Clerk, Jim Hullah, looked up at me and irritably exclaimed 'Right, Mr Brooke', giving me the necessary cue. But within a few weeks of arrival in Rochdale I had become accustomed to standing up in court and the initial terror of being on my feet had disappeared.

Court appearances covered a wide range of topics. From time to time we accessed the Court to 'section' someone under the Mental Health Act, ie require someone to be admitted to hospital against their wishes. On one occasion I applied to section a grossly obese woman who had been stuck on the lavatory for a fortnight. The toilet seat had become glued to her bottom and had to be removed together with the woman. It proved impossible to bring her down the stairs: a crane hoisted her out of the upstairs window, loo seat concealed by a blanket but still in place.

Procedure in the Magistrates' Court was informal. The chairman of the Magistrates had a habit of adding the words 'of course' to the end of every sentence, particularly unfortunate when pronouncing the verdict: 'We find you guilty – of course'. Jim Hullah, the Clerk, had a pragmatic view of his role. In one case of unlawful sexual intercourse I could not persuade the girl involved to give the crucial evidence. I dared not put a leading question on the fundamental point. After asking her 'What happened next?' several times without getting a substantive response, Jim intervened. 'Did he or did he not have sexual intercourse with you?' he asked. 'Yes, he did', she responded.

Police prosecutions were the staple court diet. Rochdale had its own police force, minuscule but enjoying the same constitution as the giant Lancashire Force which it abutted and with which it merged in 1964. The Rochdale Chief Constable (with the rank of Superintendent) reported to the Borough Watch Committee in the same way as the Lancashire Chief Constable reported to the Lancashire County Council Police Committee. Head of the CID was Chief Inspector Albert Porritt. His appearance reflected his name: thin and long-nosed, with a perpetual drip at its end. It seemed to sniff out crime.

Sixty years ago a Lancashire town like Rochdale had a self-contained criminal fraternity. There was little car ownership and the M62 had not opened up the North of England to mobile villains. In Rochdale there were five burglars. Any Rochdale housebreaking would have been committed by one of the five. Detection was relatively straightforward. When a burglary was reported five constables would be despatched to the homes of the five housebreakers. On one occasion the policeman arrived before the burglar, and was having a cup of tea with the burglar's wife when her husband returned with the swag. During the 1962-63 winter one of the burglars was tracked down by following steps in the snow back to his house.

The Rochdale Police were not always so successful. A shop in Toad Lane displayed gloves on a tray outside the shop. Pairs of gloves regularly disappeared. The shop-keeper consulted the Police. They advised him to tie the gloves together to frustrate the thief. Next day the shopkeeper rang to complain: 'Thanks to your ****ing advice', he said, 'this morning they pinched the whole ****ing lot.'

Rochdale, Sir Cyril Smith and Shrimps in the Water

There was a certain mutuality between the Rochdale police and the town's villains. They lived in the same society. They shared the same culture. From time to time a criminal appeared in court with abrasions on his face, clearly having received a reciprocal thump from the police while being arrested. From time to time a concerned lady magistrate would enquire about the bruises. It would never occur to the criminal to shop the police. 'Fell down the steps, your Honour', came the consistent reply.

In Rochdale the Napoleon of crime was Arthur Johnson (name changed). I first met him after visiting the scene of a crime with Chief Inspector Albert Porritt. Albert, nose dewdrop in place, was waiting with me at a bus stop. A sleek Jaguar drew up and gave us a lift back to the Town Hall. That was Arthur Johnson, the Chief Inspector told me. Though local tradition attributed to him every crime of significance in the town, he was never convicted.

In those days policemen patrolled the streets at night. During his nocturnal watch, one constable stopped in the small hours of the morning to enjoy an illicit cigarette. Leaning against the wall of a shop, he heard unmistakable sounds of drilling from within. Summoning assistance, he entered the shop, to find four villains excavating a hole through the wall into the strongroom of the bank next door. Chief Inspector Albert Porritt arrived. 'How did you get onto us?' asked the burglars. Speculating that such an enterprise could have been planned only by Arthur Johnson, the Chief Inspector said 'Arthur shopped you.' Incensed by this apparent perfidy, the burglars blamed Johnson for the entire scheme. Of course when the case came up at Quarter Sessions, Arthur had made the position clear and the villains retracted their confessions. Without their evidence there was nothing to connect Arthur Johnson with the burglary and he was acquitted. During the burglars' imprisonment, their families were financially supported by Johnson.

The Winding Stair

The range of crimes which I prosecuted included an extraordinary number of sexual offences, notably bestiality, an activity of which I was hitherto oblivious. Intercourse with sheep was commonplace, but Rochdalians' leisure activities included association with a cow, a bulldog and, most notably, cats. Unfortunately intercourse ended with the death of the cat. Dustbins reeked with the corpses of the unfortunate felines. Eventually the offender was tracked down. In his wardrobe was a suit with relevant traces. Questioned, the offender gave a frank reply:' That's my catting suit', he said. 'I go catting in that.'

One story in the courtroom related to a woman whose husband was addicted to urinating on the carpet. Goodness knows how much disinfectant was required to keep the house odour-free, but his wife put up with her husband's weird delinquency. But nemesis came. One day the wife achieved the summit of her social ambition – the Mayoress came to tea. Disaster struck: trembling, the wife heard the front door open and close as her husband came home early. Sure enough, a thin parabola of urine arced through the doorway, landing at the feet of the Mayoress.

My most celebrated case concerned a dust-up between young people at a night club. Innovatively, I framed a charge of riot, though unsurprisingly at Quarter Sessions the charge was reduced to one of affray. My lurid opening statement to the court attracted national publicity: 'Night of teenage terror', was the headline in *The People*. Thereafter I was known in the office as the Teenage Terror. The committal also involved me in a cross-examination which saw me at splendid cross-purposes with a witness. Having established that many of those involved were armed with bicycle chains and knuckle-dusters, I asked a girl if she had been armed. 'No', she replied, 'I wasn't 'urt at all', clearly believing that I had failed to aspirate the word 'harmed'. Further cross-examination revealed that she had hit a youth over the head with a bicycle chain. I asked her why she had done that.

Rochdale, Sir Cyril Smith and Shrimps in the Water

'Because', she replied, ''e called me a four-letter word'. 'What was the word?' I asked. 'I wouldn't like to say', she responded. 'You must tell the Court what was the four-letter word', I persisted. 'I couldn't repeat it', she said, 'not in front of all these ladies and gentlemen.' 'In order that the Court can understand the provocation,' I persevered, 'you must tell us: what was the four-letter word.' Eventually she replied: 'Bastard', she answered, bringing the house down.

My most successful cross-examination related to a burglary. The burglars had concocted an alibi which depended on their being in Manchester at the time of the offence. I remembered that around the time of the burglary there had been a great mill fire near the road from Manchester to Rochdale. In cross-examination and after a little pressure, one of the burglars said that he had seen the fire on his way back from Manchester. The production of a local newspaper established that the fire had taken place on the night after the burglary and the alibi was demolished.

My duties included briefing counsel at Quarter Sessions, though usually we sent an articled clerk to hold the nominal brief. Two regular judges at Quarter Sessions were Judges Openshaw and Stables. Stables had a mild manner but was renowned for heavy sentences. By contrast, Openshaw had a towering personality. Cowed defendants would tremble as he pronounced sentence, however light it might be. Tragically he was murdered in his garage by one of the villains he had sentenced after the latter had been released from gaol.

At this time I had my first experience of Whitehall. Around the town were a number of old mill dams, or 'lodges' as they were known locally. They regularly drowned young boys and inebriates. I was given the job of doing something about them: the local pressure was to oblige their owners to surround the lodges with a fence. Such a requirement would need legislation. To prompt action I journeyed to the Ministry of Local

Government to meet the relevant Assistant Secretary, Richard Adams, shortly to become famous as the author of *Watership Down*. Adams gave me a crash course on how to survive in Whitehall. 'I', he said, 'am *dangerous places*. But they keep on giving me *dangerous things*. I send them on sharply, I can tell you. But how can I help you?' he continued. 'How do you define your mill lodges in legislation? How do you differentiate between them and a pisspot?' He must have been attracted by the idea of educating this *naif* from the North and took me for lunch at the Reform Club, that splendid replica of the Palazzo Farnese. To my surprise it also bore a striking resemblance to Halifax Town Hall (both designed, as I later discovered, by Sir Charles Barry). Enriched by the success of *Watership Down*, Richard Adams soon abandoned Whitehall and (so far as I am aware) the mill lodges remain unfenced.

To me Rochdale seemed metropolitan, but that view was not shared elsewhere. A law clerk in Norfolk was appointed to our legal department but declined the job. He requested his expenses. In accordance with normal practice, his request was declined: expenses were paid to the successful candidate only if the job were accepted. He sued. Gordon Campbell, the head of the legal department, went to fight the case in the Norfolk County Court. Mortifyingly he lost. The candidate produced statistics showing the annual rainfall in Rochdale. The County Court Judge accepted the assertion that it was entirely reasonable for anyone from Norfolk to refuse to go to such a damp, dismal place and awarded him his expenses.

Just as I had moved to Rochdale on my admission as a solicitor, my friends Martin White and Michael Holdsworth had also crossed the Pennines. At the end of their articles with the West Riding County Council Martin went to Lancashire County Council and Michael to Cheshire County Council. County council lawyers were a cut above those working for urban authorities: they stayed with county councils. There was little movement between the different types of authorities. Though I was clearly of a lower class of local government lawyer, I kept in touch with them. They introduced me to the Local Government Legal Society, a society for local government solicitors. Although its activities were loosely aimed at professional development, the Society produced an annual book which recorded the dates of qualification of all the solicitors in local government, culled from the Law Society's register of solicitors. This enabled the ambitious to forecast the likely retirement dates and thus job opportunities in the relevant local authorities.

The Society held an annual summer school. There the great and the good of local government and the law came to share their experience and impart their wisdom. The school was attended by local government solicitors up to the level of Deputy Clerk. As well as the gain in knowledge, it gave the junior ranks a theoretical opportunity to ingratiate themselves with senior colleagues and thereby improve their job prospects. The summer school also gave me the opportunity of sizing up the likely competition in my future career. This seemed to me formidable. Martin and Michael were not the only rivals with Oxbridge degrees. I remembered the words of Michael's wife Merle: 'What a pity you can't get the top jobs because you have no degree.'

Not all the solicitors at the summer school were products of Oxbridge. On one joyous occasion I had managed to place myself at the top table with the leading lights and the day's lecturer, Professor Harry Street, famous for his book on torts. I struggled to keep up with the high-powered legal conversation as colleagues mentioned torts they had known, and discussed them with the famous professor. We had been joined at the edge of the table by an unknown and silent member. He took no part in the erudition displayed until the pudding arrived. Then his face lightened. 'Eee', he said, 'it's duff. Ah'm a fooker for duff.'[2]

The Winding Stair

My career was undoubtedly helped by the vision which these occasions gave me. An even greater help was the shortage of solicitors in local government. After eighteen months in Rochdale, in 1963 I moved on to the great city of Leicester.

---

[2] Duff is a northern boiled pudding.

7. 1963-65: Leicester, Sir Robert Mark, Skittles and Tumult at the Theatre

By 1963 the M1 stretched to the outskirts of Leicester. The city was within reach of London and it was possible to drive down the motorway and leave the car at Finsbury Park, getting the tube into central London. London beckoned, especially since I had now met my future wife Clare, a doctor then working at the Central Middlesex Hospital.

Despite its proud mediaeval background as the biggest wapentake in Yorkshire, Morley was overshadowed by the city of Leeds. Rochdale lay in the penumbra of Manchester. But Leicester was the nodal point of the region, its capital city and county town. The local authority regarded itself accordingly. There I became the second assistant solicitor, responsible for litigation, something of which I had no experience and about which I then knew almost nothing. Perched above me were the First Assistant Solicitor; the Assistant Town Clerk; the Deputy Town Clerk; and at the apex of the pyramid the Town Clerk, Sir George Ogden.

There was an unwritten convention that 'important' letters should be placed before Sir George for his signature. The importance was a matter for the originator of the letter to judge.

The Winding Stair

Other letters were signed in Sir George's name by the originator. By practice I managed to perfect a tolerable replica of Sir George's signature. This had the great advantage that my letters were believed to have Sir George's *imprimatur* by those familiar with the Town Clerk's autograph, removing the possibility of challenge or argument from the recipient. Unfortunately, I became so accustomed to writing 'G C Ogden' that I inadvertently signed Christmas cards in Sir George's name, puzzling the recipients as to why they had been favoured with a Christmas card from the great man.

In Rochdale my staple diet had been police prosecutions. Though Leicester, of course, had its own police force (whose Chief Constable was the famous Sir Robert Mark, later Metropolitan Commissioner) the police used private solicitors for their prosecutions. But Leicester carried its own insurance both for its large transport undertaking and for employers' liability. As the common law solicitor I would be in the county court regularly. Throughout my time in Rochdale there had been only one appearance in the county court. The Senior Assistant Solicitor had taken that. Though I had handled the legal affairs of the Rochdale bus undertaking, claims there had been dealt with by insurers.

In my first week I made an inauspicious start. From my limited knowledge, it seemed to me that the first case I was given was absolutely hopeless and should never have gone to court. After the departure of my predecessor as common law solicitor, proceedings had been conducted by the common law clerk, who reported to me. He was a huge man with a booming voice and carried great conviction. I was comforted by his reassurance.

Sadly he proved to be completely incompetent. He told me that the hearing of my first case was in Chambers, not in the Court itself. On his advice I arrived at the county court without gown and tabs, obligatory dress in court. The case turned out to be in open court. When my case was called I stood up. Before I could speak the judge barked 'You are improperly dressed'. I stammered an apology. 'Very well, Mr Brooke', he ruled, 'I will hear you, but I will not see you', ostentatiously shielding his eyes with his hands so that I was outside his field of vision. He also savaged the council's proceedings – as was entirely justified.

Fortunately the transport undertaking employed a very able and congenial claims supervisor, Barry Clark. He undertook all the leg work required for the transport litigation.

Interestingly, for the first time I was exposed to commercial discipline. Every year the council would procure quotes for insuring the transport fleet. The quotes would be matched against the council's costs, including Barry Clark's salary and part of my own. Fortunately during my time there we managed to keep our costs well under the commercial cost of insurers: we had the advantage that our larger claims were, given the normal delays, usually two or more years in the future. The commercial discipline was certainly effective. Given my other duties my own job might not have been at risk, but Barry would certainly have been sacked if insurers had been able to undercut us.

The discipline certainly concentrated the mind on keeping within our notional budget. There could be no question of employing additional staff or using counsel in the county court. We searched for cost-effective solutions. On one occasion a ten-year-old bicyclist was run over by a bus and lost a leg. We had evidence from an onlooker that he had kicked out at the bus and overbalanced as he kicked. If the council were held to be liable, the loss of a leg by a child of that age would lead to very substantial damages and costs. Litigation would be in the High Court. The boy was in receipt of legal aid so the claim would clearly be pursued. In order to minimise the council's liability and costs I decided to send to the boy's solicitors a proof of the evidence disclosing the kick and proposed a settlement of £500.

The Winding Stair

This is completely contrary to normal legal practice and was not in accordance with counsel's advice.

Realising I was sticking my neck out, I sent the letter to the boy's solicitors for signature by Sir George. I was summoned to the Town Clerk's office. 'Would you have recommended this if the boy had not been legally aided?' he asked. I confessed that legal aid had been in my mind. 'Was it the idea of counsel?' he demanded. The answer was no, but counsel had agreed (albeit reluctantly, though I did not tell Sir George that). After a difficult ten minutes with the great man, he signed the letter. The boy's lawyers accepted the offer, thus saving substantial costs. When we appeared in chambers to seek judicial approval to the settlement, the judge expressed great disquiet that the settlement was for such a small sum, given the gravity of the injuries. He agreed to the settlement, he said, with the utmost reluctance. Clearly my action had saved a substantial sum for the council. If the matter had gone to court it was very likely that the judge would have done everything possible to find in the boy's favour, citing, for example, the nearness of the bus to the boy as it overtook. We would never have got away with £500: the injury warranted substantial compensation. I had done a good job for the council, but I was left with an uneasy conscience.

As in all sizeable local authorities in those days, the Town Clerk was a solicitor. He exercised influence across the council's activities through the solicitors in his department. Each would be assigned committees which they would advise and attend, nominally or actually in the name of the Town Clerk. In my case I was allocated the Museums and Central Purchasing Committees, a cut above the Allotments Committee, which was the territory of the junior solicitor. Occasionally a matter was deemed too important to be left to the committee solicitor. On one occasion such a matter was before the Central Purchasing Committee. When the relevant item was reached, Sir George Ogden was summoned. As he entered all members of the

Leicester, Sir Robert Mark, Skittles and Tumult at the Theatre

Committee stood until Sir George was seated. Sir George told them what he believed that they should do and left before any discussion. When he rose to go the Committee once more stood. After his departure the Committee grumbled at his advice. He had attended in order to give them uncongenial instructions. Despite their protests, the Committee felt that it had no option but to adopt Sir George's insistent recommendation.

Leicester Museums were and still are of national importance, though the savage cuts in local government finance during the last decade have compelled damaging retrenchment. In the 1960s a dominant Museums Director had contrived to make the Leicester museums an important council service. The chairman of the Museums Committee, Mrs Monica Trotter, was a Conservative. She was an excellent and knowledgeable chairman and had been appointed when the Conservatives were in control. Because she was a good chairman, the Labour leader, Sir Mark Henig, kept her in post when the Labour party gained control. Such an action would be unthinkable now. Even without the political differences, council leaders need to distribute patronage in order to ensure their survival.

In 1962 the council had appointed only the second planning officer in the country. He was Konrad Smigielski who was nationally eminent. Leicester owes much of its present shape to Smigielski, though his plan for a high-speed overhead monorail never took off. Polish by birth, he affected imperfect control of English. So, on a cold winter day when Mrs Trotter arrived in her furs, he was able to say 'Permit me to undress you, dear lady'.

Though its museums were illustrious, Leicester then had no theatre. In 1963 the council decided to remedy the deficiency by building a small new theatre, to be called The Phoenix, in the centre of the city. It was a temporary solution until a more permanent theatre could be established. I was given responsibility for the council's share of the project. Leicester's central England rival, Nottingham, was ahead of Leicester and in December 1963 opened the Nottingham Playhouse, to be run by a triumvirate of John Neville, Frank Dunlop and Peter Ustinov. Because of my responsibility for the Phoenix Theatre in Leicester I was invited to the new theatre's opening night in Nottingham.

The evening proved one of the more dramatic and exciting nights of my life – despite the play. It was to be a glittering event, though Princess Margaret, due to open the theatre, backed out at the last minute. The opening production was *Coriolanus*, ironically a play about municipal ethics, directed by Sir Tyrone Guthrie. The cast included Ian McKellen as well as John Neville himself. At the end of the show there was a VIP reception. Anticipating that the municipal guests would have wolfed all the food before the actors had removed their greasepaint, a separate spread was installed in another room where the thespians could eat and drink their fill before joining the main gathering.

The reception provided a memorable finale to the evening. When Sir Tyrone and his company arrived they misinterpreted their direction to the separate room as a species of apartheid: they believed that they were deemed not suitable to mix with the important guests. Already irritated by the audience's unenthusiastic reception of the production, they stalked into the municipal reception and expressed their outrage. A member of the company exchanged blows with the most distinguished-looking council representative, whom he took to be the Lord Mayor – in fact the Lord Mayor's mace-bearer, a former Army sergeant. A general mêlée crowned the evening. Pork pies were hurled across the room. Cakes splattered against the walls. The word '*bunfight*' acquired a literal meaning. I shrank into a corner. The fracas certainly achieved one objective: the opening of the Nottingham Playhouse featured on the front pages of the national press next day.

Leicester, Sir Robert Mark, Skittles and Tumult at the Theatre

Life in Leicester was much more sedate, with one exception: the twice-yearly skittles match against the Leicester City Police, held in a remote village pub. Town Clerk Sir George Ogden joined his departmental skittles team. Though I was democratically elected as captain of the Town Clerk's Department skittles team, rank held in the police: Chief Constable Robert Mark (later Sir Robert and Metropolitan Police Commissioner) was by right of office captain of the police team. At that time licensing laws required pubs to stop serving at 10-30pm. The law was always ignored by the police skittles team and the drinking continued until the small hours. The only rule imposed was that everyone must leave at the same time, so as to avoid inflicting a continuous noise nuisance on the local residents. In those days there was no breathalyzer but somehow everyone seemed to drive back home without accident – something now unthinkable.

After I had spent two years in Leicester, Stockport, a medium-size county borough, advertised for an Assistant Town Clerk to take charge of its legal department, its salary a substantial increase on my Leicester pay. The vacancy was caused by the departure of John Evans, my predecessor in Leicester (and later chief executive of the City of York and North Yorkshire County Council). Despite having little more than three years qualified experience I applied for the job, thinking that at least I would gain experience of the interview process. I had cultivated the Town Clerk's secretary who slipped me a private copy of Sir George's reference. His letter said that 'Brooke is able and ambitious but far too young and inexperienced for the post, but', wrote Sir George, 'he is better than Evans whom I sent you three years ago'. Such was the shortage of local government solicitors that, to my surprise, I was appointed.

A few months later Sir George himself followed me North, becoming chief executive of Manchester City Council (and, after the 1974 local government reorganisation, Greater Manchester

The Winding Stair

County Council). Almost half the county boroughs in the country clustered round Manchester. Solicitors climbing the ranks of urban local government were almost obliged to spend some time in one or more of the Greater Manchester county boroughs. A clutch of ex-Leicester solicitors had migrated to the Greater Manchester county boroughs and Sir George took some pride in the success of his protégés.

❧

8. 1965-73: Stockport – Trouble at t'Mill and Reading the Riot Act

Stockport has a rather anonymous identity; it is often confused with Southport or Stockton. During my time there I had to chaperone an inebriated George Brown, then deputy leader of the Labour Party. Despite my interventions, throughout his speech George Brown persisted in describing the town as Stockton. Stockport's splendid Town Hall resembles its counterparts in Belfast and Durban. At its centre is the ballroom (described by John Betjeman as 'magnificent'), adorned by a superb Wurlitzer organ, the only one of its kind outside the United States. It was relocated to Stockport from the Manchester Free Trade Hall.

Stockport is unusual in one respect: the ring of local authorities around Manchester lie mostly to the east, west and north of the City. Stockport, however, is on its southern fringe, abutting Cheshire and the Peak District National Park. The town is bisected by the River Mersey, which in Old English means 'boundary river'. The historic county of Lancashire lies north of the river; to the south is the county of Cheshire. Unfortunately the Mersey now flows in a conduit under the town centre. As a result it is not easy to know whether you are north or south of the river. This is of some importance: at formal occasions north of the river the Queen is toasted as Duke of Lancaster. Omit that title in the north and howls of derision follow. Invoke the Duchy south of the river and the howls are even louder. This schizophrenia is more than symbolic: Stockport is torn between being part of the Manchester metropolis and part of genteel Cheshire. The Northern part of the town is clearly part of the conurbation. The Southern suburbs morph into the countryside.

I moved into a rented flat in Manchester, convenient for the metropolitan attractions of the city centre. But my arrival in Stockport coincided with my engagement to Clare, then a London-based Doctor. Migrating North to join me, she had no problem finding a job in Booth Hall Children's Hospital in Manchester. Clare had specialised in obstetrics but decided that married life would be more conveniently combined with the life of a general practitioner: not the only sacrifice she made to promote my career. With that in mind she chose a paediatric specialty to broaden her experience. At Booth Hall she was accommodated in the women's residential annexe, designed for six female doctors. Though Clare was then the only resident, breakfast ingredients for six doctors were left in the kitchen every evening. The free food distorted our diet: at dinner she and I would feast off the breakfast left-overs: eggs, bacon, sausages and, occasionally, kippers. If Clare were on duty, however, she would lunch and dine in the oak-panelled doctors' dining room, with waiter service – a far cry from the fare of present-day hospital doctors, lucky to snatch a microwaved snack. There was a genuine benefit in the doctors' dining room, as well as the motivational factor. The doctors did discuss patients. Specialists in one area would draw on the knowledge of consultants in another. The junior doctors learnt from the exchanges.

After our marriage, the most immediate task for Clare and myself was to find somewhere to live our joint lives. We rented a charming but moist cottage with a superb view overlooking the Goyt Valley. Fungi invaded the dank walls. We also rented a television – which most people did in those days. After six months we found that we hadn't watched it and discontinued the rental. Ten years later we were still without television. Our children went to school and found themselves culturally deprived. 'What is Sooty? Who are Bill and Ben?' they would plaintively enquire on their return from school. To overcome their cultural disadvantage, we installed a television in their playroom.

Abandoning the clammy cottage, we bought an attractive house with an equally glorious view across the hills towards the Peak District. The price was £6,995, which required the injection of all our savings to keep the repayments down to £32 per month. Soon after the purchase, annual inflation rose to 22 per cent under Denis Healey's Chancellorship. As a result the real cost of the repayments dwindled into insignificance. Like many of our generation we managed to borrow good money and repay it with bad.

Stockport was half the size of Leicester but twice as big as Rochdale. It had a population of 150,000. Like Rochdale and Leicester, it was a county borough, providing all main local government services, including its own police force. Its southern boundary adjoined the Peak District National Park. The jewel in the council's crown was Lyme Park, a stately home built on land given by Richard II to the Legh family, in recognition of services to his father, the Black Prince, at the battle of Crécy in 1346. After the Second World War Lord Newton, the senior member of the Legh family, had given the Palladian mansion, garden and park to the National Trust, but without the endowment usually required by the National Trust before taking on such responsibilities. To enable the takeover, Stockport Council agreed to take on the management of the Hall and its surrounding parkland, later made famous by Colin Firth's shirtless emergence from its lake in the BBC series *Pride and Prejudice*. In those days local authorities had the self-confidence, civic pride and resources to take on such responsibilities, as Leeds City Council did with Temple Newsam and Lotherton Hall. Today Stockport Council continues to give financial assistance, but the day-to-day management of the hall and its estate has now been transferred to the control of the National Trust.

Taking charge of the Stockport council legal department was the first time I had to manage people. In Rochdale there was always a misgiving that something might go wrong and precautions were taken. In super-efficient Leicester there was certainty that nothing would go wrong (as a result, an error in Leicester had disastrous consequences because no precautionary steps were taken to avoid a disaster). In Stockport there was spectacular inefficiency and a justified conviction that everything would go wrong because it did. Damage limitation was the order of the day.

My legal department was a complete shambles. Piles of unanswered correspondence lay neglected, in-trays an undiscovered country from whose bourn no files returned. I had always worked on the assumption that work was there to be done. In Stockport work was there to be piled up in the in-tray. As a result complications and difficulties multiplied the workload. An immediate example was in my own in-tray. These were days before the Seebohm Commission recommended merging council welfare functions in one department: the council had separate departments for young and elderly. Supervising the elderly department was the Welfare Superintendent, Harry Lunn. An old lady had died in one of our old people's homes, where she was regularly visited by her former neighbour. She had kept her money under her bed. After her death Harry Lunn handed the cash to her regular visitor. In my intray was the unanswerable claim from the old lady's son.

Asked why he had not consulted the legal department before taking unilateral action, Harry replied 'If you look deeper in your intray, you'll see the request I sent you two years ago together with five reminders. And I haven't had an answer.'

The Stockport Town Clerk, Donald Hay, had learnt the exercise of authority during the second world war, when he commanded a motor torpedo boat, 'the Spitfire of the Sea'. He was a delightful man. From him I learnt three things: one was the importance of maintaining a good relationship with all councillors, not only the leader. He cultivated councillors from all three parties, who were flattered by his attention. The second was his relations with colleagues: at 6pm every day we would gather in Donald's office and review the events of the day over a gin-and-tonic. The third was his imitation of Fabius Maximus Cunctator. As Sir Thomas Browne wrote, paraphrasing Caesar: 'Festination may prove precipitation; and deliberating delay may be a wise cunctation'. No-one could accuse the Town Clerk of festination. As a policy, he had a decided preference for cunctation. To my surprise I discovered that this proved often to be the best option: problems could vaporise over time. But Donald Hay was a human dynamo compared to my immediate superior, Derek Sculthorpe, the Deputy Town Clerk, whose inbox was a graveyard for files. Seeking his authority for action resulted always in a request to leave the file with him. Months would elapse before it could be exhumed. The effect severely hindered my attempts to instill any sense of urgency in the legal department.

The Labour-controlled council was dominated by its leader, Alderman John Holland, awarded an OBE eight years before my arrival in Stockport. An able and charismatic former headteacher, John Holland was already in his 80s when I arrived. We developed a cordial relationship based (for my part) on a high regard for his ability and experience. When I joined him on a tour of the council's old people's homes, I realised that he was older than many of the inmates. A homely philosopher, he told me in the urinal 'No matter how you shake it lad, the last drop always goes down your trouser leg. That's true of politics as well.' His other lavatorial aphorism, uttered as he emerged from a cubicle, was 'Man is a machine for turning food into shit'.

Alderman Holland had combined his leadership of the council with the chairmanship of Stockport County football team, a dual position then not uncommon among football teams in the lower divisions. Though then still in the Football League, the club was in a parlous financial situation despite a loan from the council on the security of the grandstand. The resulting purchase of a centre forward failed to improve the club's results. Its attendance continued to decline. At one stage the manager did not have enough players to make up a team. Alderman Holland resigned as chairman of the football club as I arrived in the town.

The football club's sobriquet was The Hatters. One hundred years ago the wearing of hats was compulsory. In *The Road to Wigan Pier*, published just before the Second World War, George Orwell wrote that hatless men were liable to be stoned by street urchins. Although the vogue for headgear was severely diminished by the time of my arrival in Stockport, the Christy hat company, founded in 1773, was still a major employer in the town. Its Old Etonian chairman, John Christie-Miller, dominated the town's life. As well as the board of the Christy hat company, he chaired the magistrates' bench, the governing body of Stockport Grammar School and the board of the *Stockport Advertiser*. He was also president of the Chamber of Commerce. Unfortunately for the football club, he had no interest in soccer.

Deputy Borough Engineer, Sam Marshall was as phlegmatic as his superior and, as a result, an ideal witness. At a public enquiry into the Stockport development plan, Sam was asked whether it was a good idea to locate a two lane dual carriageway next to a primary school. He answered with a simple 'yes'. Cross-examination did not budge him. For the council I had briefed Sir Frank Layfield, my first meeting with the distinguished QC. (I was to brief Frank on several occasions in the future and we became friends after he became President of the Association of County Councils.) In Sir Frank's re-examination Sam was able to dilate on his answer, free from the danger of cross-examination. Cheshire County Council had opposed elements of the development plan. Representing the county council was an ebullient young solicitor, Roger Taylor, who then specialised in social services and knew little about town planning. He was appropriately savaged by Sir Frank and decades later still talked of his mortification. Roger later became successively chief executive of the City Councils of Manchester and Birmingham. He stood down from the latter post, hubristically and mistakenly believing that the world would then be his oyster. His successors in both Manchester and Birmingham were rewarded with knighthoods.

The Stockport Children's Officer was Philippa Fletcher. She was a haughty character who made it clear that she came from a higher level of society than the other chief officers and, specifically, than Harry Lunn, the Welfare Superintendent. Addressed as Miss Fletcher by me and colleagues, she was an alcoholic who had been banned from driving but continued driving (and drinking) regardless. One afternoon Mrs Martha Grant, a Methodist Labour Alderman, was startled when Miss Fletcher's car was stopped by the police. When the driver's door was opened a drunken Miss Fletcher fell out on the pavement at the feet of the austere lady alderman. Shortly afterwards the Children's Department was subject to the annual Home Office inspection. To my surprise, the female inspector sought a confidential meeting with me. The reason, she explained, was that Miss Fletcher had made a Lesbian overture to her. I saw the Town Clerk. 'This time she surely has to go', I said. 'Certainly not', he responded with asperity: 'if councillors once get the idea that they can sack chief officers, there is no knowing where they might stop. And remember that she is Norman Hulbert's niece.' Sir Norman Hulbert was one of Stockport's Conservative MPs, ridiculed in 1963 by the satirical TV programme *That was the Week That Was* as not having spoken in the Commons since he was elected in 1959.

As in Rochdale, the council was the centre of the life of the town. It ran the public services which had the most immediate impact on its residents. They included water supply, sewerage, police, fire, public transport and public health. The only exception was the Stockport cemetery, owned by a private company. It had financial troubles: the problem with all cemeteries is that the burial fees finance the maintenance of the land. They are virtual Ponzi schemes: when the supply of burial plots is exhausted and the income from new burials stops, the company cannot continue to maintain the cemetery – a situation which had traumatic reverberations later in my career. In Stockport the council agreed to take over the cemetery and transform it into a lawn cemetery. The experience illuminated my response to the Westminster Cemeteries scandal, with which I had to deal twenty years later.

Council activities were the staple content of the Stockport Express. The newspaper's municipal reporter was a charming chain-smoking Viennese Jew, Ernest Brunert, who had escaped Hitler. He held a doctorate in law from the University of Vienna and cultivated my society in the hope of indiscretions. In 1967 he came into his own when Stockport twice hit the national news. The Roberts Arundel factory in Stockport had been taken over by an American, who sacked its male employees in order to replace them with non-unionised female labour. Unsurprisingly the unions regarded this as a test case and mobilised pickets. Demonstrations created serious disturbances. People were hurt and there were a number of arrests. Across the

Stockport – Trouble at t'Mill and Reading the Riot Act

North West 30,000 workers downed tools in sympathy for the Stockport workers. The action was the main front-page story in *The Times*.

A squad of policemen protected the detested Roberts Arundel building. On February 22, 1967, 1,500 workers from Stockport and the surrounding area met in Albert Street, a narrow road alongside the factory. As violence erupted, the Stockport Deputy Chief Constable took charge of the police squad. In the mêlée he suffered a cracked rib and retreated. A panic-stricken Chief Constable phoned the Town Clerk, demanding that the Riot Act of 1714 be read. This anachronistic piece of legislation acquired some notoriety after the Peterloo massacre in 1819. The Act required any group of twelve or more people to disperse or face punitive action after the Mayor or a magistrate had chanted the rubric 'Our sovereign Lord the Queen chargeth and commandeth all persons, being assembled, immediately to disperse themselves, and peaceably to depart to their habitations, or to their lawful business, upon the pains contained in the act made in the first year of King George, for preventing tumults and riotous assemblies. God save the Queen.' Case history determined that the precise words had to be spoken or the command was unenforceable. A slight error invalidated the whole process.

The Town Clerk had recently taken charge of the ejection of a party of travellers who had camped on council land. The operation was frustrated when the trespassers removed the key from the ignition of the council lorry which had arrived to tow away the caravans. The Town Clerk and the council workers were compelled to retreat from the fray, the jeers of the crowd resounding in their ears. This had discouraged the Town Clerk from taking charge of further field operations. He decided that it would be more fitting for me to face the rioters. I was despatched to the Roberts Arundel factory, with the Mayor primed to read the Riot Act. Clutching the text of the Act I coached the Mayor in elocution as we set off in the mayoral limousine.

A policeman stopped us as we approached the screaming crowd. 'This is the Mayor,' I yelled, 'and he is here to read the Riot Act.' The flustered constable shrieked back: 'I don't ****ing care who you are. You can't come here'. I managed to convince him of our *bona fides* and a police escort shouldered us through to the steps of the factory entrance. Unfortunately literacy was not the strong point of the mayor and he stumbled through the reading. As a result the invocation of the Riot Act was almost certainly invalid. However, the mayor's words were drowned in the roar of the crowd. I was probably the only person who could hear his speech. Further action was in any event unnecessary: the pubs had opened and the crowd dispersed. Despite the intervention of Harold Wilson, then Prime Minister, the protests proved unsuccessful: losing patience, the American shut the factory and Harold Wilson devalued the pound to $2.40. I imagine that I am the only living person to have heard the invocation of the Riot Act, which was repealed months later.

At that time both the main political parties believed in the importance of building council housing. The 1951 Conservative manifesto read: '*Housing is the first of the social services. It is also one of the keys to increased productivity. Work, family life, health and education are all undermined by crowded houses. Therefore, a Conservative and Unionist Government will give housing a priority second only to national defence.*' When he was Minister of Housing, Harold Macmillan consolidated his political reputation by achieving the construction of 300,000 council houses each year.

Under Labour control, Stockport council needed no government encouragement to replace the slums with new houses. Unlike Rochdale and other councils, Stockport refused to build multi-storey flats, believing them to be socially undesirable. However, the new Labour Government believed that the industrialised building of multi-storey flats was the only way to achieve their housing targets. They constructed a financial regime which compelled construction of high-rise flats on industrialised principles. Bowing to the inevitable and despite the opposition of borough architect John Rank, the council constructed multi-storey flats, using the industrialised 12M Jespersen system. In May 1968 a relatively small gas explosion caused the collapse of one entire corner of Ronan Point, a multi-storey tower block in Canning Town, Newham. Four people died and 17 were injured. It was clear that the system of construction was inadequate. It resembled that used in Stockport. As a result Stockport's new multi-storey flats were subject to a costly rebuild. Despite explicit instructions on the original construction from the Government regional office, Ministers refused to accept financial responsibility. The junior Housing Minister, Reg Freeson, walked out of a meeting in Stockport Town Hall when councillors of both parties pressed him for compensation.

In June 1967, a British Midland Airways passenger jet narrowly cleared the clock tower of the Town Hall before crashing on vacant land behind the building. 72 of the 84 passengers died. It was the fourth worst disaster in British aviation. The crash became the climax in Richard Francis's 2003 novel, *Prospect Hill*, which features a fictionalised version of the clash between council and Government over the flats, culminating in the air crash. As in Stockport, his council was forced by the Government to build multi-storey flats. The Minister was described as an 'odious twerp'. I recognised myself as a character in the book.

Change in local government: Athelstan Popkess

When I began to work in Stockport the key skill sought in a chief officer was the ability to spend money – not to save it. Councils wanted chief officers who would drive through their capital programme. That commitment began to change during my time in Stockport. Local government powers had already started to diminish. The first indicator was the amalgamation of police authorities. There had often been ill-feeling between the county and the borough forces. There was rivalry and not always co-operation. Indeed from time to time there was active malice. In the hope of being able to land him with a speeding ticket, the West Riding Police kept a special look-out for the car of the Chief Constable of the Wakefield City Police when it left the city and entered the county jurisdiction.

Chief Constables in the local police forces answered to the city and borough councils' Watch Committees. As a result they were extremely sensitive to local pressures. However, the spread of car ownership and the introduction of motorways made the tiny borough police forces unviable. The immediate trigger was a series of scandals. The most notorious was the case of the Chief Constable of Nottingham, the superbly named Athelstan Popkess. He was suspended by the City Council's Watch Committee when he refused to disclose a report on his investigation into allegations of corruption by councillors. Predictably details were leaked to the press on the eve of the municipal elections. His reinstatement became a political necessity and the Home Secretary, Rab Butler, intervened.

The incident triggered national change. The Police Act 1964 gave the Home Secretary powers to amalgamate police forces: the days of the tiny borough police forces were over. Stockport was on the southern flank of Manchester and its amalgamation with the other police forces in the Manchester conurbation was logical. However the Conservative-controlled Stockport Council fought doggedly for their policemen to join the Cheshire Police Force. There was some rationality in their fight: crime in rural conservative Cheshire (and therefore the cost of policing) was clearly lower than in the densely populated conurbation. The council's fight succeeded: the Stockport and Cheshire forces amalgamated in 1967. It was, however, a Pyrrhic victory. Seven years later, in the great local government reorganisation, the decision was reversed: responsibility for policing in Stockport became the responsibility of the Greater Manchester Police. The Royal Commission on Local Government in England had been created in 1966. Local government reorganisation was obviously imminent. Recognising the inevitable, Cheshire County Council established diplomatic relations with the neighbouring county boroughs. The charismatic Clerk of the Cheshire County Council was Sir John Boynton. He included adjacent county borough mayors and chief executives in the stylish county council hospitality. At Chester races, held on the Roodee, the oldest race course in the country, the county council marquee dispensed champagne and smoked salmon. The Roodee is on the banks of the River Dee: from time to time the racing was cancelled because the racecourse was flooded. County council hospitality continued unabated: duckboards gave access to the council's marquee and the partying could take place without the distraction of racing. The class distinction between county and districts became apparent when the Stockport Mayor, unaccustomed to such generous hospitality, tripped over his robe, teetered off the duckboard and had to be fished out of the ooze.

After the amalgamation of police forces, the next service to be lost by Stockport Council was transport. A Passenger Transport Authority was created to take over all transport in Manchester and the surrounding county boroughs. Stockport was proud of its buses, which enjoyed an open platform at the rear, like the old London Routemasters. Upmarket Manchester had switched to buses with rear doors. Believing rear doors to be a namby-pamby affectation and despite expostulations from Manchester, Alderman Holland made a point of buying a fleet of six open-platform buses in the last few weeks before the take-over. One of the first acts of the new Greater Manchester

Passenger Transport Authority was to scrap them and replace
them with buses with rear doors.

Like other local authorities, Stockport Council (disguised as
the Stockport Water Corporation) was responsible for supplying
water to its residents. It was also responsible for providing water
in the surrounding urban districts. The supply was drawn from
Fernilee Reservoir in the Goyt Valley in Derbyshire. A water
shortage prompted the building of a further reservoir in the
Goyt Valley, to be called Errwood. The Waterworks Manager
and the consulting engineers hit various objections and
administrative problems. The Town Clerk put me in charge of
sorting them out.

At my first meeting I was in the company of just three people:
the Waterworks Manager, the Consulting Engineer and the
minute clerk. The initial issue involved the Peak Park Planning
Board, which was unhappy about the new reservoir. On a cold
winter's day at the site of the proposed reservoir I met the
chairman, a retired Admiral, and ten or so of his members. I
encountered a style very different to the constipated municipal
scene. After inspecting the site we retired to the pub, frozen to
the bone. Counting the numbers of those present and without
further enquiry, the chairman summoned the barmaid: 'Twelve
pink gins. Large ones', he demanded.

The proposed reservoir would be a blot on the landscape,
announced the Peak Park Planning Board. The reservoir could
not go ahead in the teeth of opposition from the National Park
Authority. Landscape architects were hired to propitiate them.
At the public hearing the delights of the Goyt Valley were
trumpeted. Our landscape architect agreed that the valley was
most attractive. Asked whether there was anything which could
improve such a delightful environment, he responded 'Yes: a
sheet of water'. After negotiating a landscape scheme with them,
the Planning Board changed tack: it was not the new reservoir
itself which would destroy the tranquility of the valley, but the

flow of tourists which it would generate. The resulting traffic would mutilate the environment.

To get the scheme off the ground I had to make progress. Since the costs of delay outweighed other considerations we agreed to provide a park and ride scheme so that the Goyt valley would not be overrun by cars. Location and construction of the car park required the involvement of the Derbyshire County Council as highway authority. Meanwhile, the Nature Conservancy had discovered a colony of rare beetles. They were relocated at substantial expense. The Royal Commission on Historical Monuments (later merged with English Heritage) protested at the submersion of the 1762 packhorse bridge, which stood on an ancient salt route. We agreed to dismantle it stone by stone and re-locate it between the two reservoirs. The Forestry Commission asked for a landscape scheme to replace the trees which were to be immersed in the reservoir. In every case it was cheaper to propitiate the objectors than risk a delay to the scheme.

The numbers attending my meetings about the reservoir increased exponentially. Matching the expertise of all these outside bodies required the council to appoint its own experts. The experts came not in single spies but battalions. The numbers attending meetings swelled from the original four to nearly fifty. And – after all the objections – the tourist propaganda now describes Errwood reservoir as a 'wonderfully magical place'.

I think that Errwood was the last municipal reservoir to be built in England. The availability of clean water was a fundamental prerequisite of 19th century urban life. When he was Mayor of Birmingham in 1873, Joseph Chamberlain, made his name by municipalising the city's water supply. He insisted that the charges for water should be based not on consumption but on property values, so that larger families and the less affluent would be able to afford its use. Other local authorities followed Chamberlain's lead and assumed responsibility for water supply. The responsibility largely remained with local government until the local government reorganisation of 1974, when it was transferred to ten regional water authorities – quangoes appointed by the Minister. Local authorities had taken pride in their water supply: the Nidderdale reservoirs still rejoice in the portentous crenellated structures built by Bradford Council, each with a plaque proudly acclaiming the names of the Lord Mayor, the chairman of the Water Committee and, of course, the Town Clerk of the day. Bradford councillors were outraged when in 1975 the new Yorkshire Water Authority planned the construction of a link main to transfer water from Bradford's reservoirs to augment the Leeds supply. It wouldn't have been too bad if the Bradford water had been destined for Huddersfield or Halifax – but to Leeds! Bradfordians were still stung by the old Leeds gibe: 'The three main streets in Leeds are Kirkgate, which leads to the church; Briggate, which leads to the bridge; and Swinegate, which leads to Bradford'.

By 1980, six years after local government had lost its responsibility for water supply, investment in water infrastructure was one-third of what it had been in 1970, when local authorities were in charge. The Water Boards were unable to meet European Union water quality standards and the UK was prosecuted for non-compliance. After the 1987 election, water supply in England and Wales (not Scotland) was privatised by the Conservative government at a knock-down price – alleged to be about one-tenth of its real value. The water companies are now owned by investment companies from, inter alia, China, Abu Dhabi and Kuwait. England and Wales are the only developed countries in the world to rely on the private sector for water supply. The sale prompted Birmingham City Council to take to litigation, unsuccessfully arguing that since the assets had been paid for by the Birmingham ratepayers, then the proceeds of privatisation should be returned to them via the council.

Stockport – Trouble at t'Mill and Reading the Riot Act

My Irish mandate

After three years in Stockport as Assistant Town Clerk, I made fruitless applications for Deputy Town Clerkships with increasing desperation. I was often not even short-listed, though I was interviewed for the jobs of Deputy Town Clerk at Southend, Greenwich, Nottingham and, as a last resort, Leamington Spa, a non-county borough. Going to Leamington would have been a great come-down after a county borough – but the job was quite lucrative, the salary swollen because the job was combined with the Deputy Clerkship of the local Water Board.

I tried my luck with a county council, applying for the job of Assistant Clerk at Somerset. Unsurprisingly my old friend (and our best man) Martin White got the job: county councils always wanted county people. Remembering Merle Holdsworth's advice, I became painfully aware that my lack of a degree was a major handicap. When I was interviewed for the Deputy Town Clerkship of Nottingham City, I became aware of a further handicap: my youth. At the pre-interview lunch the councillor next to me confided his indignation at the youthful impertinence of one of the candidates, who had applied for the job at the age of 26. Presumably he did not vote for me. The pre-interview drinks and lunch was not unusual: I developed the technique of discreetly decanting my gin and tonic into a friendly plantpot.

I contemplated an undistinguished career in local government. Then my most significant break-through arrived: the Stockport Deputy Town Clerk, Derek Sculthorpe, got the job of Deputy Town Clerk of Manchester – where Sir George Ogden, my old boss from Leicester, was now Town Clerk. The appointment panel for the resulting vacancy, chaired by Alderman John Holland, appointed me. He and I had always got on well: I had a very genuine admiration for him. He clearly had a fellow feeling for me. There was no doubt that our relationship was a key factor in my appointment. The interview again reminded me of the importance of maintaining a good relationship with councillors.

Soon after my appointment as Deputy Town Clerk, the Labour Government introduced the idea of mandatory training. Every employer had to pay an impost which would be reimbursed if its employees received approved training. Having had no local government training whatsoever, I was sent off to Birmingham University on a ten-week course for senior local government officers. The course was led by Professor John Stewart, a Socratic figure who had the most profound influence on me. The course was a revelation: I began to think about local government as a community governing itself, not just as a collection of services which happened to be run by a council. I began to fit my own activities into a conceptual framework. I learnt that my job as Director of Administration was to be the Geographer of Policy Space. My thought was stimulated by the publication in 1967 of the reports of Sir John Maud (later Lord Redcliffe-Maud) and Sir George Mallaby on the management and staffing of local government. The Mallaby report pointed out that in a typical local authority 'there may be unity in the parts, but there is disunity in the whole'.

The Maud and Mallaby reports quickened the pace of change in local government management, which still enjoyed a number of antiquarian practices. In the largest local authority in the country, Birmingham, the minutes of each committee meeting were laboriously read out in full at the beginning of the following meeting. The money paid to councillors was based on the number of meetings they attended. Unsurprisingly the number of meetings mushroomed. A typical authority might have as many as 35 committees and over 400 meetings each year. Commentators ridiculed the apocryphal Rotherham Cancelled Bookings Sub-Committee, which met monthly only to confirm the minutes of its previous meeting.

Stockport – Trouble at t'Mill and Reading the Riot Act

The timing of my appointment as Deputy Town Clerk was opportune: after many years of Labour dominance, the Conservatives took control of the Stockport council in 1968. They were led by a flamboyant Rolls-Royce driving florist, Walter Knight. Anticipating Mrs Thatcher, the Conservative controlling group sought a minimalist local authority. They scrapped the council's plan for an integrated health centre, infuriating the doctors who had budgeted on going there. They abolished the mandatory requirements imposed on taxis. Believing that the residents of council houses were dedicated Labour voters, the Conservative controlling group halted the council house-building and slum clearance programmes. Following national Conservative government guidance, they instituted a programme of housing improvement areas. The council officers, led by the Medical Officer of Health, were appalled. The MoH had devoted much of his career to condemning slums and seeing them replaced by new council-owned housing. Now, he lamented, the underprivileged would continue to live in damp, sub-standard dwellings.

The council officer hierarchy was organised to cope with slum clearance, a process administered under compulsion. It had no administration or systems to create housing improvement areas, the success of which relied on involvement and agreement by residents. Organisational paralysis set in. Nothing happened. The Leader, Walter Knight, and the other members of the Tory administration became more and more impatient. Unless something did happen, heads would roll.

Thinking that I would be in line for decapitation with my colleagues, I volunteered to take over the housing improvement programme. Instead of working in a town hall office with few contacts with residents, I launched myself into a series of public meetings and private conferences. It was a sobering experience and led me to a Damascene conversion. I realised that the streets due for preservation were the home of a vibrant community. The street was a social centre for residents; older people minded children in school holidays; younger people shopped for the elderly. The community propped itself up. There would be a catastrophic loss of quality of life if residents were dispersed to housing estates on the edge of the town: social services would have to step in to support many residents. I became a passionate convert to the cause of communities and their encouragement. I read and believed Jane Jacobs's *Death and Life of Great American Cities* and its pleas for mixed uses to create a vibrant city scene. I learnt that nomenclature was key: rename 'nonconforming uses' as 'small businesses' and they became acceptable. I also dismissed the arrogant officer view that experts knew best: the councillors had been absolutely right in challenging the blinkered professional view.

Police dogs and other animals

Lack of action on the housing improvement areas was not the only problem. During my time at Birmingham University relations between Stockport councillors and officers had deteriorated: the Conservatives were disenchanted with the atrophied regime they had inherited. Officers had failed to react to the administration's policies. My absence had removed the only force for innovation in the council hierarchy. When I returned I found that Walter Knight and his Conservative group had come to believe – with some justice – that the officer structure was incapable of running the council's services in the innovative ways the Tories believed were necessary. They decided to employ American management consultants to re-animate the council's services. They chose Booz Allen & Hamilton, whose front man was then Christopher Bland (later Sir Christopher, chairman of the Board of Governors of the BBC and known to the many whom he patronised as 'Pigling'). I was seconded to work with the consultants, who quickly identified me as the agent for change (there was no competition) and keystone of their proposed structure. They recommended making me a chief officer under the title of Director of Administration. The recommendation hit a major hurdle: when the consultants put the proposal to the council leader, Walter Knight, he told them that he couldn't stand me. He said that I gave him the impression that I thought he spoke a load of rubbish. In recognising this, he revealed a percipience with which I had not credited him. Under the auspices of the consultants, Walter Knight and I shook hands and the recommendation went ahead.

With the support of the consultants and Walter Knight, a quiet revolution took place as council services were re-evaluated. I made one immediate change. At that time the agenda of the council's decision-making committees functioned without supporting written papers. The relevant chief officer would give an oral report. To the intense frustration of the chief officers, any matter of significance would be deferred. Unsurprisingly the chairman wished to consult his political colleagues before making any major decision. The majority party did not want an open debate in the presence of the opposition. The result was an agonisingly slow decision-taking process. I introduced a system of written reports. There was an immediate barrage of protests from the chief officers, who had relished the ambiguity and obscurity in which they could cloak their oral presentations and draft the subsequent resolution. But the resulting clarity and expedition of decision-taking made a spectacular improvement to the council's processes.

The recommendations of Booz Allen and the steps I had taken to implement them reverberated nationally. One consequence was to make me a regular out-of-term visitor at Trinity College, Cambridge, where I was surprised to find that basic ablutions required me to make an open-air crossing of the quad. I went at the invitation of a body called CRAC (the

The Winding Stair

Careers Research Advisory Council, still going strong in Cambridge). They invoked me in order to persuade PhD students to abandon research and become practical participants in society. I devised a couple of gaming exercises, during which participants formulated a strategy and were then swayed to abandon it as real life hit them. The end of course review, when I compared their original aspirations with the outcome, was always revelatory.

The Booz Allen report prompted the Government to commission a report on local government management, whose report largely followed the recommendations of Booz Allen – in particular propagating the idea of corporate management. It cited Stockport as a 'progressive' council which envisaged the local authority's services as an integrated package. As the main agent of the corporate management changes in Stockport I appeared regularly on the conference circuit and was assiduous in publishing accounts of the developments. As a result I became something of a national figure in the local government world. A visiting group from a German local authority was directed to Stockport, where I was disconcertingly introduced as *Der Unterstadtführer*.

My reputation spread. The Home Office despatched me to a conference in Rome to consider electoral law in the European Union. This was memorable for two reasons. The Irish delegate approached me and said: 'I hear you are representing Great Britain.' I assented modestly. 'Well', he said, 'let me give you the Irish mandate too. I think I'll get more by going round the town than staying here.' And off he disappeared. To nearly a thousand delegates I started my address by claiming diffidently that I represented the United Kingdom 'and the Republic of Eire'. My address was not a success. Thinking to lighten the leaden atmosphere, I introduced a joke into my speech. Nearly a thousand delegates greeted it with stony silence. I hastily relapsed into appropriate Eurospeak: 'This is a vitally important

114

matter which must concern all those who value democracy in our great community of Europe'. The audience greeted it with tumultuous laughter. Demoralised, I stumbled on. Only later did I realise that the 'simultaneous' translator had just caught up with me.

The Stockport Tories relished the publicity as the council acquired a reputation of being in the van of progress. At that time there was a fashion for a 'scientific' approach to management systems. One approach was the introduction of PPBS – Planning, Programming and Budgeting Systems, evangelised by the then Conservative-controlled Greater London Council. These gathered together the authority's policies and attributed costs to them – costs which would otherwise have been lost under headings like salaries, transport and cleaning. Its most famous practitioner was Gordon (later Lord) Wasserman, son-in-law of Hugh Gaitskell, who demonstrated the effectiveness of the policy by analysing spending on police dogs. The police budget revealed only diminutive canine costs. However, cross-budget analysis added the cost of manpower (the policeman at the end of the leash); premises (the kennels); transport (the van in which the dog was transported to the scene of the crime); supplies (food for the dog) etc. When all the supporting costs were aggregated, police dogs were actually quite expensive. As a one-off method the process yielded impressive results and new perceptions. An example in Stockport was the building of council estates. Unlike private estates, garages on council estates were grouped in separate blocks at some distance from the dwellings. As a result tenants preferred to leave their cars handily parked on the road outside their house, rather than trek round the corner to the block of garages. Most garages were unoccupied and attracted no rent. The analysis convinced the council either to integrate garages with the council houses or to stop building them.

The Government insisted on the 'scientific' approach to

management. They refused to sanction the borrowing of money to finance capital schemes unless they had been evaluated by operational research. The Stockport Council needed a new waste disposal depot. At Government insistence I commissioned the Local Government Operational Research Unit to evaluate and identify the best option. At the Committee the researchers demonstrated with some erudition that site A was the optimum solution. The chairman congratulated them on their presentation before asking the committee to agree to locate the depot at site B. I took the Committee more slowly through the research, but with the same result. After the meeting I asked the chairman why he had chosen Option B. 'Nay, lad', he said, 'Option A's in a marginal ward: we only have a majority of fifty there. We're not going to put a waste disposal depot there.'

As well as innovative forms of policy analysis, the council launched a productivity drive, for which there was plenty of scope. Organisation and Methods investigations improved efficiency. Work study was introduced for manual services, with spectacular gains in output. We hit one major stumbling block: its application to the employees of Lyme Park, the estate which the council then managed for the National Trust. Its workers (who lived in the cottages on the estate) had survived the transfer to the council from Lord Newton. They behaved as family retainers. Working hours had no meaning for them: after dinner they would go out into the park to tidy up after the day's visitors. Their productivity exceeded anything which could possibly be prescribed by our normal work study criteria. Our work study officer asked what we should do. Rewarding their industry would bust both the budget and the system. Taking the pragmatic view, I agreed that we would drop the work study element and simply pay them the maximum bonus possible.

Stockport – Trouble at t'Mill and Reading the Riot Act

Reorganisation 1973 and French wine

At that time there was an obvious problem with the structure of local government. Tiny local authorities, sometimes with a population of only a few hundreds, had responsibility for substantial functions. The powers of the county council did not extend into the self-governing county boroughs, the so-called 'holes in the blanket'. The 'holes' were often the county towns, the social, cultural and transport centres of the county. It was impossible for the county council to plan services like education or devise a transport strategy which excluded the county's nodal point. The county town itself would often be surrounded by suburbs which were outside the jurisdiction of its council. Local Acts of Parliament, accumulated since Victorian times, confusingly extended only within the area of the council which had originally procured their enactment.

Local government reorganisation had been in the air since the publication of a White Paper in 1945. But opposition from local government and the pressure of the other massive reforms tackled by the Attlee government frustrated further action. The problem remained. In response Harold Wilson's Labour Government appointed Lord Redcliffe-Maud (as he had now become) to head a royal commission to consider local government reorganisation. After a three year gestation period the Commission reported in 1969. The Labour Government accepted the Commission's recommendation that the country should be governed by unitary authorities, except for three Metropolitan areas (Merseyside, the Manchester conurbation and the West Midlands) which would have a two-tier system. Their decisions were reversed by the Conservative Government which came to power in 1970. That Government introduced two-tier local government throughout the country, to be implemented in 1974. To the metropolitan areas were added three additional county councils, West Yorkshire, South

Yorkshire and Tyne & Wear. [Curiously 21st century Conservative Governments are dedicated to the creation of the unitary authorities which they rejected when in power in 1970 and which the Labour party then supported.]

Under both Conservative and Labour proposals the County Borough of Stockport was to be reconstituted as a metropolitan district council within the realm of the Greater Manchester County Council. The county council would have an overall planning remit and run metropolitan wide services like transport, fire and trading standards. The remaining local government services would be run by the district councils. Stockport Council's victory in having its police service run by Cheshire County Council was short-lived. Police was to be a function of the Greater Manchester County Council. However, Stockport Council's population was doubled by absorbing from Cheshire the adjacent districts of Bredbury & Romiley, Cheadle & Gatley, Hazel Grove & Bramhall and Marple. Disley (in which Lyme Park was situated) was originally included in the new Metropolitan District but a rearguard action in the House of Lords decreed that it should remain in Cheshire.

Obviously extensive planning was required to achieve such a substantial reorganisation. A joint committee was created under the chairmanship of Alderman Knight, the Stockport leader. I was put in charge of creating the master plan, working through a string of officer working parties. From their workings came a comprehensive plan for the new authority, ranging from its standing orders and procedures to its political and officer structure and personnel policies. My experience of working in the community had reinforced my commitment to subsidiarity and my belief that decisions should be devolved to the most local level possible. I proposed a completely new idea, a series of neighbourhood councils which would have their own budgets and delegated decision-taking. Each would be served by an area coordinator. This was politically very attractive: the councillors to be absorbed from the urban district councils could see that they would not be swamped in the new metropolitan district council (as the new authorities were to be called). It had an enthusiastic reception from the councillors. The idea received national publicity and has become widely copied, though usually in an attenuated form. Evidence consistently shows that wellbeing improves where communities are empowered and enabled to take ownership of local assets. Most recently (September 2021) research by the Conservative thinktank *Onward* found that 'the most successful [regeneration] schemes focused on smaller geographic areas such as neighbourhoods'.

That was not my only revolutionary proposal: another was the proposal to transfer the youth service from the Education Department to the Leisure Department. This provoked the Director of Education into seeking support for his opposition to the proposal from the Education Ministry in Whitehall, to which Education Directors had a direct line. Both Directors and Department were united in their determination to keep councillors from 'interfering' in schools. [It is distinctly unfair to read that Sir Michael Wilshaw, when Chief Inspector of Schools, told local authorities that they had 'failed to cut the mustard in terms of improving schools in the 50 years up to the birth of the academies'. (2 December 2015, *Independent*).]

My recommendations were accepted by the joint committee. At the election on 12 April 1973 the voters chose those councillors who had been prominent on the joint committee. They then became, of course, the key members of the new Stockport Metropolitan District Council. At its first meeting the new authority adopted lock, stock and barrel all the recommendations I had drafted for the joint committee, giving it a running start as a new authority. The pecking order of councillors had already been decided, with a careful balance between those from Stockport and those from those surrounding county areas to be absorbed into the area of the new local authority – though the former county council members did not last long, unable to cope with the ungentlemanlike thrusting of the county borough members. The new council formally confirmed the officer structure approved by the joint committee and proceeded immediately to make officer appointments.

The success of any reorganisation is enormously assisted when lubricated by money. In 1973 the era of austerity was in the future. Nationally a generous early retirement package for senior officers had been agreed, the intention being to supercharge the new authorities by getting rid of the dead wood of the old guard. Almost all those eligible took advantage of the package. To Young Turks like myself it was clear that this was a unique opportunity to advance our careers. It was also clear that if I did not then make the big break-through, future opportunities for advancement would be extremely limited: the new generation appointed to the top jobs would not retire for years. For my future career it was now or never. Like most aspiring young men (there were no women contenders in those days) I put in multiple applications for any jobs which seemed suitable. My applications would be considered only if the national Staff Commission could be satisfied that no suitable candidates were available from the existing staff of the constituent councils which formed the new local authority.

Informally the members of the new Stockport council had decided to appoint the existing Stockport chief executive, Donald Hay, as chief executive of the new authority. However, like almost all his contemporaries, Donald had decided to take advantage of the generous early retirement package on offer. Jobs with the new council were ring-fenced to those employed by the existing local authorities. As a result the two obvious candidates for the chief executive job with the new Stockport authority were the Stockport Director of Finance, Arthur Wilson, and myself.

The installation of the new authority coincided with a civic visit from Stockport's twin town, Béziers, supposedly the largest wine-producing commune in France. Béziers made mostly mediocre wine, but lots of it. On the night before the appointment was the civic dinner in honour of visitors from the twin town, lubricated by our visitors' best wines. The occasion was clearly a preliminary to the formal interview. At the dinner my wife, Clare, heavily pregnant with our second child, excelled herself in persuading councillors that she was the ideal chief executive's wife. Unfortunately I was not so successful. Next day the councillors very sensibly chose the treasurer, making undoubtedly the correct choice (as I later came to believe). The only dissentient voice was the old town clerk, Donald Hay: 'They should have realised', he said, 'that the only person who could do the job as chief executive's wife was Clare Brooke'.

Interviews for the job of director of administration followed the appointment of chief executive. Given my lead in orchestrating the creation of the new authority there was an assumption that I should be appointed after my failure to be selected as chief executive. The applicants for the post included my deputy, Peter Bounds, and the chief executives of Hazel Grove and Marple, the two main urban district councils to be merged with Stockport. When it came to the interview, Peter and the two urban district council chief executives withdrew in my favour. These generous gestures had exactly the reverse effect of that intended. The interviewing panel declared that they were not going to have the officers telling them whom to appoint. They wanted to readvertise the post so that they could have a choice of candidates. Walter Knight, now leader of the new authority and (since our mediated hand-shake) a Brooke supporter, had a struggle to persuade the Panel to appoint me.

The appointment as director of administration of the much enlarged new Stockport authority was a step up from a similar post with the old Stockport County Borough, but was far from the great leap forward to which I aspired. Almost all the older chief executives had taken advantage of the generous early retirement package. Not untypical was the chief executive of Leeds City Council, who retired to the Yorkshire Dales and became clerk of Halton Gill Parish Council, thus moving from one of the biggest jobs in local government to what was certainly one of the smallest. The appointment of a new generation of younger chief executives was going to set appointments in stone for many years. Unless I made the big leap forward I would be stuck.

The national Staff Commission had laid down rules for appointments to the new authorities. The new local authorities advertised their jobs and solicited applications. However, they were allowed to offer appointments to outsiders only once when they had sampled and exhausted their local talent. Unsurprisingly most new local authorities were able to identify suitable appointees from within the ranks of their constituent councils.

9. 1973-84: Return to West Yorkshire – The Splattered Sandwich and the Mausoleum

I had applied for multiple jobs, like all those hoping for employment after reorganisation. A few days after my appointment as Stockport's director of administration, the post brought me an invitation to be interviewed for the job of director of administration at West Yorkshire County Council, one of the six new metropolitan county councils created to bring strategy to the conurbations around Newcastle, Liverpool, Manchester, Leeds/Bradford, Sheffield and Birmingham. West Yorkshire was the third largest authority in the country. The job would clearly be the great leap forward which I coveted: it would put me in the big league.

Of course, I had just accepted the job of director of administration of Stockport. I could not abandon that job on the off-chance of securing the West Yorkshire post. But I was desperate to take advantage of this one last opportunity for the big leap forward. I was clear that the new Stockport chief executive, Arthur Wilson, would insist that I had accepted the Stockport post and refuse permission to allow me to seek another job. Dodging Arthur's anticipated refusal, I visited the council leader, Alderman Walter Knight, in the evening before the West Yorkshire appointment. Walter graciously consented to my crossing the Pennines for the interview. Next day I returned from the Yorkshire interview to find that, as I expected, Arthur had persuaded Walter Knight to withdraw his consent. But by then it was too late.

Fortified by Alderman Knight's approval, I arrived at the great county hall in Wakefield, headquarters of the West Riding County Council and designated to be the HQ of the new West Yorkshire County Council. The only senior job in the new county council advertised externally was that of director of administration. The job of chief executive and all other chief officers had been filled from the ranks of predecessor authorities. Appointment to the director of administration post had been left till last. By then any local contenders for the job had managed to procure jobs elsewhere: there was no local candidate.

The princely salary offered by the county council had attracted an impressive shortlist: the external candidates more than compensated for the lack of internal candidates. The daunting competitors included Martin White and Michael Holdsworth, my old friends from the Wakefield Law Students' Society, both with a West Riding County Council pedigree. I was the only candidate without an Oxbridge degree. Curiously this boosted my chances in two ways. Cowed by the competition, I came to the conclusion that my chances were slight and as a result I relaxed, believing that I had nothing to lose. Moreover the chairman of the appointing committee was a Dewsbury trade union official who was actively hostile to the intellectual pretensions of Oxbridge. He liked the idea that I was a Morley lad who had left school at 15. He checked me out by phoning his NUPE counterpart in Manchester. He in turn phoned the Stockport Council work study officer, who gave me a glowing testimonial.

I was appointed. Immediately on my return to Stockport Jim Gardner, the chief executive of Sunderland, phoned me. He had been appointed as chief executive of the new Tyne & Wear County Council and urged me to reject the West Yorkshire job and take his old job as chief executive of Sunderland. In the reorganisation, 'leapfrogging' was not uncommon: employees would accept the first post offered but continue to seek better jobs elsewhere. I decided that backing out of the Stockport job was enough duplicity and stuck to my West Yorkshire offer. Although I would be only number two in the West Yorkshire County Council hierarchy (whereas the Sunderland offer was the top job), the county council was the third biggest authority in the country and offered an entry into the elite league of county councils.

The move had a spectacular effect on our financial position. When I had joined Stockport council seven years previously my annual salary was £2,110. My leaving salary was £6,057. At West Yorkshire it was nearly £11,000, prompting the *Daily Mirror* to carry the headline '£10,000 aged 29.' The county council had taken a policy decision to pay top salaries in order to attract the best candidates. When he saw the salary attached to the new county council's job of parliamentary officer, the West Riding Council's parliamentary officer, thought that he had been 'priced out of the market'.

It was a time of economic stagnation and dramatic inflation – so-called 'stagflation' – with wage awards reaching 30 per cent. Led by Edward Heath, the Conservative government fought inflation. In 1975 it set a target for local authorities of limiting their rates increase to 25 per cent. It established a statutory Pay Board, chaired by retired Treasury mandarin, Sir Frank Figgures. The salaries offered by the West Yorkshire County Council prompted him to announce his intention to intervene. My colleagues and I braced ourselves for the investigation. But before the Pay Board could begin its enquiry the Government fell and Harold Wilson's Labour government took over in February 1974. One of its first acts was to scrap the Pay Board.

The Winding Stair

It also established the Layfield Commission to examine local government finance, with public spending under severe pressure due to the economic crisis. Sadly the government chose to ignore Layfield's recommendation of a local income tax, perceived at that time as too radical.

I started work at Wakefield county hall in July 1973, nine months before the expiry of the West Riding County Council. In the city's civic centre, county hall's modest polygonal tower was overshadowed by the Doric portico of the law courts next door and, next to that, the Gothic tower of the town hall. Shortly after I arrived in Wakefield the law courts were the location of the trial of Judith Ward, coincidentally the daughter of a Stockport councillor, whom I knew well. Thanks to largely spurious evidence assembled by Chief Superintendent (as he then was) George Oldfield, later notorious for his role in the Yorkshire Ripper case, she was convicted of perpetrating the M62 coach bombing, when an IRA bomb killed twelve people. It took 18 years before her conviction was quashed and she was released from prison. Given the alleged IRA involvement, high security surrounded the law courts and county hall. Police snipers occupied nearby roofs. One day the buildings were evacuated when a suspicious parcel was found in the courtyard. As a cautionary measure it was exploded and a ham sandwich splattered against my office window.

My appointment in Yorkshire clearly required me to reestablish my Yorkshire roots and move across the Pennines. The choice of house was of great interest to the West Yorkshire councillors. Leader Eddie Newby, from Bradford, urged on me the then posh Bradford area of Nab Wood. The Morley councillor and Labour Whip, a gay nurse named Billy Merritt, attributed to me a desire to return to my native soil and join the Morley textile oligarchs in their traditional habitat, the Morley Rein Road. Sadly we found the area round Wakefield uncongenial. We extended our search for housing over an ever-

126

widening circle, finally hitting on a rural house at Aldwark on the River Ure in North Yorkshire. It required a long drive to Wakefield, but on rural roads. Our decision to buy was followed shortly by the oil embargo from the Organisation of Arab Petroleum Exporting Countries. It resulted in the production of ration books for petrol. Living in the middle of the countryside was no longer possible: we were obliged to relocate near a rail station. We chose to live in Ilkley, an attractive town on the edge of the Dales, mainly because it had a rail station. On its main street, the Grove, passers-by were seduced by the smell of roasting coffee from Betty's celebrated café, famously patronised by Alan Titchmarsh and Alan Bennett. The latter had been invited to become a director of Betty's, with a lucrative salary and as many buns as he could eat. He declined the offer when told that his sole duty would be to sit in the café in order that his patronage could be observed by the natives.

Our chosen residence was a substantial Edwardian house, in which we lived for five years. It had a large wine cellar with traditional stone shelving. The oil embargo had damaged the economy so that the price of our new house in Yorkshire was substantially less than we received for our house in Cheshire: we had money to spare. The economic crisis had hit businesses. It drove an upmarket local wine merchant into liquidation and we were able to stock our stone keeping cellar with fine wines, including first-growth clarets at £6 per bottle – and some 1965 Ogier Côte-Rôtie. Côte-Rôtie was then an unfashionable wine, but one of which I had become very fond.

There was a sequel forty years later, long after we had left our Edwardian house. I was then chairman of the board of the Leeds Playhouse, the theatre built thirty years previously with the funds of the abolished West Yorkshire County Council. I had reluctantly persuaded the Board to change its name from West Yorkshire Playhouse to Leeds Playhouse, in deference to the support we received from the Leeds City Council. The theatre was due for renovation and improvement. We applied to the Arts Council for a grant but were refused. Persevering, we addressed the criticisms of the Arts Council and applied once more. The chairman of the Arts Council, Sir Peter Bazalgette, was due to visit the theatre. An oenophile, Baz wrote a regular column in *Decanter* magazine, from which I knew that his favourite wine was Côte-Rôtie. Just before Baz's visit, I was telephoned by the people who had bought our Victorian house. In an inaccessible corner of the cellar they had discovered two crates of wine forgotten when we had moved house forty years previously. One crate contained the 1965 Ogier Côte-Rôtie, which was drinking beautifully. Of course, we brought out the Côte-Rôtie when Sir Peter arrived for dinner at the theatre. Our renewed application to the Arts Council for money to modernise the theatre was approved. I do not, of course, suggest that that the Côte-Rôtie was why the grant was approved – bureaucracies don't work like that – but it did make Baz's visit to the theatre stick in his mind.

We moved from the Edwardian house with the keeping cellar during the 1979 'winter of discontent', when strikes were endemic. We agreed to buy a house just below Middleton Woods, a well-known local beauty spot. Twenty-eight acres of the woodland had been given to the Ilkley Urban District Council by Arthur Hentzen, a wealthy German Bradford wool tycoon, who lived nearby. The gift included a mausoleum in which Hentzen planned to be buried next to his 'housekeeper', Miss Ellen Adams, who had died in 1935. During the war Hentzen left Ilkley to live in Switzerland and died in December 1949 in Germany. In accordance with his wish his body was brought back to the mausoleum in Middleton Woods and laid to rest next to Miss Adams.

Living next door to our new house was a delightful octogenarian, Stanley Ryder Runton. Stanley was the former owner of Wendy Knitting Wools and husband of the late County

The Splattered Sandwich and the Mausoleum

Alderman Kathleen Ryder Runton CBE. In 1941 Mrs Ryder Runton had been appointed OBE in her dual capacity as Evacuation Officer for the West Riding and Chief Billeting Officer for the Ilkley Urban District Council. She became chairman of the West Riding County Council, was elevated to the rank of Commander and became the driving force behind the County Council's 1966 purchase of the Studley Royal estate for £250,000. Once owned by the Marquess of Ripon, first Chairman of the West Riding County Council, the estate's elegant 18th century walkways, statuary and temples frame Fountains Abbey and were declared a Unesco World Heritage site in 1986. By then the estate had been inherited by the North Yorkshire County Council and transferred by the County Council to the National Trust.

Our house move was complicated by heavy snow, as well as by industrial action during the winter of discontent. The house purchase was not straightforward. A postal strike frustrated postage of the crucial banker's draft from our purchaser's solicitors in Rochester. I despatched my articled clerk to collect it. He and the banker's draft were stranded in Rochester when the railways were paralysed by strike action. My bank refused point blank to advance the amount of the banker's draft even for twenty four hours, confirming the view that banks lend money only to those who don't need it. In desperation I appealed to my father-in-law, who took the title deeds of his own house to his bank. On the strength of the deeds, his bank telegraphed through the necessary cash – which we replaced next day when the articled clerk returned with our banker's draft. During the delay our furniture van became snowbound in the long steep drive of our new house.

The heavy snow in 1979 was not unusual: in those days Ilkley was often icebound in the winter. Every year skates hissed on the polished ice of Ilkley Tarn. The swooping rhythm of the skaters is captured in *Ilkley Tarn*, the second movement of Arthur

The Winding Stair

Wood's Yorkshire suite *My Native Heath*. The suite is now famous for its fourth movement, the maypole dance *On Barwick Green*, theme tune of *The Archers*.

The regular snowfall enabled our children and me to indulge our passion for skiing: the thriving Yorkshire Ski Club was based in Ilkley. It was run by a German engineer named Gerhardt, who had a remarkable history. He had worked in Yorkshire before the War and became engaged to be married to a Pudsey girl, who worked in Leeds. As the Second World War loomed, Gerhardt returned to Germany where he became a bomber pilot. In 1944 his plane was shot down over England. After descending by parachute, he was taken by rail to Leeds en route to the prisoner-of-war camp at Butcher Hill, Horsforth. Unlike his escort, Gerhardt was familiar with the local transport system. When they arrived at Leeds station Gerhardt explained to his attendant that the best way to get to the PoW camp was on the number 33 bus. He asked if he could visit his fiancée, on his parole to appear at the bus station in an hour's time. The parole granted, Gerhardt walked through the middle of Leeds in his Luftwaffe uniform to meet his beloved. He said that people looked at him suspiciously, but, being English, were far too polite to challenge him.

After the War he remained in Yorkshire, married his Pudsey fiancée, founded a successful engineering company in Guiseley and became the mainstay of the Yorkshire Ski Club.

10. The New West Yorkshire County Council and Calculated Rudeness

Back to 1973. The key functions of the new West Yorkshire County Council were strategic planning, transport (including rail), highways, waste disposal, land reclamation, police, the fire service and consumer protection. Concurrent with the district councils, it also had powers for recreation, archives and archaeology and inherited from its predecessor responsibility for the Road Construction Unit, responsible for creating the new network of motorways in the North East. The intention was that the county council would take a strategic view of the conurbation as a whole. However, unlike its predecessor the West Riding County Council and the shire county councils, the new authority was not responsible for education, social services and libraries: those services were provided by the five constituent district councils – Leeds, Bradford, Kirklees, Calderdale and Wakefield – which also controlled local planning.

The West Yorkshire County Council had a very different gestation to that of the new Stockport Council. The joint committee set up in Stockport saw its role as preparing the way for the new Stockport Metropolitan District Council. It looked forward to the future. In West Yorkshire the great cities of Leeds and Bradford and (to a lesser extent) the county boroughs of Dewsbury, Halifax, Huddersfield and Wakefield had the opposite intent. They were accustomed to independence. They resented the creation of a county council which would encroach on their power. For many, their participation in the West Yorkshire joint committee had the objective of stifling the new West Yorkshire County Council in its infancy. Primitive action was taken: offices destined for transfer to the new county council were stripped of their furniture. The county council's highways directorate found that the vehicles they inherited from the district councils had long since lost their MoT certificates and had been preserved for the sole purpose of transfer to the new county council. The district councils had stalled legal actions against them so that liability could be passed on to the new county council. After the comprehensive and constructive planning I had masterminded in Stockport it was disconcerting to discover that, not only had little of any use emanated from the West Yorkshire joint committee, but that much had been done to frustrate the functioning of the new authority. I had to start from minus one.

In the West Riding hostility between the county boroughs and the county council was long-standing. The culture of the county council was very different to that of the plebeian urban councils. I knew that I had arrived in the county world when the chief executive of another county council wrote to me as 'Dear Brooke', the standard appellation among county clerks. There was also a political element: the county council was often of a different political colour from the districts. The county council may have been more genteel, but the West Riding county boroughs had suffered for years under the arrogant assumption of ascendancy by the County Clerk, Sir Bernard Kenyon, whose conviction of the superiority of the county council was absolute. At a meeting with the town clerks of the great Yorkshire cities – including Leeds, Sheffield and Bradford – Sir Bernard exploded:

West Yorkshire County Council and Calculated Rudeness

'What a load of bloody fools: no wonder you've have finished up where you are.' The Town Clerk of Sheffield signed off one interchange by writing to Sir Bernard: 'I must now discontinue this correspondence since I fear that I cannot match you for calculated rudeness'.

The district council chief executives were not alone in loathing Sir Bernard's overbearing manner. Sharing their view was Sir Alec Clegg, the eminent West Riding Education Director. In the full Education Committee, he referred to Sir Bernard as 'that bladder of lard across the road'. The county council had more than one hundred members, including aldermen elected by the councillors. All members of the county council were also members of the Education Committee. Refusing to recognise the suzerainty of the county council, Sir Alec built a separate council chamber across the road so that the Education Committee could feel themselves an independent authority. That attitude was shared by other departments. There seemed to be no corporate spirit whatsoever.

Though writhing in its death throes, the old West Riding County Council was still operational when I arrived at county hall in summer 1973. When petrol rationing was introduced during the oil embargo I attended a meeting of West Riding chief officers, which had been convened to discuss their reaction to the crisis. Some departments had ample supplies of petrol: others were chronically short. To my astonishment there was no suggestion whatsoever that those departments with lots of petrol should share their surplus with those who suffered from its lack. The county council departments operated autonomously and without any sense of being part of a greater whole.

It may be that their spirit of independence had been prompted by the bullying of Sir Bernard, whose presence was intimidating. He stood over six feet high and weighed over 20 stones. Despite his bulk, Sir Bernard retained his membership of the county council cricket team until the elevation of his trouser seat while he picked up a ball prompted ribald comments from miners in the watching crowd. On one occasion Sir Bernard discovered in the corridors of County Hall Raymond Gledhill of the *Yorkshire Post*, doyen of local government reporters. Sir Bernard shouted 'Why are you skulking here?', picked up the tiny Gledhill and ejected him bodily out of County Hall – a marked contrast to the deference afforded to the 21st century media. Sir Bernard did not confine his disdain to the press and the West Riding town clerks. On hearing that a chief officer was having an affair with his secretary, Sir Bernard's reprimand was 'Cats don't crap on their own doorstep'. When the West Riding Chief Constable arrived at Sir Bernard's office with his usual coterie of acolytes, Sir Bernard barked: 'Good God Scott! Have you brought the office cleaner?'

Sir Bernard had a similarly arrogant attitude towards county councillors. When John Boynton, later Sir John, applied to become Deputy Clerk of the West Riding County Council, he was nonplussed when Sir Bernard enquired: 'But if the council makes the wrong decision, would you have the courage not to implement it?' Sir Bernard's subordinates treasured the story of the newly elected county councillor, promoted by election from the pit to the gentility of County Hall. On his first visit he encountered Sir Bernard, who demanded to know who he was. 'I', responded the tiny miner, 'am a county councillor. And who art thou?' 'I', retorted Sir Bernard imperiously, 'am the Clerk of the County Council.' 'Art thou?' responded the tiny miner, putting his arm round Sir Bernard's immense shoulders. 'Then I'm thi boss'. In his early days Sir Bernard was genuinely impressive. In his latter days he relied on bluster and failed to 'do his homework' (as Steve Crowhurst, his Parliamentary Officer told me).

When Sir Bernard reached retirement age, he explained to the West Riding County Council that it could not manage without him. While he would, of course, draw the pension to which he was entitled, he was prepared to continue as clerk and to receive his normal salary in addition to the pension, provided that he was also allowed to accept outside appointments. The cowed county council accepted this remarkable arrangement. One of the lucrative outside appointments which Sir Bernard acquired was his directorship of a company run by the corrupt architect John Poulson.

When the incumbent of a post retires it is often the case that the successor is chosen with the opposite characteristics of the predecessor. The members want a change. When Sir Bernard eventually retired, the county council chose the meek and unobtrusive Peter Butcher to succeed Sir Bernard as County Clerk of the West Riding County Council. Butcher attracted national publicity on his appointment. He lived in a modest semi-detached house near the Wakefield bus station. He had bought the house when first appointed as an assistant solicitor in County Hall. When selected to succeed Sir Bernard, Butcher decided to trade up and acquired the other half of the semi. The *Daily Express* heard of this eccentricity and sent a reporter to investigate how the holder of such an important and lucrative post lived so modestly.

11. The War with Leeds, Corpses on the Bus and the House of Lords

The old West Riding County Council was one of the largest local authorities in the country. The county town was Wakefield, chosen in 1889 because of the convergence of the north/south and east/west railway lines close to the site earmarked for the County Hall. The city was embellished by a cathedral with mediaeval origins and the tallest spire in the county. The cathedral and the county council had some interaction. On my arrival in the city I was greeted by John Allen, the Cathedral Provost. John had been Rector of Chippenham in Wiltshire when the Bishop of Wakefield lunched with the Bishop of Bath and Wells at the Athenaeum. The Bishop of Wakefield explained that he needed a Provost and asked his fellow bishop if he knew a likely candidate. The Bishop of Bath and Wells commended John Allen. Invited to become Provost, John declined politely, preferring to stay with his family in charming Chippenham rather than uproot them to a mining town in Yorkshire. He was told unequivocally that God had summoned him to Wakefield. John obeyed the call, despite some surprise that the Almighty had chosen to manifest himself over lunch at the Athenaeum. Later David Hope, my contemporary at Wakefield Grammar

War with Leeds, Corpses on the Bus and the House of Lords

School, joined the cathedral and became Bishop of Wakefield, before his successive translations to London and the archiepiscopal throne in York.

The dominion of the West Riding County Council stretched from the edge of the Lake District in the North to the Humberhead plain in the South. The county council had a vision of its role commensurate with its status. Its identity was trumpeted across the county in a distinctive roundel, a hollow circle with a horizontal bar containing the name of the location and the grid reference. Together with the six legal deposit libraries (like the British Library and the Bodleian) it collected every published book – a unique collection tragically dissipated among its successor authorities. To preserve the heritage of the county, after the Second World War the West Riding County Council had acquired a cluster of stately homes, which were often turned into teacher training colleges – Grantley Hall, Wentworth Woodhouse, Wentworth Castle, Bretton Hall, Oakroyd Hall and Fountains Hall (including the Fountains Abbey and Studley Royal estate). On local government reorganisation they were transferred to the new district councils or the North Yorkshire County Council. These successor authorities could not afford such historic liabilities. They were progressively sold off or (in the case of the Fountains Abbey and Studley Royal estate) transferred to the National Trust.

The 1974 reorganisation of local government had traumatic results. Resentful Tykes were transformed overnight into Cumbrians or, even worse, Lancastrians. Historic parts of Yorkshire were transferred to Greater Manchester, Lancashire, Cumbria, and Teesside. Functions of the old county council were scattered between 55 successor authorities. As a result the new West Yorkshire County Council was a very different animal from the old West Riding County Council. The southern part of the West Riding formed the new county of South Yorkshire and its Northern part was transferred to the North Yorkshire and

137

Cumbria County Councils. The central area constituted the West Yorkshire County Council, with a population of over two million.

In some compensation for the loss of its historic inheritance, the powers of the new West Yorkshire County Council now extended into the former county boroughs which were incorporated in the new metropolitan districts of Leeds, Bradford, Calderdale (Halifax), Kirklees (Huddersfield and Dewsbury) and Wakefield. While they welcomed the expansion of their boundaries to include the adjoining areas which were formerly governed by the West Riding County Council, those members of the 'second-tier' authorities who came from the former county borough councils (which constituted a significant part of the new district councils) resented the intrusion of the county council into their jurisdiction.

The new county council, with a population of over two million people, had a very different demographic to the West Riding. Its new constituents, the former county boroughs, Leeds and Bradford being the most important, were rooted firmly in trade and industry. The landowning classes, who had been prominent in the old West Riding, did not appear in the new county council, which started its life firmly under Labour party control. Within the Labour party councillors competed for seniority on the new authority. The jobs were shared out according to political realpolitik. The leader of Dewsbury Council, Hector Nunn, an old trade-union official, was made chairman. The chairmen of county councils, usually long-serving, had been hitherto regarded as grandees, their names automatically included in *Who's Who*. Hector was duly included. But the new county councils operated the municipal system of Buggins' turn. The chairmanship switched annually. *Who's Who* soon changed its policy.

The former leader of Bradford City Council, Eddie Newby, became the leader of the new county council. He was a mill worker, who worked nights so that he could participate in local government during the day. Salt of the earth, Eddie lived in a terrace house, had no car, and travelled the twenty miles to County Hall by bus, presumably catching up on his sleep during the journey. His genial personality made him as popular with the opposition parties as with the Labour Group. Moreover he had a clear liking for me, my working class background no doubt establishing a bond. Unlike Stockport, where councillors from different parties detested each other and did not socialise, the West Yorkshire councillors mingled in the members' dining room and bar. There was mutual goodwill. On one occasion the Conservative Whip heard of disreputable behaviour by a Labour councillor in a Leeds nightclub. He did not publicise the episode, but told me privately, so that I could alert his opposite number to warn the errant councillor about his future behaviour.

Some extremely able Labour councillors joined the county council, attracted by its powers over strategic planning, highways and transport. The council's deputy leader and chairman of its Planning and Transportation Committee was Ken Woolmer from Leeds. An academic, young and outstandingly able, he became an MP and would have become a Minister had he not been ousted from his seat by boundary reorganisation. Instead he became a prominent member of the House of Lords. We became personal friends. The planning and transportation powers attracted other talented young councillors as well as able and experienced Leeds councillors. There was a smattering of women, though no councillors from ethnic minorities: in those days their absence raised no eyebrows.

An immediate point of conflict was the choice of the HQ of the new county council. The debate echoed that in 1890, when Wakefield was chosen as headquarters for the new West Riding County Council in preference to Leeds. The West Riding County Hall was an impressive art nouveau building, its copper light switches featuring scantily-clad nymphs. Its council chamber had served as a model for the Middlesex Guildhall in Parliament Square. But Leeds City Council was determined that Leeds should dominate the new West Yorkshire County Council. Hubristically they earmarked for the county headquarters an office building in central Leeds. The specification included a double-height room for the county council's council chamber. The new West Yorkshire councillors had no intention of being subjugated to Leeds. They chose the old county hall in Wakefield for the headquarters. With County Hall also came the splendid staff club and the extensive sports facilities which a benevolent county council had provided for its employees.

The clash between Leeds and the rest of the county continued with the appointment of the Chief Constable for the new county. There was considerable discord between the Leeds and West Riding Police Forces. Moreover, shortly before reorganisation Chief Constable Ron Gregory of the West Riding Force had attracted substantial criticism after an investigation disclosed that he had used his police car and driver to make regular visits to his mother in Wales. His defence was that he was visiting the Police Dog Training Centre, which was located a few miles away, and he had called on his mother while he was in the area. The implausible excuse for these multiple excursions was accepted. In the competition to become Chief Constable of the new County, he contended with the Chief Constable of Leeds. Determined not to see the county dominated by Leeds, the Police Committee stuck to the county man despite his unlikely interest in police dogs.

The appointment of the chief executive of the new West Yorkshire County Council caused yet another skirmish between councillors from the old county boroughs and the former county council. West Riding county chief executive Peter Butcher faced competition from his lively and able deputy Tony Mallett, as well as from Ken Potts, the ebullient 17-stone chief executive of

Leeds. The new councillors chose Butcher as Chief Executive. Deputy county chief executive Tony Mallett was far more able, but choosing him would have risked splitting the anti-Leeds vote. Mallett was then appointed as chief executive of the South Yorkshire County Council, which took over the southern part of the old West Riding.

Incensed by his rejection and loath to see the City of Leeds obliged to accept the ukase of the county council, Ken Potts thereafter waged unceasing war on the county council. The astute Potts appreciated that the county council had a major role in equalising resources. Leeds provided much of the revenue of the county council. Its rateable value subsidised services in other parts of the new county. It was cheaper to provide services in Leeds than in the spread-out areas of Calderdale. Leeds did not have the extensive areas of derelict land left behind by the coalfield in the south of the county. It did not have the upland Pennine areas of Kirklees. Surprisingly the other district councils in West Yorkshire failed to appreciate the cross-subsidy engineered by the county council. They also resented the warmth which the parish councils developed towards the county council compared to the chilliness of their own relationship with the parishes. Unlike the district councils, the county council presented no danger to the exercise of powers by the parish: grandparents are always less threatening than parents.

Eventually the overweening Potts engineered his own downfall. The Leeds City Council had a useful practice: when Leeds councillors went on overseas excursions, they took with them the editor of the *Yorkshire Post* or a senior journalist, thus assuring that there would no adverse press publicity about council 'junkets' when they returned. Surprisingly Potts did not learn from this. As with Sir Bernard Kenyon and other powerful men, Ken Potts believed that he was above suspicion. He was compelled to resign when he accepted a freebie to South Africa from the computer company which had sold a mainframe to the city council. I greatly missed my jousts with him: after years of skirmishing, his last words to me were 'You and I would have gone on well if we had been working together'.

Peter Butcher had a baptism of fire in his role as chief executive of the new county council. Unlike Stockport, no-one had drafted standing orders for the new authority. At the first meeting, held in the West Riding County Council chamber, Peter persuaded the chairman to announce that the meeting would be conducted under the standing orders of the county council. During the meeting a vote had to be taken. The West Riding County Council practice aped parliamentary procedure: councillors were expected to proceed through Aye and Noe division lobbies. The newly elected councillors refused to subject themselves to such an archaic system. They insisted on a simple show of hands, Butcher bleating helplessly as the members jeered.

Further humiliation awaited Peter Butcher. On the evening before the appointment of the county council's passenger transport supremo, Butcher was at an event in Leeds. There he encountered the favoured candidate, Tom Lord, director of the Leeds transport operation. As was his usual evening practice, Tom Lord had imbibed generously, relying on the driver of his official car to get him home. Sighting Peter Butcher, Tom Lord summoned him for a drink. The straitlaced Butcher replied: 'Don't you think you have had enough?' Incensed, the jocund Lord responded explosively. Next morning Butcher sought a private meeting with the interviewing panel for the county council transport job. He related his experience the previous evening and explained that Lord was clearly unsuitable for the job. To his mortification, the interviewing panel exploded with laughter as they imagined the exchange between the prim Butcher and the piratical Lord. Familiar with Tom Lord's nocturnal imbibing, they duly appointed him, as they had already decided. The incident dealt a mortal blow to Butcher's self-confidence and convinced him that the county council had been taken over by the jacquerie. Thenceforth he avoided county councillors whenever possible. The practical result was that the controlling Labour Group treated me as the de facto chief executive, with Peter Butcher marginalised.

Tom Lord was not the only pre-determined appointment. The allocation of jobs in the new local authority had been subject to negotiation between the different interest groups within the Labour group, balancing appointments between the predecessor authorities. The key functions of the county council were transport (including highways) and planning. The West Riding had an eminent county surveyor, Tony Gaffney, later President of the Royal Institute of Chartered Surveyors. Leeds also had a prominent transport engineer, Eddie Naylor. A structure was evolved which would accommodate them both. There was a strong belief that transport and highways must follow from town and country planning. In order to accommodate this principle, the different contenders for the jobs and the balance between former authorities, a Byzantine bicephalous structure was articulated, named the Department of Planning, Engineering and Transport. Joint heads were the Directors of Engineering and Planning. Symmetrically, each would have beneath him two departmental heads, for engineering and transport in one division; and for strategic planning and local planning in the other.

The county council's planning role was strictly strategic: the district councils were responsible for local planning within the county council's structure plan. Its planning department was grossly over-staffed, with a Director and two heads of department, one of whom, Martin Bradshaw, later became President of the Royal Town Planning Institute. In the engineering division Tony Gaffney was supremo; below him Eddie Naylor took on transportation and Tony Gaffney's county council deputy, Joe Sims, the engineering function. This included responsibility for the regional Road Construction Unit. This had attracted some prominence: Colonel Maynard Lovell, Tony Gaffney's predecessor as West Riding County Engineer, had achieved notoriety by refusing to accept the Ministry of Transport specification for the Tinsley Viaduct on the M1 outside Sheffield, believing, correctly, that it was inadequate. As a result and uniquely in Yorkshire, it was not designed by the county council's Road Construction Unit. As Colonel Lovell had foreseen, it was soon judged unsafe and had to be reconstructed at a cost of £82m, fourteen times the original building cost.

Uniquely, and by common consent, it was agreed by the county councillors that there was no suitable local candidate for the job of Director of Administration – hence the national advertisement and my own appointment. But, to my surprise, I found that, before my appointment, patronage from councillors had filled all the senior posts in my future department with staff from the constituent authorities. I was to have no part in choosing my own senior staff. However, the planning and transport lawyers had been imported from Leeds at the instance of the talented chair of the Planning and Transportation Committee, Ken Woolmer. He had made sure that he brought with him an outstanding officer, David Ansbro (later chief executive of Leeds and Pro-Chancellor of Leeds University), who in turn brought with him an able complement of lawyers for the planning, highways and transport section of my department. In reciprocation county councillors had secured the appointment of two generalist lawyers from the county council who were delightful people, but completely incompetent. Casting back my memory, I remembered that in Morley the Town Clerk had consulted me over the meaning of some of the impenetrable legal opinions emanating from County Hall. I had then been overcome by the profundity of the lawyer who could deal in such obscurity. I now realised that the emanations exhibited only confusion. It was a lifetime lesson: able people clarify obscurity. I arranged for the early retirement of the two ex-county council lawyers as quickly as I could.

The munificent salaries offered by the county council attracted other able people. Tony Gaffney and Martin Bradshaw were not the only chief officers to have the distinction of being elected President of their professional body. The Director of Finance, Geoff Pollard, became President of the Chartered Institute of Public Finance and Accountancy. In my own department Elizabeth Berry became President of the Society of Archivists, Richard Dalley President of the Association of Public Analysts and Douglas Smith President of the Chartered Institute of Legal Executives. I took great pride in the appointment of six county council officers as presidents of their professional societies.

Council meetings, staffing and alligators

My basic responsibilities as Director of Administration were the articulation of the county council's decision-taking process and the control of its legal work. One of my first tasks was to procure a coat-of-arms for the new County Council. This required my attendance on York Herald at the Royal College of Arms, an elegant 17th century building near the Thames, now enveloped by city skyscrapers.

After considerable discussion York Herald suggested *For the arms: Or two Piles Azure a Rose Argent barbed and seeded proper; and for the crest: on a Wreath of the Colours a Mural Crown Or standing thereon a Lion rampant guardant per fess Gules and Tenne crowned Or bearing in its forepaws a Rose Argent barbed and seeded proper; and for the supporters: Dexter a Lion rampant guardant per fess Gules and Sable armed and langued Azure crowned and charged on the shoulder with a Sun in splendour Or sinister a Lion rampant guardant per fess Tenne and Vert armed and langued Gules crowned*

The Winding Stair

Or charged on the shoulder with a Rose Argent barbed and seeded proper, the whole upon a Compartment representing the Pennine Hills; and for the motto: 'By effort achieve'. A dazed county council agreed with the recommended insignia.

There were more immediate and practical issues. Given the complete absence of any useful guidance from the joint committee, I set to producing standing orders and procedural rules for the council's governance. After his failure to impose authority at the inaugural meeting of the county council, Peter Butcher decided to leave the conduct of the council meetings to me. He assumed a back seat in the gallery and thus symbolically confirmed to the councillors that I was in charge. The council meetings became highly structured: before the meeting the three party Whips would meet the chairman of the county council and myself when we would agree an order of speakers. The Whips discouraged any speakers who had not sought their permission to speak and the chairman would do his best not to call them. This procedure established my importance in the eyes of the county councillors, since I would prompt the chairman whom to call. It also gave the meeting a sense of shape and drama, most vividly realised by me when our two children, then aged 7 and 9, visited. After half an hour, fearing that they would become irritable and raise a commotion, I commissioned one of my staff to take them to the bar and buy them a drink. They were furious and refused to go, so engrossed were they in the drama unfolding before their eyes. Not all was high drama in the council meetings: low comedy also played a part, when one councillor said 'If these allegations are being made, then I want to know the alligators.'

My job attracted an odd bag of other responsibilities as well as responsibility for law, administration and procedure. Some had a synergy with law or administration (like parliamentary work, accommodation, public relations, telephones, catering and cleaning). Others simply did not fit in elsewhere. They included

Top row: Mary, Harry, Alfred, Edward and Amy, my mother. *Front row*: Ethel, grandfather, grandmother, and Edna – a family photograph taken on 20 July 1929.

Right: Uncle Harry and his wife, Fay, return to Australia in 1959.

Below: The angelic author, aged 9, in 1948.

Below: Enjoying an Austin 7 sun-roof with girl-friend in 1962.

Left: I met Clare in the Aegean, June 1966.
Above: More dramatic transport that year.
Below: Our wedding day.

Above: The professional, 1974. *Below*: Meeting the Prince and Princess of Wales: Diana hovering in the background as usual.

Above: Mrs Thatcher: the Prime Minister in uncharacteristically friendly mode.

Above: Ceremony in St James's Palace. Note the white gloves, one carried, an essential part of court protocol.

Above: Lady Porter and I make the front pages. My departure opens the door for the homes for votes scandal and the £45m surcharge on Shirley Porter.

Right: A publicity shot by the River Wharfe for my book, *The Environmental Role of Local Government*, which sold 20,000 copies when the Government quoted it extensively in the first ever White Paper on the environment.

Left: Invitation to a reception with French President François Mitterand in October 1984. Note the special permission from the Élysée Palace to wear black tie with decorations, a concession from the rigid French protocol.

Health chief off to new job

Above: The *Telegraph & Argus* reports on my resignation as chairman of Bradford Health Authority to take up the role of secretary with the Association of Metropolitan Authorities, as shown by the *MJ*'s front cover

Right: Order of events for HM The Queen's Golden Jubilee celebration.

THE QUEEN'S GOLDEN JUBILEE

CEREMONIAL

A THANKSGIVING SERVICE AT ST. PAUL'S CATHEDRAL

at 11.30 am
Tuesday 4th June, 2002

Left: The Dolphin Square row hits the news – usually because of its tenants, who included a drunken Sarah Churchill, Mandy Rice-Davies, Christine Keeler, Vassall the Admiralty Spy and Princess Anne.

Entre nous
Rodney Brooke reveals the stories behind the headlines

"I London mayor Ken Livingstone is not running the Greater London Authority as expected — he has some outsiders in his cabinet.

This raises some ethical issues. Do they have to sign up to the same code of conduct as councillors? How will the rules on declaring interests work?

Consider the mayor's regeneration adviser, architect Lord Rogers. His influence on development policy could bring him long-term benefits. He may be able to attract briefs because he has the mayor's ear.

Expert outsiders in cabinets are a good idea — it could be copied by other councils — but the ethical issues involved require more discussion.

Ken: singing his own song

In the pipeline: Yorkshire residents have their reservoir back, but at a price — £2bn of debt

Waterworks for Yorkshire

Water privatisation gave the government a windfall from the sale assets originally paid for by ratepayers. Birmingham City Council made a heroic, but unsuccessful, attempt to reclaim the proceeds.

Now a third way has been found. Kelda, owner of Yorkshire Water, planned to transfer its reservoirs, sewers and pipes back to the consumers. A mutual company would buy them at their regulated value — £2.4bn.

So Yorkshire consumers could find themselves once more owning the assets seized from them in 1989, but saddled with a £2.4bn debt. For consumers it would be an expensive circle. What's more, Kelda plans to appoint the directors of the new company.

Ofwat regulator Sir Ian Byatt gave the plan the thumbs-down, but the idea is certain to be revived. Deciding on the issue will be new water regulator Philip Fletcher, deputy secretary in the Department of the Environment when water was privatised. Now he will be able to reverse the process.

At last councillors are to be properly rewarded. Independent panels are recommending reasonable rates. Even in Scotland the Kerley Committee has proposed £12,000 a year for backbenchers and £40,000 for top leaders.

Councillors will now get pensions. The government had planned to confine them to cabinet members. But, already smarting over the stripping of their powers, backbenchers revolted over this further separation into sheep and goats. The government caved in.

Expect scandals about abuses. The local government scheme is based on final salary. After 30 undistinguished years on the council, old Bill will suddenly find himself elevated to the cabinet for his last year's service. Officers have worked this dodge for years. It's standard practise for hospital consultants, whose merit payments arrive in time for pension calculations.

Meanwhile the government looks set to strip councils of social services and education powers. How ironic that councillors will be adequately paid just when there's nothing left for them to do.

Spin attracts public scorn, but the more it's discussed, the more important it becomes. Lobbying and PR agencies are the place to be. Taking the message on board are Rob Colmer and Brendan Murphy.

Mr Murphy left *The Sun* to become the Local Government Association's chief press officer. He brought with him a tabloid newspaper perspective. Mr Colmer turned the LGA's Conservative office into a professional operation. Now both are leaving the LGA to join the sultans of spin at PR consultancies.

Rely on LGA public affairs chief Phil Swann to use the growing local government diaspora. Networking has always been part of his strategy.

Feelers out: the LGA's Phil Swann

Westminster's animal magic

Press officers at Westminster City Council have much to do with the animal kingdom. Pigeons in Leicester Square are just the start.

In the days of Dame Shirley Porter the City Hall press office launched the pooper-scooter. People

Left: In 2000, I found myself reincarnated as a gossip columnist for the *Local Government Chronicle*

Above: Receiving my knighthood from Prince Charles in 2007 in Buckingham Palace.

Above: The family at daughter Antonia's.

Right: cricket on the lawn, at home in Ilkley.

the police prosecution service, archives, estates, the public analyst, emergency planning, the archaeological service and the rent officer. I also had responsibility for the administration and finance of the Coroners' and Probation services. In addition – as West Yorkshire was the largest authority in Yorkshire – responsibility for Yorkshire-wide bodies fell on me. They included administrative responsibility for the Yorkshire Tourist Board and the Yorkshire and Humberside Development Association, both of which had their own chief executives and boards, of which I became clerk.

The staffing of the West Riding Clerk's department was idiosyncratic. It included no graduates. Staff were recruited at school leaving age and allocated to one of eleven committee secretariats after a year or two of obligatory service in the post room. They stayed in the same section, slowly ascending the promotion ladder until they retired fifty years later as head of section. Every secretariat was an island entire of itself. The secretariats produced the minutes of their respective committees in different idioms. Each section had its own separate contract with a private company for printing those minutes. There was no interchange between sections.

Sir Bernard Kenyon inherited the system when he succeeded Sir Charles McGrath as clerk of the county council in 1943. On his appointment Sir Bernard indicated his firm intention to change it. But the following day he decided that it should continue. It was still in place in 1973. Surprisingly it had nurtured some extremely able people. I quickly realised that Harry Townsend was a brilliant manager and put him in charge of the secretariats. One thing I did change: the printer who produced the minutes of the county council itself was about to retire and close his works. The Department's Chief Administrative Officer, Bill Shearman, put forward a plan for the county council to take over the printing works. I adopted it nervously, but it was enthusiastically welcomed by the controlling Labour county group. It proved a successful move both financially and operationally, an unusual example of de-privatisation.

Corpses on the bus, the Winter of Discontent and the House of Lords

My Administration Department included a Parliamentary section, which dealt with the West Riding's local legislation, as well as with the interpretation of national legislation. The section was headed by Steve Crowhurst, an outstanding figure. He had left school at age 13 but would clearly have taken a First at Oxbridge had he had the opportunity. Crowhurst paid me the most valued compliment of my career. When he eventually came to retire, he told me 'I've worked hard for you, Mr Brooke – because I thought you were worth it'.

A thicket of local legislation faced Steve Crowhurst. In Huddersfield, for example, a local Act forbade citizens to take a corpse on a bus without first informing the driver. In neighbouring Dewsbury, like Huddersfield now part of Kirklees, no such communication was required. Huddersfield householders were required to whiten the step outside their front door before 8am each weekday. Failure attracted a fine.

Dogs were forbidden to bark during the hours of darkness by County Council regulations made in 1911. The regulations applied only in the West Riding area and even there excluded boroughs having a population of 10,000 or more in 1881.Ossett, for example, did not receive its borough charter until 1890, so that the West Riding law applied. After dusk Ossett dogs had to maintain a Trappist silence. In boroughs with an earlier charter and a sufficient population dogs could howl defiance with impunity, provided that they stayed on the right side of the ancient frontier. Some historical investigation was required before the dog wardens could quell nocturnal yowling.

War with Leeds, Corpses on the Bus and the House of Lords

Many public general Acts of Parliament had their origin in local legislation. The vital Clean Air Act of 1956, for example, was copied from a Manchester Act. But much of the old West Riding legislation was archaic, obsolete or had been superseded by public legislation. Considerable research was required to exhume and re-enact useful clauses and repeal the others or allow them to lapse. There were also new problems. The County needed the statutory power to enter on private land to repair burr walls – those that support the highway. The Pennine town of Hebden Bridge required special provision. In its steep-sided valley space was limited and there was little flat land. This led to the building of 'upstairs-downstairs' houses with so-called 'flying freeholds'. They were known as 'over and under' dwellings. Rather than the back-to-back houses built elsewhere in the Yorkshire mill towns, in Hebden Bridge houses were built one on top of the other. The upper houses were entered from the hill and the lower ones from the valley, with their back wall against the hillside. This could lead to great problems: the lower houses relied on the upper houses to keep out the rain; and the upper houses relied on the lower houses for structural support. The West Yorkshire Bill aimed to confer reciprocal rights on the owners of the two dwellings. To demonstrate the need for the clauses I had to display photographs of the houses to the House of Lords Committee which examined the legislation.

The West Yorkshire Act became a precedent for other local legislation. We published a manual to help other local authorities through the parliamentary process. As one of the first examples of local legislation after local government reorganisation, our Bill did not have an easy passage. In the hearing by the Private Bill Committee in the House of Lords I was interrogated by the Committee for three days. Justification was sought for every clause. Provisions which became standard and later went through on the nod were scrutinised intensely and had to be justified. The Lords committee studied the difference between retaining walls and burr walls and the need for the county council to have powers over them.

But – having survived the scrutiny of the House of Lords – the Bill hit a major obstacle in the House of Commons. Dr Edmund Marshall, Labour MP for Goole, persisted in blocking it (which he could do by simply shouting 'object'). His motive was unrelated to our Bill: he wanted to intimidate British Rail into installing a barrier at a level crossing in his constituency. This happened several times until the MP for Wakefield, Walter Harrison, the Labour Party's Deputy Chief Whip, leant powerfully on Dr Marshall. Walter took over the Bill and shepherded its progress through the Commons. The Bill left one unexpected legacy: I had suggested to the Lords Committee the need for a proper catalogue of local legislation, much of which was inaccessible. The committee adopted my suggestion. Nearly twenty years later I was invited by the then Lord Chancellor to a reception in the House of Lords to celebrate the completion of the index.

The West Yorkshire Bill was before Parliament at a time of high drama: it was there during the Winter of Discontent in 1978-79, when the Labour Government under Jim Callaghan tried to reduce inflation through wage restrictions for public sector workers, causing a wave of strikes. The problem of our house move was not their only impact. Rubbish piled up on the streets. Corpses were unburied. The strikes impacted on me in several ways. I have a vivid memory of driving Dennis Healey, then Chancellor of the Exchequer and a Leeds MP, to Leeds Station and being lambasted by him for my defence of 'profligate spending' by local authorities.

For me the most enduring effect of the Winter of Discontent was an aversion to using lifts. During the disruption I was summoned by the Monopolies and Mergers Commission, which (like most public bodies) has been regularly supplanted – initially by the Competition Commission and later by the

Competition and Markets Authority. Among the duties of the Commission was to inquire into the performance of public sector bodies. Specifically it was concerned about the possibility of anti-competitive practice, because the county council used its statutory powers to prescribe a standard fare structure for bus services in the county. On the day of my evidence to the Competition Commission the weather was both wet and swelteringly hot. Public transport was crippled by industrial action. There were no underground trains and no buses. The roads were paralysed by private cars. When my taxi was immobilised in the traffic, I baled out and sprinted through the drizzle and heat into the Competition Commission's office in Carey Street. Wet and sweating heavily, I crowded into a lift designed to hold eight passengers. I shared it with seven other sweltering people. It broke down. The temperature rose unbearably as we steamed and sweated in the stifling heat of the cramped lift. We were reassured by staff that an engineer had been summoned. 'Where', we asked, 'is he coming from?' 'Cricklewood' was the answer. Though none of us knew where Cricklewood was, the engineer clearly faced a protracted journey. For nearly two appallingly claustrophobic hours we were confined in the tiny, airless lift until release came.

The Winter of Discontent destroyed the Labour Government. With a wafer-thin majority, Prime Minister Jim Callaghan clung desperately to power. As Deputy Chief Whip, Walter Harrison was key to the Government's survival: he would grab recalcitrant Labour MPs by their lapels and threaten their testicles if they hinted at failing to vote. Undermined by events, the Callaghan government faced a motion of 'no confidence' in March 1979. Alfred 'Doc' Broughton, MP for my hometown of Morley, was on his deathbed when the crucial vote was called. Walter Harrison approached Bernard Weatherill, the Conservative Chief Whip, to allow 'pairing', that is to identify a Conservative MP who would join Doc Broughton in not voting.

The Winding Stair

Weatherill could not find a Conservative MP who would agree to pair: the convention had not been intended for such a critical situation. Doc Broughton said that he was prepared to come down to London by ambulance and be carried into the precincts of the House, where by convention he could be nodded through the lobby. After reflection, Weatherill said that he would abstain himself rather than force a dying man down to London. Such an action would have destroyed Weatherill's political future. Walter was so impressed by Weatherill's honourable behaviour that he refused to accept the offer. The Conservative motion was passed with 311 votes for and 310 against: the Labour Government fell. This drama was played out when I was in Parliament with the county council's Bill, often accompanying Walter Harrison, one of nature's sergeant-majors, as he strong-armed Labour MPs into the lobbies. The episode was transformed into *This House*, a brilliant play by James Graham which had two sell-out runs at the National Theatre. Sadly, Walter died just a few weeks before the play's first night.

12. Death in Jeddah: The Helen Smith Case and emergencies

One of the first duties in my new job in West Yorkshire was to fill the posts of coroner, of whom there were three within the county. The three current incumbents were all experienced and perfectly competent. There was no reason why they should not be re-appointed. However the posts had to be advertised and a number of applications were received. The county council was the appointing body, but the consent of the Home Secretary had to be procured. The law relating to coroners was anachronistic. In 1965 the Home Secretary had appointed a committee, chaired by Norman Brodrick QC, to modernise the law. After an elephantine gestation the committee had eventually reported in 1971, but no action had been taken to implement its recommendations.

The county council leader, Eddie Newby, chaired the interviewing panel for the coroners' appointments. I prepared a list of appropriate questions, concentrating on the recommendations of the Brodrick Committee. Realising that the interviewing committee would be perplexed both by the questions and by the answers, I prepared model replies against which the committee could judge the response of the candidates.

The Winding Stair

Eddie came in late, just as the first candidate was due. Waving away my introduction, Eddie invited the first candidate into the room. Seeing the papers in front of him, he chose the model answers and read the first out to the candidate. Though his mistake soon became obvious, Eddie continued to read to the end of the model response. 'Now', asked Eddie, 'what is the question to which that is the answer?'

The Committee duly agreed to re-appoint the three postholders and I despatched their recommendations to the Home Secretary for confirmation. The then Home Secretary was Roy Jenkins, whose diligence in tackling his red box was famously limited. The appointment of coroners in West Yorkshire was not at the top of its contents and for several weeks Jenkins failed to delve down and reach the papers which required his signature. Eventually my increasingly desperate pleas to the Home Office impelled his Private Office to move the consents towards the top of the red box. Jenkins counter-signed the appointments only hours before the coroners were to take office.

Unpredictably the county council's responsibility for the coroners' service precipitated it into a scandal of national interest – the inquest on Helen Smith. The Helen Smith case was front-page news for months. She was a nurse from Guiseley, near Leeds, who worked in Jeddah, Saudi Arabia. In 1979 she went to a drink-fuelled party and was found dead next morning, having dropped from a seventh-floor balcony onto spiked railings below. Her knickers were partly removed. Next to her was the body of a Dutch tugboat captain, also a guest at the party. The official Saudi investigation concluded that the couple had fallen from the balcony while drunk, possibly during or after a sexual encounter. Six post-mortems reached differing conclusions. Her body had been returned from Jeddah without several organs and now lay in a mortuary within the jurisdiction of the Leeds coroner, Philip Gill. Helen Smith's father, Ron

Smith, a former policeman, believed firmly that she had been raped and murdered. Because the death had occurred abroad, Coroner Gill refused to hold an inquest. Believing this to be an establishment cover-up, Ron Smith challenged that decision in the Divisional Court, where he was represented by Stephen Sedley, later a distinguished member of the Court of Appeal. Gill's decision was upheld, with references to the propensity of corpses to migrate around the world and the difficulty of establishing the cause of a death which took place in another continent. An uproar followed. The investigative journalist Paul Foot and *Private Eye* magazine took up the cudgels.

John Gunnell, leader of the county council, joined the county council's Conservative opposition spokesman in supporting Ron Smith in his quest for an inquest. The county council, anachronistically responsible for financing the Coroners' service, instructed me to withdraw the money for legal support to Philip Gill. It pressed for a public enquiry. Ron Smith appealed and this time was successful: the Court of Appeal ruled that coroners in England and Wales must hold an inquest into a death overseas if the body is returned to the coroner's district and the circumstances are such that an inquest would have been required if the death had occurred in this country.

Of course any relevant evidence lay in Saudi Arabia. A key witness was the host at the party, Dr Richard Arnot, who had been sentenced to thirty lashes for supplying illegal drink at the party. Dr Arnot refused to attend the inquest unless his expenses and the cost of legal representation were paid. The county council agreed to fund them. Arnot chose to be represented by the flamboyant Sir David Napley, who had represented Liberal Party leader Jeremy Thorpe in his trial for conspiracy to murder. Sir David's fees of £164 per hour, paid by the county council, were deemed outrageous by the national press. Each day Sir David arrived at the inquest in his golden Rolls Royce, ensuring that the case made the front page of the dailies. The hearing in

1982 was billed as 'the inquest of the century'. Despite the urging of the coroner, the jury declined to find accidental death and came to an open verdict. The verdict hardened Ron Smith's cussedness and made him more inflexible than ever. He declared that he would never bury his daughter because one day her body would provide the evidence that she was murdered.

Paul Foot published a four-hundred page book on the saga, *The Helen Smith Story*, in 1983. Nothing happened for thirty years. It was very clear that no further evidence would be forthcoming. The body – its vital organs long since eviscerated – began to deteriorate and (at the expense of the county council) had to be placed a special sealed casket. Shortly before he died and at the pleading of his wife, Ron Smith finally relented and the body was cremated. Helen's ashes were scattered from the Cow and Calf rocks in Ilkley.

The Helen Smith case was distressing but enabled the county council to take advantage of its rather peripheral role to secure good publicity, making it clear that it was on the side of the angels and completely opposed to a cover-up. Of course, I was piggy-in-the-middle, Since the finance for the Coroner's service was in my departmental budget Coroner Gill looked to me for support. The county council expected the contrary.

Archives, the Guillotine, emergencies and rotten cod

Implausibly, archives caused another battle. They were a shared responsibility between the county and the district councils. Included in my job specification was the setting up of an archives service. The West Riding was the only county council not to have had an archives service. When he was the West Riding County Council Clerk, Sir Bernard Kenyon had boasted that he had not been taken in by 'those charlatans of archivists'. The county council was, however, the custodian of significant records. *Inter alia*, they included lists of inmates of the county asylums and an explanation of their disability – their insanity usually attributed either to alcohol or sex.

Together with the county of Middlesex, the West Riding also inherited a forerunner of registered land: the registry of deeds, in which all transactions in real estate had been recorded since 1704. The records also contained the journey log of Barbara Hepworth's father, appointed West Riding County Surveyor in 1921. During school holidays she accompanied him as he inspected the rural roads. Her diaries record her impressions of the limestone country through which they journeyed and the rocks which influenced her sculptures.

The county council also kept the archives of the Quarter Sessions, on behalf of the lord-lieutenant as *Custos Rotulorum*. The archives explained the Yorkshire Beggars' litany '*From Hull, Hell and Halifax may the Lord protect us*'. The Hull magistrates were exceptionally severe. The need to evade Hell is self-explanatory. But why avoid Halifax? The court records normally recorded executions as 'John Smith, *hanged* this xth day of 16xx'. The rubric was different in Halifax where the records read: 'John Smith *topped* this xth day of 16xx'. In Halifax the gibbet was not a gallows but a guillotine, a Yorkshire invention described dramatically in 1727 by Daniel Defoe in his *Tour thro' the Whole Island of Great Britain*. Any thief who stole goods worth 13½ pence or more was beheaded three days after being caught. If the thief had stolen a horse, sheep or cow, the animal would be attached to the pin holding the blade of the guillotine so that it could personally despatch the thief.

A visiting Edinburgh citizen noted the efficiency of the contraption and copied it. In Edinburgh it was observed by a French visitor, Doctor Guillotin, who was appalled by the erratic impact of beheading axes. He imported the contraption to France as a painless and foolproof method of execution. Sadly there was no patent protection in the 18th century or Yorkshire could have netted substantial royalties during the French

Revolution. A replica of the Halifax guillotine now stands in the town centre.

The county's fascinating archives had languished for lack of a keeper. Local academics, led by the eminent Professor Maurice Beresford, were determined that the new county council should remedy the West Riding's failure to provide an archives service and had lobbied effectively. Having a blank sheet of paper, I made a proposal to councillors for the appointment of a County Archivist and the establishment of an archives department. I was told firmly to go back to the drawing board: my proposals were totally inadequate both in the salaries I proposed and in the department's staffing. My revised proposals were princely and attracted applications from the best archivists in the country, eager to gain fame and found a service in virgin territory. The appointee, Elizabeth Berry, created an outstanding service (sadly now severely run down, thanks to the financial privation imposed on local authorities).

Strangely custody of archives supplied another battlefield between county council and district councils. The district councils also enjoyed statutory powers to run an archives service. Leeds City Council, in particular, had a very important, though underfunded, archive service. Formerly a Cinderella service, the thought of the county council taking over prompted the district councils to take an immediate interest and to encourage a spirit of antagonism in the field. Archivists competed in their search for material. The archival rivalry prompted the intervention of the Home Office, which had overall responsibility for archives services. Ministerial intercession unified the district services with the county service, a move heartily disliked by Michael Collinson, the Leeds archivist. The relationship required great tact. There was also an ethical issue: the Wakefield archivist, John Goodchild, had a substantial private collection of archives. It was unclear which archives had been given to the archives service and which to

Goodchild. The issue was resolved after his death: all the archives, including Goodchild's, are now in the West Yorkshire Archives Service.

Surprisingly the activities of the County Council's Public Analyst provided yet another bone of contention with the district councils. Responsibility for the Public Analyst had been placed in my department for want of a better home. The incumbent was Richard Dalley, doyen of Public Analysts. The public health inspectors of the district councils would send samples to the Analyst to investigate for a specified substance. It was Richard's practice also to analyse the samples for whatever substance he thought appropriate. He developed ground-breaking methods for detecting additives, fakes and counterfeits. Regularly his analyses uncovered undesirable foreign substances which Richard would reveal to the local press. His discoveries attracted national fame and prompted new practice in the field. The kudos he acquired not only robbed the district health inspectors of the credit but also implicitly censured their failure to require a test for the relevant foreign body. Richard made one unexpected contribution to the department. My PA would circulate my weekly diary so that my colleagues could tell me of any issues they might have with those whom I was to meet. Unsurprisingly there was rarely an overlap between my diary and Richard's activities. But from the Public Analyst would come pregnant messages to my secretary: 'I see Rodney is going to lunch with the XXX on Tuesday. Tell him not to have the cod.' His analysis of its perils removed cod from my personal menu. Sadly economic privation ended the funding of the West Yorkshire Public Analyst in 2012.

My responsibilities included planning to cope with emergencies. One major emergency was a chemical explosion at the huge chemicals plant of Hickson & Welsh on the River Aire at Castleford. The explosion caused toxic liquid to flow through the town and over an allotment. At the public meeting called to assure residents that all was safe, Noel Cooper, the Chair of the West Yorkshire County Council Fire Committee was challenged to eat a rhubarb pie made from rhubarb grown in the allotment. Nobly, he obliged (and seemed to suffer no ill effects). Fortunately the incident had been the site of a practice exercise shortly before the emergency and was dealt with competently by the Fire Brigade.

Competence was not in evidence during a dummy disaster arranged by the district council in Bradford – which, in common with other metropolitan district councils, had emergency planning responsibility for local incidents. The dummy incident was instigated without notice by the ebullient Bradford chief executive, Gordon Moore, and resulted in a local Ragnarök. When the alarm was given, panicked staff could not find the key to the Emergency Control Centre in the Town Hall. In desperation the City Engineer smashed a window to gain access, severing a blood vessel in so doing. The pseudo emergency became real as the ambulance siren shrieked and paramedics rushed him off to hospital.

13. Death in the Afternoon –
The Bradford City Fire and Corruption

The real Bradford disaster happened on 11th May 1985. With a game to spare, Bradford City won the Third Division football trophy, their first silverware for 56 years.

A capacity crowd of 11,000 came to the club's Valley Parade ground to witness the last game and celebrate the club's triumph. The Bradford *Telegraph & Argus* brought out a special edition. Representatives from Bradford's three twin towns, Verviers (in Belgium), Mönchengladbach and Hamm (Germany), came over to join the celebration. Halfway through the game, panic spread when fire broke out in the old wooden main stand, built in 1911. TV cameras captured the harrowing detail as spectators leapt onto the pitch to escape the flames. Fifty-six spectators burned to death in the conflagration.

Almost a year earlier, on 18th July 1984, the County Council's Chief Fire Officer, Kevin Horan, had come to see me.

This was a unique visit: the Fire Service was competently and independently run and had little interaction with the rest of the county council, except at budget time. Kevin had instigated an inspection of the Bradford City football stand. Below the stand's wooden superstructure there was an accumulation of paper and other inflammable debris. Kevin believed that the stadium presented a substantial fire hazard. He had sent a letter to the football club warning them of the danger. They took no notice: the wooden stand was due to be replaced at the end of the 1984-85 season. Deeply concerned at the hazard, Kevin called upon me to sign a further letter. This specifically highlighted in full the improvements required and emphasised the fire risk at the stand. He asked me to sign it, believing that a warning from the County Council's chief executive would carry greater weight. I signed and despatched the letter. The club still took no action. Shortly afterwards I left the employment of the county council.

The county council had no statutory duty to inspect football stands and no power to enforce its recommendations. It could rely only on persuasion. The football club had received the specific warning but took no action. At the inquest, coroner James Turnbull recommended a finding of death by misadventure, which the jury adopted. Litigation followed. The judge criticised the club: no one in authority, he said, had given my letter the attention it ought to have received. As a result he found the football club two-thirds liable for the heavy damages arising from so many deaths. Despite the absence of a statutory duty or any relevant powers he found the county council one-third responsible. The county council, he ruled, had 'a common law duty' to the spectators.

It is a judgement which I still find difficult to understand. Over what issues does that common law duty extend? Should the London Fire Service have inspected the escalator at King's Cross station, where a conflagration caused the deaths of 31 people? And – given that the county council did identify the fire risk at the stadium and warned the club twice – what more could we have done in the absence of statutory powers of enforcement? The only possible action would have been to bring pressure to bear by publicising the warning in the press. Would I have done that had I remained with the county council?

Death in the Afternoon – The Bradford City Fire

After a few weeks in my post with the county council I realised that I had not been shown a large part of my department's allocated office space. I discovered that it was occupied by Deputy Assistant Commissioner Jim Crane of Scotland Yard (later Sir James and HM Chief Inspector of Constabulary). Jim was investigating the influence of the shady architect John Poulson, whose arrest in 1973 had immediately preceded my arrival in Wakefield.

Poulson had dispensed in the public sector the same patronage which is customary in the private sector. He saw nothing improper in his activities and kept a meticulous record, which emerged during his bankruptcy proceedings. Within his net were Reginald Maudling (then Home Secretary), Members of Parliament, civil servants and T Dan Smith, charismatic leader of Newcastle Council and leading light of the Labour Party in the North of England. Guests at Poulson's opulent house included Sir Cyril Smith and Sir Jimmy Savile. When the scandal was exposed Maudling resigned. T Dan Smith and others were imprisoned. Also within Poulson's network was Sir Bernard Kenyon, ex-Clerk of the West Riding County Council. The scourge of venality in others, Sir Bernard, knowing himself to be incorruptible, did not hesitate to become a director of one of Poulson's companies at the same time as he continued to function as clerk of the county council. His signature appeared on planning permissions obtained by Poulson. The investigation into Sir Bernard clouded his later years and was discontinued only on his death.

Sadly, the popular Eddie Newby, leader of the West Yorkshire County Council, was implicated in the Poulson affair. Members of all three political parties mingled on a friendly basis in the County Hall members' bar and Eddie held court among them. While he was leader of Bradford Council, Eddie had been lured by T Dan Smith to inspect housing in Paris. Given T Dan Smith's dominance in the Northern Labour Party, this was tantamount to an instruction. Eddie thoroughly enjoyed what he saw as a free weekend of hospitality, well beyond his extremely limited budget. The bill was met by Poulson and the weekend earned Eddie a suspended prison sentence which required his resignation from the county council. As he stood up to leave for ever, all members of the county council rose to their feet to applaud him out of the chamber. A tear glistened in every eye.

Poulson's legacy to me was a rigid approach to the acceptance of hospitality. I imposed a strict regime on the county councillors. Shortly after my appointment the civil engineering contractors responsible celebrated their achievement in building the longest continuous section of motorway in the country, part of the M62 transPennine route. Since responsibility for the motorway road construction unit was with the county council I had responsibility for organising a suitable event to mark the royal opening.

The road construction unit had excelled itself in the design of the last stretch of the M62 transPennine motorway. It is famous for a number of ingenious features: the wall of the Scammonden Dam carries the motorway; when it was constructed, the Scammonden Bridge was the longest single span non-suspension bridge in the world; and, uniquely, Stott Hall Farm is marooned between the two carriageways. When the stretch of motorway linking Yorkshire with Lancashire was completed the Queen came to cut the tape. The county council entertained Her Majesty and guests with tea and buns in an appropriate tent. Down the road the contractors provided lavish hospitality in a magnificent marquee. To widespread resentment, I vetoed invitations from the contractors to county councillors. My action was justified when within days the county council awarded the contract for construction of the Leeds inner relief road to the same contractors. Had our councillors been seen to wolf down the contractors' champagne and caviar, then *Private Eye* would have had a field day.

Death in the Afternoon – The Bradford City Fire

Shortly afterwards my personal rectitude was tested. The *Egon Ronay Good Food Guide* declared the Box Tree Restaurant in Ilkley the best restaurant in Britain. The *Guide* was then sponsored by Dunlop. To celebrate the award a splendid banquet was to take place at the restaurant. We were invited to it by a friend, Roy Marsh, who was a Director of Dunlop. I was severely tempted to accept. My invitation stemmed from my friendship with Roy and had nothing to do with the county council. Luckily I stood firm and declined. Returning from the feast, Roy took much pleasure in describing lovingly the gastronomic and oenological delights which had been enjoyed. A month later Slazenger, a Dunlop subsidiary, applied for planning consent for a development in the West Yorkshire motorway box, created by the intersection of the M1 and the M62. The decision was extremely sensitive. I had a pivotal role in promoting the award of planning consent. Had I accepted Dunlop hospitality I should have had to disqualify myself from participating and my credibility would have been badly damaged.

14. The Airport, Skating, Opera and Geoffrey Boycott

In 1974 party politics were not recognised in the formal framework of local authorities. In law decisions were taken by the council. Officers served the council as a whole, not just the members of the majority party. In practice key decisions were taken by the controlling political group on the council. To overcome the problem the Labour administration of the county council adopted the usual practice in municipal authorities of arranging political group meetings before each decision-taking committee. Those meetings would effectively take the decisions which would be announced at the full committee, where they could be debated and challenged by the opposition parties. I took the (then unusual) view that I should be present where decisions were taken in order that those taking them were fully briefed. At the invitation of Eddie Newby as leader of the council, I attended the Labour group meetings. I made it clear that officer advice was also available to the minority groups. When Eddie Newby was obliged to resign from the county council, his successor as leader, Ken Woolmer, continued the practice. Taking charge of its administration, I became the key actor in framing and implementing county council policy.

The Airport, Skating, Opera and Geoffrey Boycott

Ken Woolmer soon made his presence felt. One key local controversy was the future of Leeds/Bradford airport, half owned by the county council and half by the five West Yorkshire district councils. Located in Leeds, the airport's very existence was opposed by its local residents, whose champion was the Leeds City Council. However, the shortness of its runway severely limited the capacity of the airport. It became clear that its survival depended on lengthening the runway. The County Council's Labour Group decided to back the runway extension. My only personal stake in running the airport was as secretary of the Airport Consultative Committee, which included members of parish councils and the local community. Administration of the airport had been allocated to Bradford Council, whose City Solicitor proposed to entrust the forthcoming planning enquiry to Roger Suddards, a local solicitor.

Roger was a charismatic and able lawyer. But he would not have the support which I could command from the county council's resources. I also wanted to be in the centre of such a key process. I persuaded Ken Woolmer to get the county council to entrust the job to me, which they did. I immediately retained my old professional colleague Sir Frank Layfield, by then the foremost planning silk of the day. As key witness on the financial viability of the development, I requisitioned Ed Anderson, an extremely able young accountant in the county council's Finance Department. [Ed so impressed the airport director that he became the airport's accountant, a first step towards a dazzling career which culminated in his becoming chairman of National Savings and lord-lieutenant of West Yorkshire.]

Frank Layfield was the most demanding taskmaster imaginable. At the end of each day's hearing, he would spell out the research he required for the following day. The team which I had assembled had to produce the answers that evening. When they were complete I would take them over to Frank's hotel –

on one occasion at 2am, being received by Frank in his dressing gown. The following morning he would know the briefing notes better than those who had written them. Frank destroyed the opponents of expansion. The Leeds planning witness, Clive Brook, was an able planner but no expert on airports. He was brutally crushed by several days of Frank's relentless cross-examination. Frank specified 22 points which had to be established. The first three points consumed three days of relentless questioning; the last 19 took forty minutes. The success cemented my own reputation for effectiveness: failure would have been extremely damaging.

The highly controversial affair taught me a lesson about the media. During the public enquiry I was interviewed on television while I was standing at the end of the runway. I was asked about noise nuisance from the airport, just as a heavy lorry went past. 'The decibel level from aircraft will,' I said, 'be no more than that created by this lorry.' As I spoke an aircraft came in to land. The interviewer pointed the microphone at the aircraft and an ear-splitting noise drowned my words. This was the first of several experiences where I found that the manipulation of the television process can give an entirely false impression. Viewers are oblivious of the artifice which doctors the message received by their eyes and ears.

In 1977 control of the county council changed: the Conservatives took power which, as normal, they replicated on every committee. Their leader was Tom Batty, former leader of the West Riding county council. Tom had one organisational requirement: he asked me to devise a committee structure which would provide a position of responsibility for every one of the 56 Conservative councillors. This was achieved, even if some had to be satisfied with the post of vice-chairman of a local road safety sub-committee.

The change of power provided me with an immediate ethical problem. The Co-operative Society had applied for planning permission for a large store in Ilkley. The county council had raised no objection to it on grounds of traffic. The public enquiry into the planning application was due to take place on the Tuesday after the election. The county council's standing orders prevented any formal meetings for a week after the election. The local Conservative county councillor, Harry Haddrill, whom I admired and counted as a friend, was bitterly opposed to the application, the Co-operative Society being regarded as an offshoot of the Labour Party. He and Tom Batty, the new leader, came to see me on the day after the election to ask me to arrange representation at the enquiry from the county council as highways authority and to oppose the application vigorously. It was clear that there were no highways grounds on which we could reasonably oppose the application, That, however, was not the point. There was no constitutional provision which would enable me to obtain a formal decision from the county council before the start of the planning enquiry on Tuesday. I had no option but decline their request. The Conservative Group reported me to the Ombudsman who, however, supported my decision. In the event the store was never built.

Despite this initial set-back, my relations with the new controlling Conservative party were cordial. They soon needed my help. A delightful old-style politician, Tom Batty refused point-blank to hold one-party meetings before a committee. As a result he hit a problem. Early in his administration the Mecca Group decided to close their plush Bradford ice rink, which rejoiced in coloured lighting in the barriers, sparkling chandeliers over the ice and a stylish bar and restaurant. The issue was considered by the recreation & arts committee, under the chairmanship of a Mrs Suttenstall. On the committee's instruction, I met Eric Morley, chairman of Mecca. He offered to keep the ice rink open if given an annual subsidy of £10,000 from the county council. The recreation & arts committee decided that it would be a good thing for the county council to preserve the ice rink by providing the subsidy. They agreed to seek the sanction of the finance committee for the spending. Mrs Suttenstall appeared on local television and radio to glorify the beneficence of the county council in preserving such a valuable amenity for the youth of the county.

The finance committee, however, took a different view and refused to allow the spending. The chairman of the finance committee, Peter Hartley, in private life chairman of Hillard's supermarkets, appeared on local television and radio to justify the decision of the finance committee not to waste ratepayers' money on the ice rink. When the committee's decision went to the county council, the full Conservative group decided to reverse the decision of the finance committee and to provide the necessary subsidy. Tom Batty then had to appear on the media to explain why, after all, it was a good idea for the county council to intervene to keep the ice rink open. The episode convinced him that a one-party decision-taking body was necessary. He also realised that one-party groups before each committee would not operate to prevent policy reversals like the ice rink. Together we set up a one-party strategy meeting to develop and frame policies. Including all committee chairs, it became the key body in the county council's policy-making. Despite change in political control, it endured until the county council's abolition.

The opera was an immediate issue faced by the Conservative group after it took control. Living in West Yorkshire was George Lascelles, 7th Earl of Harewood, then managing director of the English National Opera. He had an ambition to found a northern branch of English National Opera in Leeds, with the support of Leeds city council. The city council's chief executive, Ken Potts, advised Lord Harewood to see me to gain county council support. Lord Harewood duly came to county hall to solicit my backing. I managed to persuade leader Tom Batty to support the initiative, though, with his Bradfordian aversion to Leeds, his first inclination was to wish the opera anywhere other than Leeds. Convinced, he launched a successful appeal to the other Yorkshire county councils to put money into the opera. The matter of financial support from the West Yorkshire county council was considered by the Conservative group on a murky night at a party meeting at Leeds/Bradford airport, isolated on its plateau and the foggiest airport in the country. Tom's supporters were unable to find their way through the fog and the backbench Tories who did get there declined to give money to the opera. So, to Tom's mortification, the West Yorkshire County Council was the only one of the Yorkshire county councils to refuse financial support to (what became) Opera North.

Unexpectedly Tom Batty died suddenly. He was replaced by Royston Moore, formerly principal of Bradford College but by then Chairman of the Bradford Health Authority (a position in which I succeeded him twelve years later). Surprisingly Royston and I found ourselves in a clash of interests when the County Council rationalised its fire cover and decided to sell the Baildon fire station. Royston's Bradford Health Authority wanted the site for a clinic; the medical practice in which my wife Clare was senior partner sought it for a surgery. Royston and I scrupulously declared our interests and a transparent process was formulated which excluded both of us from any participation in the council's decision. Clare's practice made the higher bid and the building became their Baildon branch surgery.

In 1981, after four years of Conservative control, the Labour party regained control of the county council. Ken Woolmer had been elected to the House of Commons in 1979 and was succeeded as leader by another Leeds University lecturer, John Gunnell, elected only in 1978. He was extremely able but without experience of running a council. John and I became firm friends: so much so that on his death I delivered the memorial speech at his obsequies. Approaching the 1982 county council election, John asked for my help in framing the Labour party manifesto. I consulted Conservative leader Royston Moore, citing the Westminster convention that the main opposition party could draw on the advice of civil servants in framing their manifesto. Royston agreed and the Labour manifesto took shape with my input.

I regard myself as a devotee of opera. But John Gunnell was even more dedicated. In his poverty-stricken days as a junior academic in America, he would stand in the gods at the Metropolitan Opera through the longer Wagner operas. Unsurprisingly, the Labour manifesto we produced included a firm financial commitment to Opera North. A Labour party manifesto is sancrosanct. From time to time during the ensuing Labour administration, councillors grumbled about the amount of money going to the opera. I had a simple answer: 'It's in the manifesto'. More populist pledges in the manifesto were improvements to public transport and the construction of new stations to encourage commuters to travel by train.

The manifesto was put into effect: the 1981 election brought a big swing to Labour. The Labour councillors who had previous experience of control were insufficient in numbers or competence to govern the county council. It was clear that the new administration would have to include newly elected councillors. As a routine I met all the new county councillors to welcome them and induct them into basic systems. Since John Gunnell had not met many of his new colleagues he consulted me on the appointments. The new crop included some outstandingly able people like Ken Patterson and Wayne Jenkins, who became key figures in the new administration. In particular, John asked me if I had come across a possible chairman of the Finance Committee. I had been greatly impressed by one new member, John Harman. Since he was a mathematics lecturer at Barnsley College, I thought he might have the necessary skills to be finance chairman. Indeed he did.

The Airport, Skating, Opera and Geoffrey Boycott

An immensely impressive man, he was in due course appointed chairman of the Environment Agency by Conservative Secretary of State John Gummer (now Lord Deben) and knighted. Sadly he failed to find a Parliamentary seat: he would have made an impressive Minister.

Another new member, whom I misguidedly failed to esteem, was Fred Pennington. Fred was a cobbler from Castleford. Like all shoemakers he was slowly spoken. It took him a long time to decide to say anything and even longer to say it. Enlisted in 1939, he had become a Bren gun carrier in the War. He was chosen, he said, only because he was the only member of the platoon strong enough to carry it. Fred commanded respect among the councillors in the south of the county. Despite my low esteem but because of his support in the south, John Gunnell made him chairman of the Highways Committee, thought to be a routine committee with limited discretion. When the Labour Group took control I suggested that the leading members and the officers' management team should have an awayday. The intention was not only to establish the direction of policy but also to establish constructive personal relationships. We stayed overnight in a local hotel. After dinner we played bridge. I drew Cobbler Pennington as my partner. I played the Acol system. Fred used some pre-Acol system completely unknown to me. As a result I had no idea what we were doing, except that Fred clearly did. He controlled the play superbly and routed the opposition. I then learnt that Fred, the Castleford cobbler, had won the national *Daily Mail* bridge competition in 1938. It taught me a lesson: I acquired a proper regard for Fred, though I had to be patient to hear what he had to say. Interestingly his daughter had married a Nepalese. When she wanted to return to England to see her father, Fred had to canvass my support. I had to make a statement to the Nepalese authorities that he was a suitable person to take care of his own daughter.

The Winding Stair

The employment of Geoffrey Boycott was one immediate issue for the new controlling Labour Group. Five days before the election the Conservative chairman of the economic development committee had engineered a decision to hire the famous Yorkshire and England cricketer as an ambassador for the county council. For the relevant fee we were entitled to a certain number of hours of Boycott's time. We were to use them by stationing Boycott on the county council stand at economic development events. The Labour opposition was bitterly opposed: Boycott's xenophobic image was not one they wished to connect with their administration. It was clear that Labour would win the election and they declared their refusal to use Boycott as publicity for the county council. Within the law, it was my duty to implement the decisions of the county council. Despite the imminence of the election, I obeyed the wish of the Conservative majority on the county council and rushed through the contract with Boycott. The post would have been too slow: I got Boycott to come to my office to sign the contract (idiosyncratically bringing his own teabag) where I found him as uncongenial as his reputation. But - bearing in mind the likely view of county council after the election in three days' time – in the contract I defined Boycott's obligations as widely as I could. As expected, the new controlling Labour group refused to use him for publicity purposes, but extracted value for money by using the contract to oblige him to give cricket coaching to disadvantaged children in the inner cities.

15. Defenestration, Promotion, Police and the Miners' Strike

Peter Butcher was still the titular chief executive of the county council, though I had become *de facto* chief executive,. After six years as director of administration in West Yorkshire I was headhunted for the job of chief executive of Birmingham City Council. Clearly this was one of the biggest jobs in the country and I let my name go forward. My interview for the job went well and on my return home I was telephoned by the Birmingham administrator, who told me privately that the job was mine, but that formal authority was needed before an official offer could be made. Next day was the meeting of the West Yorkshire policy committee. I took advantage of the opportunity to brief the leaders of the three parties – John Gunnell (Labour), Royston Moore (Conservative) and Trevor Wilson (Liberal) – that I was due to leave the county council. At the end of the meeting I went home as usual.

Soon after my return the phone rang. It was John Gunnell. He told me that the three political groups on the policy committee had met after the meeting and unanimously decided to impose early retirement on Peter Butcher and to appoint me as chief executive in his stead. Shortly afterwards an irate

The Winding Stair

Butcher also phoned. While privately delighted at ending his uncongenial stint at the county council, he was, understandably, rather chagrined by his abrupt and unexpected defenestration. I assured him that the development had been as much a surprise to me as to him. Next day I was telephoned with premature congratulations on my appointment in Birmingham by the Chief Constable of the West Midlands, Sir Philip (later Lord) Knights. After I withdrew my application, the Birmingham job went to the ebullient Tom Caulcott. Tom put Birmingham on the international map – his critics would say at the expense of the council's services. Under Tom's guidance, Birmingham Council built the International Exhibition Centre and the new Symphony Hall. He recruited Sir Simon Rattle to conduct the City of Birmingham Symphony Orchestra, which took up residence in the new hall. He even lobbied – unsuccessfully – for Birmingham to stage the Olympic Games.

A couple of my West Yorkshire colleagues were understandably chagrined that they had not been given any chance of being considered for the job of chief executive. I went some way to mollify their feelings by remaining in my old office. As chief executive of the county council, it would have been natural for me to move from my office in the administration department into the office formerly occupied by Peter Butcher and his formidable predecessor, Sir Bernard Kenyon. But that office had one substantial drawback. County hall boasted a roofscape of many chimneys: it was built in the days before central heating. In those days every office had a coal scuttle to fuel a live fire, together with a firescreen to deflect and spread its heat. An army of attendants circulated County Hall to replenish the coal scuttles. When central heating had been installed in the building, Sir Bernard refused to have it in his room. As a result the central heating pipes made a dog-leg round his office, which retained its fireplace and coal scuttle. On my desk as chief executive were two hand bells: one to summon my secretary and one to summon the man who mended the fire. Unfortunately the services of the man who mended the fire had long been dispensed with and the coal scuttle had also disappeared. The coal fire had been replaced by two-bars of an electric fire, which were completely inadequate for their task of warming the cavernous office. Having frozen in my first day in the office, I hit on the solution: I returned to my former office and redesignated the chief executive's office as a room for the county councillors. This provided them with a facility which they had not previously enjoyed, though it meant that in winter they could not spend substantial lengths of time in county hall without contracting hypothermia.

Being now in charge in name as well as *de facto* presented me with the opportunity of changing the county council's structure. The hydra-headed department of highways, engineering and transportation clearly required rationalisation. The two equally ranked chief officers, one for planning and one for highways and transport, each had two senior deputies. The structure had been devised in the interests of symmetry rather than practicality. It was completely out of balance: while the responsibility for highways, traffic and transport was substantial, the strategic planning function did not demand anything like the same level of activity. The weekend after the announcement of my appointment, I took my annual walk round the Yorkshire Three Peaks – Pen-y-ghent, Whernside and Ingleborough. As I went I dictated the bones of a new organisation structure for the county council. Among other proposals, I included a double promotion for a planner called Brian Briscoe, who had impressed me greatly. Later he became Sir Brian and the first chief executive of the Local Government Association.

I also immediately promoted David Ansbro to my former job of director of administration. In his place as head of legal services I appointed an impressive applicant, Basil Smith. When David Ansbro left to become chief executive of Kirklees, I had a dilemma: should I appoint Basil Smith, who was extremely competent, or an outsider? One of the candidates for the job was Gordon Johnson, who later became chief executive of Lancashire county council. To the disappointment and surprise of Basil Smith, I appointed Gordon. I felt guilty at overlooking Basil, who was extremely competent, but took the view that a third internal promotion would be too incestuous: the office should have an outside stimulus. Basil duly left and became chief executive of Avon county council.

The county council was then responsible for the criminal prosecutions service. The West Riding County Council prosecuting service was led by the flamboyant Maurice Shaffner. To Maurice's pride, it was the only local prosecuting service licensed by the Director of Public Prosecutions to handle murder cases. Determined to protect the independence of the service from the police, county councillors had very deliberately decided to place it in my department, with Maurice as head of prosecutions. While Maurice resented his administrative subservience, he welcomed his independence from the police and my protection of his departmental budget. On one occasion a solicitor member of his prosecuting team had been revealed as gay. The police refused to work with him. Maurice needed my support to induce the chief constable to reverse the decision. Sadly the gay prosecutor quit rather than face the obloquy which gay people then encountered. When Maurice retired his deputy, Richard Otley, was appointed to replace him. Sadly the abolition of the county council in 1986 coincided with the establishment of the national prosecuting service. Things went downhill rapidly. Policies were imposed from London and had no sensitivity to local circumstances and sensitivities. There was no flexibility: bureaucracy ruled. Richard Otley could no longer even respond himself to letters from local MPs – they had to be composed in London.

As well as chief executive of the county council, I was also clerk to the police committee. Though county councillors formed the majority of the committee, it also included representatives of the magistracy, who were, at least in theory, non-political. The Police had a disconcerting lack of respect for the law. Suspecting something amiss, on one occasion they searched the flat of a county councillor and discovered, the chief constable told me, a 'rubber woman'. He also told me in confidence that the chairman of the police committee had exposed himself in a public convenience and received a police caution as a result. I asked the chief constable's permission to tell the leader of the county council, who would certainly have removed the chairman from that position, given his resulting vulnerability to pressure from the police. The chief constable told me that I must honour his confidence, which I felt obliged to do. The result was that the chairman of the police committee continued in office.

A later and Conservative chairman of the police committee was a pompous and unpleasant man, disliked by all who knew him and hated by his wife. In his public utterances he would refer to 'my force', which infuriated the chief constable. Relationships between the two were stormy. At the usual dinner at the end of the annual inspection by (later Sir) Lawrence Byford, the inspector of constabulary, the chairman rose to make what I assumed would be the usual speech of thanks. Instead he demanded the sacking of the chief constable. Lawrie Byford turned to me: 'Is that the view of the police committee?' he enquired. Spluttering over my coffee I could only stammer that the issue had not been considered by the police committee.

When he became leader in 1981, John Gunnell asked my advice on the committees on which he should serve. I told him to ignore the police committee: service there would be a waste of his time, since the chief constable had complete control of all operational matters and the committee was a relatively powerless institution. It was, John Gunnell said, the only piece of bad advice I gave him. Fortunately he rejected it and joined the committee, immediately encountering an ethical debate. To enable the traffic lights in the city centre of Leeds to be operated most efficiently, the traffic engineers had installed video cameras, which were monitored from an eyrie above the Headrow, the main traffic axis. The police asked to have access to the video cameras. After much debate about this incursion into individual privacy, it was eventually agreed that the police could have access to the observation post – but only in pursuit of an actual named incident. Has there been any such debate over the surveillance from video cameras which is now a matter of routine in city centres?

A succession of high profile issues made the police committee the focus of national attention. John Gunnell reaped the political benefit. The Helen Smith case had enabled him to mount a national stage and secure excellent publicity for the county council. Most fundamental was the miners' strike of 1984-5. Hostile to the power of the National Union of Mineworkers, Mrs Thatcher's government announced its plan to close over 70 pits. The union mounted a strike, seen as a personal campaign against Mrs Thatcher. It was led by the Yorkshire miners' leader, Arthur Scargill, who alleged that the government had a long-term strategy to destroy the industry by closing pits every year. This was denied by the government, although papers released in 2014 under the thirty years rule confirm that Scargill was correct. The strike polarised the country. The strike was widely seen as a challenge to the Thatcher government: the mineworkers' union had been credited with bringing down the government of Edward Heath in 1974.

The scale of the miners' strike meant that the local constabularies, including West Yorkshire, had to call on the Metropolitan Police to assist them in maintaining order. Relationships between the miners and the West Yorkshire police force were largely characterised by good-humoured raillery: the miners and the police came from the same social background.

Defenestration, Promotion, Police and the Miners' Strike

The arrival of the Met changed the atmosphere: where London police were present the picketing of collieries resulted in violence. Serious disturbances resulted, notably the so-called Battle of Orgreave in South Yorkshire in June 1984. This was a violent clash between pickets and the police, a defining moment that changed forever the conduct of industrial relations. Tristram Hunt described the confrontation as 'almost mediaeval in its choreography…at various stages a siege, a battle, a rout and finally a brutal example of legalised state violence.' Shown on television, it polarised the country between those who supported the miners and those who supported Mrs Thatcher's government.

At every police committee the chief constable, Ron Gregory, accounted to the councillors for the actions of the West Yorkshire police force. Of course the Labour members were sympathetic to the miners' cause. However, there was no criticism of the behaviour of the West Yorkshire police. I believe strongly that the reason was the direct accountability of the chief constable to the elected members. The strike was a close-run thing but ended with the defeat of the miners and the end of the British coal industry. It also marked the end of the power of the trade unions.

16. Death on the Streets:
The Yorkshire Ripper and Willie Whitelaw

The police committee had a key role when West Yorkshire became the centre of world attention - thanks to the so-called Yorkshire Ripper. For five years, between 1975 and 1980, a Bradford resident, Peter Sutcliffe, murdered 13 women and attacked at least another seven. Except for two in Manchester, his crimes were all committed in West Yorkshire. Most (though not all) of the victims were sex workers, but his last victim was 20-year-old Jacqueline Hill, a student at Leeds university, murdered on 18 November 1980. The Ripper's doings terrorised the region: women were advised not to venture out alone at night. Sexual harassment increased in Yorkshire while Sutcliffe was at large. An atmosphere of fear permeated the county. Innocent men were accused by those who thought them suspicious: actress Pat Phoenix, famous as sex symbol Elsie Tanner in TV soap *Coronation Street*, indicted her chauffeur. Clues abounded and, in the days before computerisation, were recorded on card indices. The accumulation of evidence overwhelmed the police. The floor of the incident room in police headquarters at Millgarth, Leeds, had to be strengthened because of the weight of physical documents. The several leads to Sutcliffe (who was interviewed by the police on nine occasions) were lost in the welter of data.

The Home Office despatched a posse of Scotland Yard detectives to review the handling of the case. They failed to make any breakthrough. The inability of the police to detect the murderer became a national scandal. An explosion of Prime Ministerial anger followed the murder of student Jacqueline Hill. Home Secretary Willie Whitelaw and several senior officials were told to present themselves in Mrs Thatcher's private office to explain what they proposed to do. According to the Downing Street minutes: 'The Prime Minister said that since the local police had so far failed totally in their enquiries into a series of murders which constituted the most appalling kind of violence against women, it was now a question of public confidence. There were doubts whether the investigation was being conducted as effectively as it might be, and something needed to be done to restore the faith of the public in...the police.' Mrs Thatcher was on the brink of taking charge of the enquiry herself. Willie Whitelaw summoned the chief inspector of police, now my old friend Sir James Crane, and warned him that drastic action was required, immediately. Sir James got straight on to Lawrence Byford, told him to get to the headquarters of the West Yorkshire police first thing in the morning and do whatever he thought necessary.

Predictably, intervention by Lawrie Byford and his team from Scotland Yard did not identify an avenue to a breakthrough. In charge of the case was George Oldfield, by now the assistant chief constable in charge of crime detection. By this stage of the Ripper hunt George was getting through a bottle of whisky a day. False loyalty prevented chief constable Ron Gregory from replacing him. In March 1978 the police had received a letter from a man claiming to be the Yorkshire Ripper. He followed it up a year later with a tape recording spoken in a strong Wearside accent. The police did not reveal the existence of the tape. But a few weeks later, in June 1979, the *Sunday Times* was tipped off and planned to publish details of the tape the following weekend. The police had to decide whether they should authenticate the tape. Ron Gregory telephoned to invite me to police headquarters. There Ron, George Oldfield and I listened in silence to the eerie tape of the jeering voice. It referred to a murder in Preston in 1975 which had not previously been linked with the Ripper, though the police believed that it probably was his doing (in the event it proved not to have been committed by the Ripper). But the key connection between the tape and the Ripper was the saliva on the envelope of the 1978 letter. It came from someone with blood group B, shared by only eight per cent of the population. It was also that of the Yorkshire Ripper.

After listening to the tape, one immediate question came to my mind: 'Other than the dubious connection of the Ripper with the Preston murder, was there anything in the tape which had not been in the press?' I asked. George admitted that everything in the tape had been reported. Specifically, at the time the tapes were received a woman called Yvonne Pearson had been murdered but her body had not been discovered. This struck me as strange: had the tape been made by the Ripper he would surely have said 'And there's one more you haven't found yet.' When I raised the issue George shrugged it off. Ron and George felt that the intervention of the *Sunday Times* required them either to confirm or deny that the tape was from the Yorkshire Ripper. The coincidence of the blood group panicked George Oldfield and his deputy, chief superintendent Jim Hobson, into authenticating the tape and informing the press. They said that they were 99 per cent sure that the tape was from the Yorkshire Ripper. This identification was fatal to any chance of identifying Peter Sutcliffe: anyone without a Wearside accent was immediately excluded from the investigation. The several clues which led to Sutcliffe were discarded. The policeman who last interviewed Sutcliffe had recommended further investigation. The false trail to Wearside meant that his recommendation was ignored.

With hindsight it was, of course, easy to trace the paths which led to Peter Sutcliffe. It was not so easy before his identity was established. In the days before computers, tens of thousands of punched cards were produced in the hope of finding symmetry. Though the West Yorkshire Police attracted the blame, the cream of Scotland Yard and the police inspectorate had also failed to make a breakthrough. The 'Ripper tape' had destroyed any chance of tracing Sutcliffe. No detectives ever identified Sutcliffe: on a routine police patrol he was caught in possession of the sharpened screwdriver and the ball pein hammer which he used for his murders. To my great apprehension, and before I could intervene, Ron Gregory, George Oldfield and Jim Hobson went on television to gloat over Sutcliffe's capture, almost certainly damaging the chance of a fair trial. Ron Gregory contrived to attract more criticism when it was revealed that during the trial he planned to go to Atlanta to advise on child murders there.

Such was the public concern that the Attorney General, Sir Michael Havers, insisted on prosecuting the case in person. At the trial he attracted censure by saying of Sutcliffe's victims that 'some were prostitutes, but perhaps the saddest part of the case is that some were not. The last six attacks were on totally respectable women,' rather implying that killing prostitutes was acceptable. Sutcliffe's solicitor brokered a plea bargain with Sir Michael. The bargain was that Sutcliffe would be immured in a secure mental home, would have no trial and his confessions to all the murders would be accepted. The Judge refused to accept the plea of insanity. This disqualified Sir Michael from presenting the prosecution case, which thus fell to his junior silk, Harry Ognall (later Sir Harry). In eleven hours of brutally effective cross-examination Harry Ognall demolished psychiatrist Hugo Milne's argument that Sutcliffe was a schizophrenic. By a majority the jury found Sutcliffe to be sane. Three years later, in March 1984, he was diagnosed with paranoid schizophrenia and transferred to a high-security psychiatric hospital. He remained there for 32 years until a Mental Health Tribunal ruled him sane enough to be transferred back to prison. He was kept in chains until shortly before his death in November 2020 after he has refused treatment for Covid-19.

Unsurprisingly there was a considerable aftermath to the Ripper case. The mother of Jacqueline Hill, the Leeds University student who was Sutcliffe's last victim, announced that she would take legal action against the West Yorkshire police for negligence in their failure to identify Sutcliffe. Had they been competent, she claimed, her daughter would still be alive. Chief Constable Ron Gregory asked me to accompany him for the harrowing task of interviewing Mrs Hill. The reason for the visit was partly to apologise for the police failures but mainly to persuade her not to take legal action. In the event I couldn't make the date for the visit. Ron failed to persuade Mrs Hill not to litigate. Her case went to the House of Lords where it was decided that there was no duty of care owed to the individual by the police in the detection of crime. The key judgement said: 'A great deal of police time, trouble and expense might be expected to have to be put into the preparation of the defence to the action and the attendance of witnesses at the trial. The result would be a significant diversion of police manpower and attention from their most important function, that of the suppression of crime. Closed investigations would require to be reopened and retraversed, not with the object of bringing any criminal to justice but to ascertain whether or not they had been competently conducted'.

The West Yorkshire police committee had been understandably critical of the investigation. They commissioned an investigation by Colin Sampson, the assistant chief constable, later Sir Colin and chief inspector of constabulary for Scotland. He pulled no punches, ruthlessly identifying the missed clues which could have saved lives. Not unreasonably, given the public concern, Home Secretary Willie Whitelaw decided that an external investigation should also be carried out. He commissioned Lawrie Byford (later Sir Lawrence), who produced his report in record time, since he had the benefit of Colin Sampson's report.

There was heavy snow on the day that Lawrie Byford was to present his report to the police committee. Roads were impassable. I phoned chief constable Ron Gregory to say that I couldn't get there. A Police Range Rover was immediately despatched and roared down the middle of the carriageways, like a Russian autocrat's ZiL limousine, to get me to county hall to defend the West Yorkshire force. My presence was unnecessary: when Lawrie Byford presented his critical conclusions to the police committee, the members responded magnificently by springing to the defence of their force: 'Tha's been inspecting this force for t'last seven years Sir Lawrence', they said. 'If tha thought it were such a cock-up, why the bloody 'ell didn't tha say so before?' A good question, given that Lawrie Byford had failed to identify any break-through in the investigation when he had reviewed it on the Home Secretary's instruction. Neither had the high-powered Scotland Yard team, despatched on Mrs Thatcher's orders.

Lawrie's report had other reverberations. Immediately after its publication I was summoned to meet Home Secretary Willie Whitelaw at his office. We met at 6-30pm. To my surprise and contrary to the ministerial code, there were no civil servants in the room. In my experience that was unique. If I wanted to see Ministers without civil servants I had to arrange to meet them in the House of Commons. Willie Whitelaw gave me a gin and tonic – and after a friendly chat asked if the West Yorkshire police committee would agree to the sacking of the chief constable. I told him that the police committee felt defensive about their Force. Senior Scotland Yard detectives and the inspector of constabulary had been summoned to help and had made no impact on the investigation. It was only with hindsight that the path to catch the Ripper had been obvious. The police committee would not agree to sack the chief constable. In any case he was due to retire within weeks. Willie Whitelaw changed the subject and I heard no more about it.

A few weeks later my reply to the Home Secretary would have been very different. Ron Gregory retired and immediately sold his memoirs to the *Daily Mail* for £40,000. They were based on Colin Sampson's report. This act provoked absolute and justified fury in West Yorkshire: Ron Gregory was banned from the police mess, excluded from lieutenancy events and spent the rest of his life as an outcast in Spain.

Twenty-five years later there was a codicil to the Ripper case, when DNA tracked down 'Wearside Jack', the maker of the tape. He was John Humble, a Sunderland alcoholic. In 2006 he was sentenced to eight years in prison for the hoax which had allowed Sutcliffe to continue his murders.

17. Germany, Nudity, Plum Cake, Parliament and the Nuclear Holocaust

One of my first duties in West Yorkshire was to organise a visit to Germany. The West Riding County Council, one of the most populous counties in England, had twinned with the Landschaftsverband Westfalen-Lippe. The Landschaftsverband was the governing body of Westphalia, the most heavily populated region in Germany. Its members wanted to continue the relationship with Yorkshire. The main successor authorities, the county councils for West, South and North Yorkshire, agreed to replace the former West Riding and the three councils nominated a group to make the visit to Westphalia. It included Conservative North Yorkshire councillors, who were typical county gentry; Labour South Yorkshire councillors, mostly ex-miners; and Conservative West Yorkshire middle-class councillors. I went as their chaperone and discovered that the North Yorkshire Tory and the South Yorkshire Labour councillors got on like a house on fire: the South Yorkshire miners had been the batmen of the North Yorkshire councillors during the War or national service and were beaters on their grouse moors. The *déclassé* West Yorkshire Tory councillors had nothing in common with either group.

The Winding Stair

The visit was bibulous in the extreme. The first shots of alcohol were consumed shortly after breakfast. After a day of continuous refreshment came a visit to the Münster Opera House, where the *Dreigroschenoper* was showing. To my consternation Polly Peachum stripped stark naked preparatory to donning her wedding dress for the *Hochzeitslied*. Knowing my accompanying councillors to be strait-laced, I feared a walk-out. I need not have worried. When I looked along the row, every councillor was fast asleep.

We had another charming inheritance from our West Riding predecessor. In the 1920s a member of the West Riding County Council had left £100 in his will, the income from which was to be used to provide good plum cake and wine at the county council meeting immediately before Christmas. Sadly the income from the inheritance no longer covered the cost of the plum cake, let alone the wine. Nevertheless the legacy was an excuse for the members of the West and South Yorkshire County Councils to continue the custom of the West Riding County Council and to have a joint bash immediately before Christmas.

More significant county-wide jobs came my way. I was the County Emergency Planning Controller for the four counties – West, North and South Yorkshire together with Humberside. The Cold War was then at its height. There was genuine fear of a nuclear attack.

Under the Pennines near Halifax was a shelter to which I was to flee when nuclear war broke out. I had to take with me three senior councillors so that we could restore democratic authority after the atomic radiation had died down. The shelter was equipped with sufficient food and drink to keep us alive for a few weeks as well as with body bags so that we could tidy up the corpses after it was safe for us to emerge. The post was equipped with a ground zero indicator which would indicate the strength of the weapon and its distance from the machine. A bomb power indicator would show the 'blast peak overpressure of the explosion'. A survey meter would measure the radiation level of the fallout.

Labour councillors did not take this seriously. Ideologically they believed that the very existence of the shelter was an incitement to World War III by implying that civilisation could survive a nuclear holocaust. Indeed it was implausible to think that we could restore the authority of the county councils if there had been a nuclear attack. But as county controller I was required to undertake training at the aptly-named Hawkhills, the national civil defence training centre at Easingwold in North Yorkshire. In the grounds of the Georgian house was Doom City, a mock-up of a bombed town where trainees could learn how to deal with the aftermath of a nuclear attack. There members of its staff would sidle up to me and in hushed voice brief me that there was reliable information that the Warsaw Pact countries were making preparations for a nuclear war which was expected to start within the next month. The Hawkhills is now a conference and wedding centre, privatised and run by Serco. *Tempora mutantur.*

I enjoyed other, more practical, roles which extended over the four counties. One was the clerkship of the Yorkshire Tourist Board (rebranded in 2009 as *Welcome to Yorkshire* and credited with bringing the *Tour de France* to the county). Its chairman was then the patrician leader of North Yorkshire County Council, Colonel Lawrence Jackson, who limped from the wound he received on D-Day. To the upright Colonel Jackson's disgust, the Director of the Tourist Authority was detected in fiddling his expenses and was sacked and prosecuted. Until his successor was appointed I functioned as acting director. At a Tourist Board reception for those active in the Yorkshire tourist industry I noticed a guest with a straggling moustache who had not joined the general throng: he stood alone. I took him to be the steward of a landed estate in the county. As acting host, I introduced myself. 'My name is Miles', he responded. He revealed in conversation that, as well as his place in Yorkshire, he also had a place at Arundel. I recalibrated my conversation.

Colonel Jackson's plan was to appoint the Duke of York as President of the Tourist Board when the Duke came of age. [Subsequent events revealed that the Duke of York would not have been a wise choice.] But the advent of Thatcherism and the miners' strike disturbed the political equilibrium. Alarmed that the *sansculottes* might appoint Arthur Scargill as president, Colonel Jackson hastily arranged the election of my acquaintance, Miles Norfolk. A genuine Yorkshireman, the Duke lived at Carlton Towers near Selby long before he inherited the Dukedom of Norfolk. He was Major-General Sir Miles Fitzalan-Howard until he acquired the title Baron Beaumont from his mother. Then his father died and he became Baron Howard of Glossop. Finally, after a second cousin died, he became Duke of Norfolk. As Colonel of his regiment, he had to speak at the Regiment's annual dinner. His favourite story was to tell how in year one he spoke as Major-General Sir Miles Fitzalan-Howard; the following year as Major-General Lord Beaumont, when he overheard a guest saying that he had never heard of this Major-General Lord Beaumont but at least he could not be as bad as the fellow they had the previous year; then similarly the year after when he spoke as Major-General Lord Howard of Glossop; and again the following year when he spoke as Major-General His Grace the Duke of Norfolk.

Coincidentally I also had to remove the Director of the Yorkshire and Humberside Industrial Development Association. *Faute de mieux*, I temporarily functioned as head of that organisation. As a result I represented the county at an exhibition in London which trumpeted the charms of Yorkshire and Humberside. To my incredulity I was approached by two McKinsey consultants who told me that they represented a company which required a site on which to create 10,000 jobs. 10,000 jobs! Could I help? The company was Nissan. After much heart-searching it was decided that the Yorkshire region's most suitable site was near Hull. However the Tyneside chief executive, Jim Gardner, articulated a more convincing bid. He corralled the unions into agreeing a one-union shop and Nissan chose to locate their factory in Sunderland.

While the Director's post was vacant I also voyaged to Scandinavia to attract investment in the county. There we were successful in attracting a number of companies to locate in the former coalfield area. Taking three potential investors to the legendary Operakällaren restaurant in Stockholm landed me with the most spectacular restaurant bill of my life, prompting me to seek a personal interview with the Director of Finance before I presented my expenses claim.

Trips to Scandinavia were rare. But deputations from the county council made regular journeys to Brussels and Strasbourg, in quest of the European crock of gold. George Thomson (later Lord Thomson of Monifieth), the EEC Commissioner for regional affairs, was a former Labour MP and welcomed visits from party colleagues from West Yorkshire. We would be joined by the County's MEPs, one of whom, Tom Megahy, was housed in a county council office across the road from county hall, and formed a very convenient conduit. At each year end Tom would announce how much money he had left from his entitlement to EEC expenses and we adjusted the rent of his office so that the remaining funds were transferred to the county council: better the money in Yorkshire than Brussels, believed Tom.

Contrary to popular prejudice, the Brussels bureaucracy is tiny compared with Whitehall. Officials are very open to argument, lap up information enthusiastically and are most responsive. Acting on the advice freely available from George Thomson and his staff, we were able to secure substantial European funds for the county. One day, out of the blue, I received a telephone call from the EEC audit department. We had secured an EEC grant to resurface three roads in inner Bradford and the auditors wished to inspect the finished works. I phoned the county surveyor and asked him to make the necessary arrangements for the visit. Half an hour later a panicked county surveyor phoned back. 'We got', he told me, 'the grants to make up A Street, B Street and C Street. But', he said 'they weren't ready, so we made up D Street, E Street and F Street instead'. Fortunately we hit on a strategy. We changed round the nameplates on the three streets during the two hours of the auditors' inspection.

Arrangements for the visits to Brussels did not always go smoothly. On one occasion the county council delegation arrived at our Brussels hotel too late for food. The only place where nourishment was available was the hotel casino. To overcome the problem I used county council funds to buy gambling chips so that we could enter the casino and access the free food. Having eaten our fill, we then started to use the gambling chips. Desperate to lose so that we could go to bed, we encountered an incredible spell of good luck. The roulette ball repeatedly landed on our chosen numbers: we kept winning. Eventually abandoning the attempt, we cashed in our chips and went to bed. I had the delicate task of fabricating an expenses claim which discreetly netted off the gambling winnings from the expenses.

Our hotel was near the red light district, where semi-clad girls displayed their charms in the windows of the street. Next morning at breakfast one councillor, a NUPE trade union organiser, tackled me. 'I've just been up that street over there', he said, 'and it's disgusting.' I assented, mildly. 'Yes', he continued, 'Them girls were on last night: they're working a double shift. It's disgusting'.

The offices of the EEC were not the only corridors of power tramped in the interests of the county council. From the creation of the county council we arranged meetings between our councillors (chaperoned by me) and the Members of Parliament who represented the county. They began unsuccessfully: the MPs failed to turn up. Even the MP who had organised the meeting did not put in an appearance. The key to success, we found, was to offer them food. The dinners were a great success. It enabled us to canvass the county's interests with leading politicians, who relayed Westminster gossip.

West Yorkshire MPs included Denis Healey, then Chancellor of the Exchequer, and Merlyn Rees. When Jim Callaghan became Prime Minister he appointed Merlyn as Home Secretary. They had a close relationship: Merlyn had been Minister of State in the Home Office when Callaghan was Home Secretary. Immediately after his appointment as Home Secretary Merlyn hit a controversial issue when the USA Government requested the deportation of Philip Agee and Mark Hosenball. Agee was a former CIA agent who had moved to London to denounce the agency's support for authoritarian governments in Latin America. Hosenball had revealed the (then theoretically unknown) existence of GCHQ in *Time Out* magazine. The request for extradition was hotly resisted by many Labour MPs. As had been his practice when he was Minister of State, Merlyn went to see Callaghan to ask him what to do. Disconcertingly Callaghan refused to give a view. 'Merlyn, it's a matter for you as Home Secretary', he said. 'And if you get it wrong, Merlyn, I can always get another Home Secretary.'

The only regular absentee among the West Yorkshire MPs was Sir Keith Joseph. A man of natural austerity, he had no time for dinners. When the Conservative party romped to their great Parliamentary victory in the 1979 General Election, Sir Keith was the principal guest at a dinner given by Leeds Conservatives to celebrate the occasion. It was famously opulent: *Pâté de Foie Gras aux truffes* was accompanied by Chateau d'Yquem and Mouton Rothschild followed with the main course. The ascetic Sir Keith allegedly confined himself to a boiled egg and a glass of water.

The Winding Stair

The doyen of Yorkshire's Conservative MPs was Sir Donald Kaberry, MP for Leeds North-West for over thirty years. The junior Conservative MP was the idiosyncratic Geoffrey Dickens, a former heavyweight boxer, who campaigned, inter alia, for the return of hanging, the recriminalisation of homosexuality and the banning of teddy bears. He once held a press conference to announce that he was having an affair without first mentioning it to his wife. When his West Yorkshire seat was abolished he managed, amidst general incredulity, to secure a safe seat across the Pennines in Littleborough. At one county council dinner, after he had secured the Littleborough seat, he said that he regarded himself as an honorary Yorkshireman. 'And,' sniggered Sir Donald, 'we are much looking forward to your becoming an honorary Lancastrian'.

18. Testicles, Brontës, Eurovision, Snow and a Swan

Poulson, the Yorkshire Ripper, the Miners' Strike, Helen Smith and the airport runway extension dominated the political agenda but were diversions from the day-to-day business of the county council. As it grew in confidence the county council managed to insert itself into the lives of many people. I realised its importance when a Yorkshire Mrs Malaprop wrote to complain that 'the county council is spreading its testicles all over the county', coupled with a threat to report me to the 'omnibusman'.

When it regained control of the county council, the Labour party sought a role in the economic development of the county. The Greater London Council (GLC) under Ken Livingstone had created the Greater London Enterprise Board, designed to invest and provide jobs by implementing the council's economic development strategy. The West Yorkshire Labour group wanted to create a similar body for West Yorkshire. The GLC's Enterprise Board had made several unusual investment decisions characterised by the press as typical of the 'loony left'. I was extremely nervous of the proposal – partly because of the 'loony left' reputation and partly because I was acutely conscious that the county council had no relevant commercial expertise, either among its officers or its councillors. I also believed – erroneously – that the banks would finance any business which looked likely to be successful. I dragged my feet in developing proposals for an enterprise board.

A visit to the enterprise board created by the Lancashire County Council converted me. Two of its schemes stuck in my mind. One was the financing of a fish-processing plant at Fleetwood. The local trawlers brought in large quantities of white fish – but there was no market for the fish unless they were cod, haddock or another recognised species. The county council's enterprise board financed a fish processing plant which transformed perfectly wholesome but unknown white fish into fish fingers, fish pies and other saleable products. The other Lancashire project which caught my eye was in the Rossendale valley, the location of many small manufacturers in the boot and shoe trade. Each was too small to market its products effectively – but the Lancashire County Council created a marketing organisation to boost the sales of their various products. Convinced, I facilitated the launch of the West Yorkshire Enterprise Board and recruited a private sector financier to head it. A typical case was that of a successful and profitable company which was destroyed when a major customer defaulted on a £600k debt. Despite the basic profitability of the company, its bank refused to bail it out. The West Yorkshire Enterprise Board stepped in with an investment and enabled the successful company to continue trading. The success of the Enterprise Board exceeded anything we could have expected and (like the GLC's Enterprise Board, now prospering under the name of *Newable*), it survived the abolition of the county council.

A more mundane responsibility of the county council was road maintenance – in winter clearing snow off the highways. Its performance attracted seasonal publicity, most notably when a county council snow plough charged into a particularly obdurate snowdrift only to find that it concealed a Mini. In the 1970s and 1980s heavy snowfalls regularly blanketed the county, particularly in the Pennine uplands. Attempting to return home in Ilkley after one blinding blizzard, I had to abandon my car in Otley, seven miles away, and walk home in my office suit and shoes. Up in the Pennines the county council hit on the ingenious plan of giving the upland farmers snowploughs to fasten to the front of their tractors. This was magnificently effective. The farmers were themselves immobilised until they had cleared the local roads. Moreover their neighbours knew whose job it was to release them from their incarceration. Snow clearance also cropped up at question time at the county council meeting. 'Why', demanded a councillor, 'is the road outside the house of the chief executive cleared before any others?' 'Because', came the plausible answer, 'his wife is a doctor and the roads outside doctors' houses are cleared immediately after the bus routes'. The question alerted me to the scrutiny devoted to my private life.

In the south of the county were spoil heaps, dunes of barren debris excavated from the abandoned coal mines. Incapable of supporting vegetation, they desecrated the landscape. Though the county council had access to a specific grant for their removal, it was grossly inadequate: the spoil heaps seemed destined to disfigure the countryside for decades. In 1978 the Labour Secretary of State for the Environment, Peter Shore, visited the county. The county council chartered a helicopter and I flew with Shore over the spoil heaps. Effusive in condemning them, Shore did absolutely nothing to speed their removal. Six months later the Conservatives came to power in Westminster and Shore was replaced as Secretary of State by Michael Heseltine. I repeated the helicopter flight with Heseltine. Unlike Shore, Heseltine said absolutely nothing as I pointed out the desolation below. But that year the announcement of the Government derelict land grant was delayed for three months.

Heseltine had been appalled by what he saw. Determined that something should be done, he wrangled with the Treasury until the derelict land grant was quadrupled. Thanks to Heseltine, drivers up the M1 in West Yorkshire now see pleasantly undulating country at the side of the motorway. The action was typical of the career of Michael Heseltine; he reacted strongly to injustice and tried to do something about it.

Anomalously, the favourable publicity which the county council attracted came mainly from its responsibility for leisure services, which overlapped with that of the district councils. The county council's leisure projects were often more newsworthy than the opening of a new rail station. In the very early days of the county council, leader Eddie Newby canvassed the idea of the county council acquiring the Denton Hall estate in Wharfedale, historic home of 'Black Tom', 3rd Baron Fairfax, parliamentary commander-in-chief during the civil war. Tutor to Fairfax's daughter was the poet Andrew Marvell, who elegised the floods upon the River Wharfe below the Denton Hall grounds:

> No serpent new nor crocodile
> Remains behind our little Nile,
> Unless itself you will mistake,
> Among these meads the only snake.

Prince Rupert of the Rhine, the royalist commander, camped at Denton Hall on his way to defeat at Marston Moor. The Prince refrained from spoiling it (his usual custom when staying in Roundhead houses) because its walls were furnished with portraits of Fairfaxes who fought for his father, the Elector Palatine, during the Thirty Years War. Designed by the famous Yorkshire architect John Carr, the present Denton Hall has a lake, woods and extensive grounds which give onto the moor where King George VI came to shoot. Leader Eddie had a vision of the estate as a glorious recreational facility for the people of West Yorkshire, who would be taken to the estate by a shuttle bus from Ilkley station. The idea was too bold for the Labour group at the time and they rejected the offer. Had it been launched a few years later when their confidence had grown, then it might well have gained their support.

One county council project which did go ahead was the creation of public access to wetlands at Fairburn Ings (now under the care of the RSPB), legendary site of the battle of the Winwaed in 655 when King Penda of Mercia was killed and paganism eradicated. The opening ceremony was enlivened by the spectacle of an irate swan chasing Mrs Suttenstall, chairman of the Leisure Services Committee, around the lake. Creation of the Calderdale Way, a 50-mile long-distance footpath around the South Pennines, was another county council initiative.

Encouragement of tourism was included in the leisure portfolio. The county council sponsored the Eurovision song contest when it was held in Yorkshire. As a result my wife Clare and I were invited to a reception at Castle Howard. As we ascended the imposing steps, we were surprised to see the television cameras apparently focused on us. We smiled nervously. We need not have bothered: the cameras were aimed at the British contenders who were immediately behind us.

The jewel in the West Yorkshire tourist crown was Haworth Parsonage, home of the Brontë sisters. To promote tourism and boost the local economy, the Conservative Mrs Suttenstall championed the opening of a tourist information office at the top of the main street in Haworth. Surprisingly the locals opposed it bitterly. They mounted a vigorous protest at the competition the shop presented because of its sale of postcards and Haworth memorabilia. The controlling Conservative Group was torn between those who supported Mrs Suttenstall and those who were opposed to public sector competition with local tradespeople.

The Winding Stair

In 1983 British Rail served a notice to close the spectacular Settle-Carlisle railway, alleging that the thirteen arches of the awe-inspiring Ribblehead viaduct were in danger of collapse. They claimed that repairs would cost £7m. The line was, they argued, an expensive and unnecessary duplication of the West Coast main line. A charismatic defender of the Yorkshire Dales and member of the National Park Authority, Colin Speakman, came to see me to enlist the county council's support to save the railway. I had no problem persuading John Gunnell, the leader of the county council, to help: the county council responded enthusiastically. Working with the Ramblers'Association to achieve maximum publicity and secure political commitment, the county council financed a steam locomotive journey from Leeds to Carlisle. At every station – including those which had been closed for years - the train collected the local MP, who naturally supported saving the railway.

Fortunately the Minister of Transport at the time was Michael Portillo. Though he was then known as an arch-Thatcherite, he was also a railway aficionado, later famous for his televised rail journeys round the world. Under his ministerial pressure British Rail discovered that the Ribblehead Viaduct could be made safe for far less than £7m. The line was saved and all the long abandoned stations between Leeds and Carlisle were re-opened. They included Dent, at 1150ft the highest mainline station in England. During the electrification of the West Coast main line the Settle-Carlisle line became for a time the main route from London to Glasgow. As well as the tourist traffic on the line, it is also a main artery for the transport of freight – coal, gypsum and cement - which would otherwise have violated the quiet roads through the Dales. At one stage British Rail even claimed that the Settle/Carlisle route was the most profitable line in the country.

The County Archaeologist, Phil Mayes, was surprisingly a regular source of favourable county council news. As well as his skills as an archaeologist, Mayes had a genius for self-promotion. His activities attracted more good publicity for the county council than any of its other functions. Excavating Roman remains was his staple diet, but his entrepreneurial bent extended into very different areas. In the churchyard in Ilkley were three increasingly weathered Saxon crosses. To halt their erosion and with my enthusiastic encouragement, he arranged their rehousing within the tower of the parish church. Stimulated by his Deputy, Margaret Faull, he persuaded the county council to take over Caphouse Colliery when it closed in 1985. The Caphouse mine was sunk in the 1770s and had the oldest working mine shaft in the country. It took on a new lease of life as the National Coal Mining Museum (the only mine now left in Yorkshire), with a £3m annual budget and a staff of over 100. Margaret Faull led it from its setting up by the county council in 1985 until her retirement in 2015.

John Gunnell, leader of the council, was deeply impressed by the excellent publicity secured by Mayes. It redounded to the credit of the county council. To most politicians good publicity is as catnip to cats. Unfortunately Phil Mayes was not sufficiently sensitive to share some of the glory with Councillor John Sully, chairman of the Leisure Services Committee, whose resentment at his exclusion from the limelight developed into deep hostility towards Mayes. Eventually Mayes overreached himself. Between the River Aire and the Aire & Calder Navigation lies the eighteenth century Thwaite Mill, perhaps the finest water-powered mill still in existence in this country. Phil Mayes engineered the county council's involvement. In the course of the takeover by the county council the Victorian portico of the mill was removed, revealing its Georgian predecessor. The mill was scheduled as an historic building and (however beneficial) alterations at a listed building without consent are a criminal offence. They prompted Leeds City Council to prosecute the county council. I had no option but to subject Mayes to disciplinary proceedings. John Sully, of course, wanted Mayes sacked. On the other hand John Gunnell, the leader, wanted to continue the employment of someone who had consistently procured such favourable publicity. Before I could deliberate and decide on the question of culpability, Mayes told me that he had no intention of waiting for me to sack him: he resigned.

There was a curious coda to the episode. Over a decade after I had left the county council, I was returning to Yorkshire on the train from London. That evening I was due to go to the speech day of my daughter's school, where she was head girl. On the train I received a phone call. 'Phil Mayes here' I heard. 'Tonight', he said 'we shall meet. I want you to know that there will be no recrimination. I shall speak to you perfectly politely'. After a mental struggle I remembered who Phil Mayes was. His daughter was a deputy head girl and we were to meet at the gathering after the school speech day.

19. Royal Undies, London and Mrs Thatcher

Still attached to the job of chief executive of the county council was the clerkship to the lieutenancy. In 1973 the lord-lieutenant was Brigadier Hargreaves, who succeeded in the post five Dukes, two Marquesses, and 12 Earls. Brigadier Hargreaves, though an imposing figure, was the first lord-lieutenant of the West Riding who had been in trade: he was one of the mining magnates of the Yorkshire coalfield until its nationalisation in 1946. His successor, Sir William Bulmer, was a leading figure in the textile industry. 1977 was the year of the Queen's Silver Jubilee and the lord-lieutenant had a leading role in fund-raising to mark the occasion. In West Yorkshire the principal beneficiary was to be the Nell Bank Centre for young people in Ilkley. The deputy lieutenants were pressured into fund-raising and contributing to the appeal. Shortly after the funds were raised the Prince of Wales decided – laudably – that the trustees of the Silver Jubilee Trust (and his own Trust) should be more representative of the people than was the lieutenancy. The excluded deputy lieutenants were understandably aggrieved, having leant on their friends to part with their cash (as well as parting with some of their own). The outcome was that I became chairman of the Prince's Youth Business Initiative in West Yorkshire – and, when I went to London, of the East End Committee of the Prince's Trust.

One of the duties of members of the royal family is intermittently to grace the country with their presence. The lord-lieutenant has responsibility for organising the royal visits to the county. As clerk to the lieutenancy I had to put the programme together. Nothing leaves behind such a trail of ill feeling as a royal visit. Those not presented to the visiting royalty are deeply affronted. Those who are presented complain that they did not have appropriate precedence. The recriminations can last for months. The problems start with the arrival of the royal visitor. As the Queen's representative, the lord-lieutenant takes precedence over all except members of the royal family themselves. But when a royal visit was arranged, the City of Leeds argued vigorously for the precedence of the Lord Mayor of Leeds. They argued that the lord-lieutenant could not then be representing the Monarch because the Queen or a member of her family would be present. To avoid unseemly disputes, I established the convention that the lord-lieutenant would greet members of the royal family on the platform of the station or by the runway of the airport terminal. The Lord Mayors would welcome the royal visitor outside the building, where they could enjoy the admiration of the crowd and the full glare of publicity.

Usually the easiest part of the job was looking after the member of the royal family. Princess Anne had at one stage a reputation for acerbity, especially when falling off her horse in equestrian events. But she proved both extremely charming and exceptionally conscientious. During her first visit to the county, the lord-lieutenant took me aside and said with some surprise 'Gosh! She is really a very nice person'. (I got to know her quite well during my time in London, when she became a tenant at Dolphin Square.) One April I had the job of accompanying Princess Diana round Roundhay Park, Leeds, in an open Land

Rover. 'I do hope, Ma'am,' I said, 'that you will be warm enough.' 'Don't worry', she responded, 'Damart from here to here', her hands indicating the extent of the royal underwear.

The only bad-tempered royal I encountered was Princess Margaret. On a blustery day the lord-lieutenant, myself and others awaited her arrival outside the terminal building at Leeds/Bradford Airport. Obviously in a bad mood, she stalked past us without saying a word. When she came to depart in the afternoon we had laid on tea and buns. Noting her expression as I invited her to a cup of tea, I had a brainwave. 'Or, Ma'am, would you prefer a glass of whisky?' I asked. She brightened up and we all drank whisky.

The Association of Metropolitan Authorities

In London lurked a leprechaun called Tom Caulcott, who was private secretary to George Brown, Secretary of State at the Department of Economic Affairs. Brown blew up when he discovered Tom sitting in his, Brown's, chair. Tom promptly resigned and joined the Association of Metropolitan Authorities (AMA) as Secretary. (He later went to Birmingham as chief executive after I withdrew my own application when I was appointed as chief executive in West Yorkshire). The AMA represented at national level the 36 metropolitan districts, six metropolitan counties, 32 London boroughs and the Greater London Council.

The Policy Committee of the AMA was shadowed by a Committee of the leading chief executives of the Metropolitan Authorities, who dispensed advice and told the Secretary what to do. This was not Tom Caulcott's view of his job. He immediately sacked the committee of chief executives but then encountered a problem: who would do the work? He looked for lawyers, one rung below chief executives and without the *folie de grandeur* of the great men. His eye fell on me. He appointed me as adviser to the Policy Committee, the key committee of the AMA.

Summoned to London for my first meeting, I was properly nervous. My Parliamentary department had dissected the Policy Committee's agenda. They supplied me with a folio which matched every item on the agenda. I brought with me the relevant volumes to back my view. Arriving in good time I was surprised to find the Policy Committee room deserted. I took the opportunity to spread my books and papers around the table so that they would be readily available when I needed to cite them in support of my opinion.

For some time I was the sole occupant of the room. No-one arrived until a few minutes before the Committee was due to begin, when one man entered. I recognised the most senior local government officer in the country: Maurice Stonefrost, chief executive of the Greater London Council (a delightful man and later a great friend). Maurice took one look at me and summed up the situation. Without in any way condescending to this *naif* from the provinces, he explained to me that officers (a) were not expected to sit at the table of the Policy Committee; (b) would occupy the seats at the back of the room; and (c) would not be required to speak. And I should remove my books before the members came in. Sure enough, at 11.00 precisely, the members trooped in from their group meetings. To my astonishment, the chairman announced the decision on every item without opening the issue for discussion. Occasionally the leader of the Conservative Party spoke to indicate dissent. Even the secretary, Tom Caulcott, did not speak. The meeting ended thirty minutes after it started, having disposed in short order of twenty or more agenda items, many of national importance. The Committee then broke for lunch.

All the legal work and discussion had been put to bed well before the meeting. As the Policy Committee's newly appointed adviser, it was my job to articulate advice to the officers of the

AMA which they would use in the drafting of the report. They could then be sure that they would not be shot down by the Policy Committee members, who would have shared the papers with their officers. The members might have been given a rival opinion by their own legal advisers, smart Alecs keen to put a spoke in the establishment and establish their credibility with their own councillors. Any discussion would take place in the party groups.

The Node and Mrs Thatcher

Tom Caulcott clearly regarded me as a protégé: I was not one of the chief executives who wanted to tell him what to do. It was through Tom that I became involved in the Node. The Node had started in the early 1970s when the Labour Government became concerned about the lack of communication between the top civil servants and the leaders of the private sector. They did not know each other socially nor were they on the same wavelength conversationally.

CP Snow's *Two Cultures* related not only to science and the arts, but also to the private sector and government. To combat this, the Labour Government established the Node – the name of a country house which provided a fortnight's residence for the brightest sparks of the civil service and the rising stars of the private sector. The civil servants would normally be Assistant Secretaries who were expected to rise higher. The private sector participants were at or just below Board level but expected to become major players in the economy.

A retired senior civil servant chaired the event. In my case that was Sir Frank Figgures, to me the former bogeyman in charge of the Prices and Incomes Board, but reincarnated as a paternalistic godfather to the Node members. The intention was that the participants would stay in touch after the Node course ended, share mutual problems, provide cross-fertilisation of ideas and attitudes between the sectors and deliver active collaboration.

No-one from local government had ever been invited to the Node. But - to the astonishment of the civil servants - the private sector participants felt little necessity to be closer to civil servants but were clear in their need to be close to their own local authority, with which they had daily dealings. As a result it was decided to invite one local government officer to the Node. The civil service organisers surveyed the unknown landscape of local government. As their guide they identified Tom Caulcott – who, as a former senior civil servant, could be trusted to understand the requirements of the situation. Tom was asked to identify a suitable local government officer who could hold his own in a country house in high-powered company and would know which cutlery to use. He nominated me, his young protégé.

Off I set to the Node, to share a fortnight with the young Turks (well, forty-year-olds) of the civil service and the rising stars of the private sector. They were, of course, all male. Coincidentally they included Brian Willott, my former competitor for the form prize at school in Wakefield. Brian was then an Assistant Secretary in the Department of Trade and later became chief executive of the Export Credit Guarantee Corporation and the Welsh Development Agency. The Node protagonists also included Bernard Ingham, the former Yorkshire journalist who, with me, had interviewed the talking dog at the Spotted Cow in Drighlington. Bernard had joined the civil service and was then responsible for promulgating energy saving on behalf of the Department for Energy. At the Node there was a three line whip for top brass to come to address us – they included the Cabinet Secretary (then Sir John Hunt) and the Director-General of the BBC (Alastair Milne). We were each asked to identify a problem which we faced and to expose it for discussion in the group. My memory is of Rodney Royston, a

Director of a major drug company and in charge, *inter alia*, of its South American operation. The question which he asked us to consider was: should his company pull out of its business in Bolivia? I had a mental vision of a llama with drugs on its side saddles being flogged up the Andes by a sweating salesman – while in a stately home in the Home Counties a group of English gentlemen decided his future.

The fortnight was delightful. Since the Node was intended to be the base of continuing relationships, there was a deliberate amount of free time - when we could play squash and tennis or walk round the grounds. Surprisingly my subsequent jobs gave me occasion to meet professionally every Node member from the private sector. The most remote in terms of interest was Denis Cassidy, chairman of BHS and Mothercare at the time of the course, but later chairman of the board of a brewing company. One Friday he rang me at 7-30am. He wanted to take over a rival brewery. The key shares were held by the South Yorkshire County Council pension fund. Could I induce them to discuss the takeover with Denis? I persuaded them to talk to Denis. They told him they weren't interested – but at least they talked to him.

Only one of the civil servants achieved the rank of Permanent Secretary, though all but one became Deputy Secretary and were appointed as Companions of the Bath. Six of the 25 Node members were awarded knighthoods – Bernard Ingham (who became Mrs Thatcher's press spokesman and was knighted on her retirement), Robin Mountford (Second Cabinet Secretary), Brian Hill (with whom I had much to do when he was chairman of the Building Employers' Federation), Humphrey Maud (the first UK Ambassador in Argentina after the Falklands War), David Kelly (chairman of the Conservative Party) and myself.

After we left the formal Node course, the biannual reunions were initially something of a duty, given the pressure on our respective diaries. But over the years we established lasting friendships and social relationships outside the main Node meetings. Our meetings were infiltrated by our wives, whose presence solidified relationships. When we retired from our main jobs, exotic excursions were arranged. After he left the Ministry of Agriculture, Bill Mason became a director of Allied Lyons, which then owned Maison Latour. Their wines embellished our lunches. Denis Cassidy was a director of Compass Catering. Among their establishments was the Victorian Baroque Michelin-starred Train Bleu restaurant at the Gare de Lyon in Paris – where we had a splendid day trip and lunch. Waiting at Waterloo (then the terminus) to catch the Eurostar train to Paris, Denis conducted his flock for a bacon sandwich in the Compass Catering outlet, while Bernard Ingham – then a director of the British branch of McDonald's – led his rival troupe for a breakfast burger. The reunions lasted for forty years until death ended them, as it does most things. The Node was, I think, an excellent idea, now sadly discontinued.

I continued publishing papers and speaking at public events during my time at the county council,. I became a Senior Visiting Fellow at the School of Public Policy at Birmingham University; and chairman of the Public Management Centre at Durham University, where Sir Kenneth Calman was then Vice-Chancellor. When I went up to Durham my accommodation was usually in the Bishop's bedroom in the Castle. The bedroom enjoyed its own reception room, which could accommodate fifty guests. In contrast, the en-suite toilet was up a narrow metal winding staircase. Going to the loo required a considerable amount of foresight when I had a broken leg, an aftermath from skiing.

At one academic event I achieved a substantial own goal, which had lasting consequences. I had delivered a paper at the Centre for Environmental Studies, established by the Harold Wilson government and run by Professor David Donnison. At lunch I sat next to Derek Senior, the *Guardian*'s local government correspondent, who had written the dissenting report in the Maud report on local government reorganisation. He also wrote the *Guardian* columns on gardening and bridge. I particularly wanted to quiz Derek about care of lawns and his latest bridge problem. On my other side was a woman who persistently disturbed my conversation with Derek in order to discuss with me the paper which I had read. Eventually common courtesy required me to respond. 'And who are you? And what do you do?' I enquired politely. 'My name', she replied icily, 'is Margaret Thatcher. And I am the Shadow Secretary of State for the Environment.' In times to come I would meet Mrs Thatcher fairly regularly. She retained this memory of our first meeting. Our relationship never recovered from its initial setback. When she came to power one of the first things she did was to abolish the Centre for Environmental Studies.

The advent of Thatcherism

Conflict was the result of Margaret's Thatcher's victory in the May 1979 General Election: she regarded local authorities as the enemy within, banished one-nation Tories, repudiated the post-War consensus and replaced citizenship by consumerism. Her Government distrusted the public service and the professional ethic, believing them to be a dissimulation of inefficient cartels and an abuse of monopoly power. Competition was the answer: the purchaser/provider split underpinned Conservative thinking over the next decade. Consumer choice was an essential ingredient in achieving efficiency and responsiveness.

An immediate target was frugality. The 1979 Conservative manifesto stated that 'Any future government which sets out honestly to reduce inflation and taxation will have to make substantial economies, and there should be no doubt about our intention to do so.' The Conservative Government avoided unpopular spending cuts on the National Health Service and social security. Cuts in the defence budget were ideologically unthinkable. As a consequence the cuts fell primarily on local government. Among other policies, the Government declared that all public transport should operate without subsidy. To Mrs Thatcher was attributed the quote: 'Anyone on a bus over the age of 25 is a failure'.

Michael Heseltine, the new Secretary of State for Local Government, promised a 'bonfire of regulations'. After much consultation the only visible result was a revision of the Rag Flock and Other Filling Materials Regulations. Heseltine was also charged with decreasing local government spending. Reluctant to trammel local autonomy, Heseltine introduced a new system of local government finance. It was intended to ensure that any local authority spending more than the Government's estimate of what it had to spend to provide an average standard of service would have to do so at the direct expense of the local ratepayers: there would be no Government subsidy.

It was easy for the Government to manipulate the grant to local authorities, although it was supposed to be an objective measure of need. The grant took into account the money which the council received from the local rates and the amount which a hypothetical council would have to spend to achieve a standard level of service in its area. This was based on a complex formula which was supposed to assess the needs of the area. It was based on hundreds of factors, including assessments of social deprivation. One component, for example, was the assessment of need for the maintenance of roads in winter: temperature was the criterion for calculating the grant. Under that head, chilly northern local authorities would expect to receive more than those in the balmy south. If the temperature used to calculate that element of the grant was ground temperature, then rural councils benefited: urban highways were warmer than rural roads because of the underground pipes. If, on the contrary, the temperature used was air temperature, then urban authorities would gain. The Government changed the criterion according to which councils were facing elections: if the county councils, then ground temperature would be used; if the urban authorities were facing the electorate then the thermometer would be shifted skywards. To a large county council like West Yorkshire the change from air to ground temperature meant a loss of nearly £3m. For three successive years the Government changed the criterion from ground to air temperature and back, according to which authorities were facing elections.

Despite the endless possibilities for manipulation, the Government's new system was conspicuously unsuccessful in cutting local government spending. A bewildering series of controls were introduced but no matter how the ratchet was tightened, local authorities continued to spend – until universal capping of local authority budgets was eventually introduced. The Government continues to lay down the limit which a council can raise from the council tax and the business rate.

Mrs Thatcher's contempt for bus passengers was a prime cause of a constitutional crisis. Cheap bus fares had been the key policy of South Yorkshire County Council since its inception. Effectively they were financed by the better-off through payment of rates. A typical journey in the county cost between 2½p and 5p – a fraction of the cost elsewhere. The policy was remarkably successful. A consequence of the low fares and frequency of service was that most residents chose to travel into Sheffield and round the county by bus rather than use their car. A further consequence was that buses were able to move around relatively freely since they were unimpeded by cars. The scheme attracted favourable national publicity, notably in the columns of Robin Pauley of the *Financial Times* (later its Managing Editor). The success of the policy was held up by other Labour councils as an example of what could be done with the will and the money. The Government's financial stringency failed to change South Yorkshire County Council's commitment to cheap transport. The county council ignored Government policy and Irvine Patnick, Sheffield's lone Conservative MP, denounced the county council as 'The People's Republic of South Yorkshire'.

Down in London Sir Horace Cutler, the flamboyant Thatcherite leader of the Greater London Council, became notorious for dialling at random a county hall telephone extension and sacking any respondent whose job title had the word 'liaison' in it. Cutler believed that the GLC should be abolished and commissioned Lord (Frank) Marshall, former Conservative leader of Leeds City Council, to report on how to remove it. In his report Frank, a natural moderate with a commitment to local government, did not support abolition, believing that London-wide issues required a democratically elected authority.

Inspired by the South Yorkshire lead, the London Labour Party fought the 1981 election to the Greater London Council with the slogan 'Fares Fair', a policy to reduce public transport fares in London by one-third. On the day after the election the moderate Andrew Mackintosh was deposed as leader of the Labour Party in London's county hall and replaced by the left-wing Ken Livingstone. 'Fares Fair' was the cornerstone of Livingstone's policies, but he also introduced other 'left-wing' policies like negotiating with the IRA and equality for LBGTs. County Hall's Masonic temple was handed over to the women's unit. Livingstone taunted Mrs Thatcher: draped over the façade of county hall a provocative banner faced the Houses of Parliament. Symbolising his battle with the establishment was the decision by the House of Lords to rule the 'Fares Fair' policy as illegal: the GLC had been acting beyond its powers in subsidising the fares. In a confused judgement the main ground of the decision seemed to be that the GLC had regarded itself as bound by the Labour Party's manifesto and had not formally considered the implications of the policy before adopting it. This appeared to most people as a strange decision, given the usual complaint that political parties fail to deliver on their manifestos. But the GLC was compelled to act on the decision. As a result fares immediately doubled.

Unemployment increased. The economy went through a recession as the Government tackled inflation and fought the power of the trade unions. Mrs Thatcher became increasingly unpopular. Her reign was rescued from an unexpected source. In 1982, three years after her accession to power, came the invasion of the Falkland Islands by the forces of the Argentine, whose premier General Leopoldo Galtieri hoped to strengthen his precarious dictatorship by a victory in the south Atlantic. In response Mrs Thatcher personified determined retaliation: the P&O liner *Queen Mary* was commandeered as a troop ship and the Argentinian flagship *Belgrano*, a superannuated ex-US cruiser, was (controversially) sunk with the loss of 323 lives. The Argentinians were expelled from the Falklands at a cost to the British taxpayer estimated at £1m per Falklands islander.

20. Abolition
and Ken Livingstone

Thanks to the victory in the Falklands, Mrs Thatcher was the new Boadicea. Rejoicing in her popularity, she prepared for a general election.

Despite the House of Lords judgement, the GLC had found a legal way to cut fares and Ken Livingstone's banners on the façade of county hall still infuriated the Prime Minister. Discussing the election manifesto in Cabinet, she had a brainwave at the end of the meeting: 'Let's abolish Ken Livingstone', she is said to have declared at 12-25pm. '*And* the metropolitan authorities as well. Let's have lunch'.

There was some later debate as to what she meant by 'the metropolitan authorities'. The metropolitan authority with the main reputation for extremism was Liverpool city council, led by Derek Hatton, a member of the Trotskyist Militant Group. He threatened to sell the art treasures of Liverpool's Walker Art Gallery to finance the city council's policies. But sober reflection convinced the Government that it would be far too difficult to get rid of the metropolitan district councils. Instead the Walker Art Gallery was nationalised and the axe reserved for the six metropolitan county councils and the Greater London Council.

Riding on the tide of her victory in battle, Mrs Thatcher triumphed in the May 1983 General Election. With 362 Conservative MPs, she had the biggest Conservative majority since 1924. The Opposition vote was split between the Labour Party, led by Michael Foot, and the Alliance, led by Roy Jenkins and David Steel. Though the Alliance won over 25 per cent of the votes (almost as many votes as the Labour Party) it won only 23 seats. The Conservative manifesto firmly pledged the abolition of the GLC and the six metropolitan county councils. It was followed in the Autumn of 1983 by a White Paper, *Streamlining the Cities*, with its blueprint for the abolition. 'With a scratch of her pen, Margaret Thatcher ended the democratically elected self-government of English cities. She did it because some of the six (*sic*) 'metropolitan authorities', London especially, were daring to pursue their own un-Thatcherite policies.' [Neil Ascherson, *London Review of Books* 24 September 2020]. The decision marked a development in Conservative party thinking: 'Ever since... the abolition of the Metropolitan Counties and the Greater London Council in 1986, Tory governments have shown a flinty hostility to the power and independence of local government [Ferdinand Mount, *London Review of Books*, 2 July 2020].

The manifesto was a body blow for me: I believed passionately that the West Yorkshire County Council was playing a significant part in improving the lives of its residents. I felt emotionally that the council was my creation: I had devised its systems, appointed many of its officers and worked in partnership with its politicians to develop its policies. The manifesto pledge seemed to me so illogical that (naively) I believed that common sense would prevail and a campaign would persuade Mrs Thatcher to change her mind. With the other five other metropolitan county councils tagging along, we launched a campaign to save the metropolitan county councils. I recruited as chief aide-de-camp a bright young lawyer from

South Yorkshire County Council, David Henshaw (later Sir David and chief executive of Liverpool City Council).

To plan the campaign in Westminster we employed a firm of Parliamentary lobbyists, GJW, named after its three principals, Andrew Gifford, Jenny Jeger and Wilf Weeks. Chaperoned by Jenny Jeger, I spent much time in the Houses of Parliament, trying to rally support. Jenny's elderly aunt was Baroness (Lena) Jeger, a former Guardian journalist. One day Lena was holding forth in a House of Lords Bar, complaining: 'Every man I have ever slept with is dead.' From a corner came a quavering voice: 'Oh Lena – you haven't forgotten that afternoon in 1938?' It was at the time of the activities of Cynthia Payne, who ran an upmarket brothel at 32 Ambleside Avenue, Streatham. Commenting in the Commons tearoom on the goings-on, an MP said: '£25 for a three course meal, a bottle of wine and a woman. That's not bad.' Across the tearoom came the response: 'I shouldn't think the wine was up to much'.

To reinforce the parliamentary crusade, I cultivated the national press by the strategy of taking the leading scribes out to dinner. 'Rodney's eat for victory campaign', mocked my colleagues in Yorkshire. The crusade captured the media. The determination of a Conservative government to abolish seven Labour-led local authorities smacked of totalitarianism. Invited to speak at a Conference of the German Länder, I was asked by puzzled Germans: 'How can the county councils be abolished? Were they not democratically elected?' Of course the Government maintained the fiction that abolition had nothing to do with their politics. Irwin Bellow, by then Lord Bellwin, former leader of Leeds City Council and Mrs Thatcher's long-serving Minister for Local Government, rather demolished that argument when he declared that 'If all the Metropolitan Counties had been like West Yorkshire, they would not have been abolished.' The abolition of the Metropolitan County Councils prompted Irwin's resignation as Minister of State. I kept in touch with him and over the years we met regularly for dinner in the House of Lords.

Mrs Thatcher's vendetta against the GLC cemented Londoners support for Ken Livingstone. The new leader of the GLC Conservatives, Alan Greengross, had been given only three days' notice of the manifesto pledge. Indignantly, he produced plans for a smaller GLC, and denounced the Government's plans as 'a bureaucrat's dream and a ratepayers' nightmare'. [He was right: after abolition of the GLC a tower block by Vauxhall Bridge was populated by civil servants who ran the capital without any electoral mandate.] With colleagues I regularly met Alan Greengross privately to discuss tactics. Interestingly the notes of our meetings with him found their way to Kenneth Baker, who had replaced Patrick Jenkin as Secretary of State for the Environment. Of course we also worked with Ken Livingstone to fight abolition. On one occasion I walked with him from county hall across Westminster Bridge. Livingstone's popular support was extraordinary: from their ladders window cleaners yelled 'Keep it up Ken'. Bus drivers wound down their windows and cheered as we passed. GLC posters proclaimed '74 per cent say yes'.

The chairman of the West Yorkshire Conservative party was Yvonne Jackson, a former rally driver, married to one of Morley's former textile magnates. She was also a member of the county council and ensured that the Tory group on the county council adhered publicly to the party line on abolition – though most privately opposed it. The opponents included the leader, Royston Moore, whom I briefed confidentially on the county council's campaign with, of course, the full knowledge of the Labour leadership. At every county council meeting Royston mollified the party loyalists by complaining about the campaign despite the fact that he had, of course, been fully involved. The Labour party members maintained the fiction that he was kept in ignorance.

The Winding Stair

The Greater London Council and the six metropolitan county councils were due to have elections in 1985, the year before their abolition. The Government proposed that the elections be cancelled. The functions of the GLC and the county councils were to be transferred to a committee nominated by the London borough councils in London and by the metropolitan district councils in the six metropolitan areas. This destruction of democracy was too much for Parliament to swallow and the Government suffered a series of humiliating Parliamentary defeats. Despite the defeats, it became clear that our campaign to save the metropolitan county councils was doomed to failure.

Fortified by her triumph in the Falklands, Mrs Thatcher could not be stopped. We set to salvaging what could be saved. Tony Harrison, the chief executive of the Greater Manchester Council, transferred the council's semi-commercial operations to private companies, of which he, of course, was a director. This was a futile gesture: the Government included in the abolition legislation power to seize all such operations and assets. Tragically Tony committed suicide. Though the West Yorkshire district councils, led by Leeds, had welcomed the abolition of the county council, none of its services would be transferred to them: a variety of quangoes and joint bodies took over the functions. The net result was a diminution of accountability and above all, a loss of the wider perspective. Regional planning was set back for at least 30 years. The problems grew until, in 2014, a 'West Yorkshire Combined Authority' was created to assume some of the functions of the former county council. In 2021 an element of the democratic base was restored by the election of a Mayor for West Yorkshire.

It became clear that our campaign against abolition was unsuccessful and that the death of the county council was certain. The leader, John Gunnell, asked me what would happen to the county council's balances. Given the capriciousness of the Government grant, we had reserves of several millions, as did any prudent major local authority. I told John that the money would be shared out among the five district councils who were our successor authorities. 'Bugger that', said John, 'do something good with the money.' I put together 32 schemes to use the money. Not all were successful: two endowments which would fund the arts in the county in years to come were declared illegal. Unfortunately the GLC had developed similar ideas: they had set up a fund to establish a housing charity in London. This was prohibited by the courts as trying to spend money after the authority itself had been abolished – the so-called 'tombstone funding'.

One of the most successful schemes was the provision of money to build a permanent theatre in Leeds, where the Leeds Playhouse had camped for a decade in a prefabricated building on the site planned for a Leeds University gymnasium. The Playhouse had had an inauspicious beginning. Tony Robinson (later Sir Tony) starred in the first production – which caused the Tory MP for Pudsey, Joe Hiley, to walk out, complaining of its vulgarity: 'It were nowt but knickers, nipples, bottoms and bloodies', he told the press as he denounced the show. The Lord Mayor of Leeds agreed with him.

It was then a time when shock waves were part of the way theatre thought it would make itself relevant. One Leeds Playhouse production was Barry O'Keefe's update of Thomas Middleton's play *It's A Mad World My Masters*. The Huddersfield Methodist Chapel Mothers' Union had a block booking for the Playhouse. Will Weston, the Theatre's Director, telephoned them to make them aware that the play was rather ribald and they might wish to miss that production. The Mothers' Union proclaimed their broad-mindedness and kept their booking. The show started with an old lady massaging her genital area and saying '*Ee it's ****ing cold. My ****'s got icicles on it.*' The Huddersfield Mothers tittered. At the beginning of the second Act a mock Angela Rippon descended the stairs while reading the news, stripping off garments until she was naked. The Huddersfield Mothers' Union laughed their heads off. At the beginning of the last Act the Queen descended the stairs and exclaimed *'Oh, horseshit.'* To a woman, the Huddersfield Mothers' Union got up and left. Nudity, blasphemy, obscenity yes – *lèse-majesté* no.

The county council's provision of money to build a theatre meant that the new theatre was named the West Yorkshire Playhouse. Thirty-five years later I became chairman of the theatre's board and, with some sadness, saw the name changed back to Leeds Playhouse to honour the commitment by the Leeds City Council to the theatre. But we retained the West Yorkshire inscription on the lintel in the main entrance. In the theatre the Brooke Room commemorates my contribution to the theatre.

21. Departure from West Yorkshire: The Fridge/Freezer and Dame Shirley

In the Autumn of 1983 a White Paper, *Streamlining the Cities*, followed the Conservative manifesto. The White Paper confirmed that the powers of the metropolitan county councils were not to be devolved to the metropolitan district councils but transferred to a series of quangos and joint bodies. By the beginning of 1984 there was no doubt that the Government was committed to abolition and that our fight for survival had failed.

As I began to contemplate my future I was approached by five different headhunters. Three canvassed real possibilities. One was the chief executive's job at Kirklees Council; another the chief executive's job at the Yorkshire Water Board; the third the chief executive's job at Westminster City Council. I dismissed the first two: going to Kirklees would be a move from the third biggest local authority in the country to a metropolitan district council. That would clearly be a big step down: from strategic thinking to relatively parochial concerns. As for Yorkshire Water: water supply had been just one of the departments of Rochdale and Stockport Councils and I saw that also as a big step down – though had I taken the job, the 1989 privatisation of water at a scandalously low price would have made me a multimillionaire. The third possibility was to go to the City of Westminster. Westminster was (and is) an authority with immense status, at the historic heart of government. Becoming a candidate for the chief executive job there was not an easy decision. The news that I, who had led the campaign against abolition, was moving to another post (particularly to Conservative-controlled Westminster) would signal the death of the county council. It would destroy morale among the West Yorkshire staff.

There was one big advantage of the job in Westminster. In a traditional district authority the chief executive was expected to live in the area of the authority and to be prominent in the town's social life. At the annual Mayor's Ball the Mayor would expect to lead the Town Clerk's wife in the inaugural veleta, while the Town Clerk steered the Mayoress. That would not be not the case in Westminster, I was assured by the upmarket Westminster headhunter. He was baronet Sir John Trelawney, employed by American headhunters Korn/Ferry. The council would accept that my family would stay in Yorkshire and that my weekends would be spent there. During the week I would occupy a *pied-à-terre* in London. That was the pattern expected of London gentry: at the weekend Westminster Tory councillors themselves left London for their country residences. I consulted my family. Our two children, Magnus and Antonia, were both settled in their schools en route to Cambridge. Clare was the senior partner in a large medical general practice and did not relish moving. The job in Westminster would mean that they could all stay in Yorkshire while I commuted weekly down to London. Clare, always supportive, took on the job of raising the children during the week, grappling with the logistics of their schooling.

I put my hat in the ring for the Westminster job. My pay as chief executive in West Yorkshire had risen to £37,539 pa. The Westminster basic salary on appointment was not much greater – £40,572 pa – but, anomalously, the job attracted pay at time-and-a-half for attendance at evening meetings. This gave a substantial boost to earnings.

Headhunter Trelawney explained that Westminster had a new leader, Shirley Porter, wife of Tesco chairman Sir Leslie Porter. She was the daughter of Tesco founder Sir Jack Cohen, who had started his career as a market trader and had made Tesco the biggest supermarket company in the UK. Would I meet Lady Porter in her Hyde Park flat rather than City Hall? Lady Porter was contemptuous of the conventions of local government, where interviews for jobs were multi-party and conducted in the local authority's offices. I agreed, though with reservations about the venue.

I arrived at the Porter flat. The maid showed me into a lavish drawing room, incongruously littered with dolls and soft toys. A substantial wall was taken up by a leather-bound set of the works of Sir Walter Scott. This cheered me up no end: I am one of the few who like Walter Scott's works and can plausibly claim to have read all his novels. Clearly the presence of his books was a good augury for my relationship with Lady Porter. After a few minutes Shirley made a studied entrance. After introductions I remarked that she or her husband were clearly devotees of Walter Scott. 'Walter Scott? Walter Scott? Walter Scott?' queried Shirley. Clearly the name meant nothing to her. Dismissing the subject she offered a gin and tonic, pressing a button which caused the leather spines inscribed Sir Walter Scott to slide back and reveal a cocktail cabinet.

Shirley filled a glass with gin and tonic and smugly showed me a new fridge, installed only that morning, a gift from the manufacturers. Clearly the chairman of Tesco received largesse in kind from the company's suppliers. The feature of the new fridge – the first of that type I had seen – was that it dispensed ice externally when a lever was depressed. Shirley held the glass of gin and tonic under the ice dispenser and pressed the lever for its baptism. A cascade of ice filled the glass and deposited the gin and tonic on the floor. Despite that setback the rest of the interview went well. My appointment was processed and approved by the conventional two-party interview in City Hall. I was to be Thomas Cromwell to Shirley Porter's Henry VIII. Cromwell lasted rather longer than I did.

I broke down when I announced my resignation to the county council's strategy board. I regarded the county council as my creation. Desertion seemed an act of betrayal. When my departure was announced staff said 'Then we've lost'. I insisted that there should be no leaving present. But in a thoughtful gesture Denis Healey gave me a farewell lunch in the House of Commons.

In retrospect, it was clear that our fight to save the county council was doomed to failure. A commitment included in the election manifesto at the request of the Prime Minister could not be abandoned. As my successor, the county council rejected Geoff Pollard, the council's director of finance, and instead appointed Bill Miles, chief executive of Gateshead, to whom the attraction of the job was its termination in 1986 and a premature pension.

The Westminster Culture and Dame Shirley

I prepared myself for the cultural shift from Yorkshire to the metropolitan ethos. The demography of London borough council members was very different to that of county councillors. County council meetings were held during the day, because of the geographical extent of a county, As a result county councillors were usually retired, self-employed, or of private means. Labour members were often employees in the public sector or unions, granted time off with pay for local government service. Because of their restricted geographical territory, London boroughs could meet in the evening, permitting their councillors to undertake 'normal' jobs during the day. As a result London borough councillors were much younger than their county council peers. They also tended to serve for much shorter periods.

Westminster council had a history of patrician leadership: the Duke of Norfolk was the first mayor of the Westminster metropolitan borough council when it was created in 1900. Former leaders of the council included Sir Hugh Cubitt, cousin of HRH the Duchess of Cornwall and great-great-grandson of the Thomas Cubitt who had been commissioned by the (then) Marquess of Westminster to build Belgravia and Pimlico. Hugh Cubitt was also chairman of the Housing Corporation and the Peabody Trust. When he was leader and a new policy was to be developed, Sir Hugh would broach it over lunch at Boodle's with the leader of Westminster's opposition Labour Party, Illtyd Harrington (ex-Paddington Council and later Ken Livingstone's deputy at the Greater London Council). Hugh Cubitt's predecessor as council leader was Group Captain Sir Gordon Pirie, a King's Scholar at Eton, who had a distinguished career in the RAF. Sir Hugh's successor was a City lawyer, David Cobbold, Charterhouse and New College, Oxford, limping from a war wound inflicted in Burma. The senior Tory backbencher was Tony Prendergast, wealthy husband of Dame Simone Sieff, granddaughter of Michael Marks, founder of Marks & Spencer. Tony's Savile Row suits creaked.

Westminster town clerks were almost as distinguished as the council leaders. In 1900 the borough's first town clerk was Sir John Hunt. The portrait of his successor, Sir Parker Morris, is in the National Portrait Gallery. Sir Parker became famous as the chairman of the 1961 Committee on Space Standards in Public Housing. Parker Morris standards improved public housing for almost twenty years until they were abolished by the Thatcher government in 1981. Sir Parker was the father of Dame Jennifer Jenkins, Chair of the National Trust and wife of Roy Jenkins, who became President of the European Commission after his distinguished career in British politics. Sir Parker had an authoritative style: he insisted that his successor, Alan Dawtry, should address him as *Sir Parker*.

In due course Alan Dawtry was himself knighted. He became a great friend and throughout my time in Westminster was a pillar of support. Like many of his generation, the shape of his life had been dictated by the War. As a member of the Territorial Army, he was called up at the outset of war and was an officer in the British Expeditionary Force in France in 1940. After the collapse of the French Army and the evacuation from Dunkirk, he was ordered to get back to England as best he could. Alan and his men trekked to their nearest port, Cherbourg, where the harbour was deserted, except for a small NAAFI supply ship. Alan and his men boarded the ship. Below decks was the captain, dead drunk. Alan arrested the captain and steered the ship as best he could across the Channel back to England. Later he took part in the landings in Algeria, Salerno and Anzio, where he and Denis Healey were both awarded the military MBE. At the end of the war Alan was a Lieutenant Colonel and Town Major of Milan. In April 1945 Mussolini and his mistress, Clara Petacci, were caught by partisans and executed. Alan's staff sergeant reported that their bodies were suspended upside down from a girder outside a petrol station in the Piazzale Loreto in Milan. Alan gave the order to cut them down.

Unlike many, Alan Dawtry was able to adapt back into civilian life and rose rapidly through the ranks of local government. As Chief Executive of Westminster he functioned as secretary of the London Boroughs Association. In that capacity Alan was a mastermind behind the reorganisation of London government in 1966, when plebeian Paddington and Marylebone were incorporated in the City of Westminster. In due course he became a centenarian. Shortly before his 101st birthday Alan telephoned Heston Blumenthal's Michelin two-star restaurant *Dinner* to book a table for a celebratory lunch. He was told that there was a six-month waiting list. 'Six months!' exploded Alan. 'My life expectancy is less than that'. They gave him a table.

Westminster council's most successful employee was Sir Donald Gosling. After leaving the Navy he became a clerk in the highways department. There he had the job of renting out bomb sites for car parking. He left the council's employment and took on the leases himself. Starting with a site in Holborn, he finished as the billionaire chairman of National Car Parks, entertained the Queen on his yacht and was made a Knight Commander of the Royal Victorian Order.

Westminster abutted the City of London, steeped in its mediaeval tradition. Its Town Clerk, Geoffrey Rowley, told me that he once received a letter from a firm of solicitors beginning 'We do not seem to have received a reply to our letter of 21st July 1876', to which Geoffrey replied: 'I am sorry that you have not received a reply to your letter of 21st July 1876, but I have been on holiday'. The boundary between the two cities bisected the Law Society's Hall, where it is possible to dine with your feet in Westminster and your bottom in the City. My suggestion that the boundary between the two cities should be rationalised provoked an indignant refusal from the City of London Council: the boundaries had been fixed in Saxon times and were not to be altered for petty logistical reasons in the twentieth century.

The Westminster Council culture was very different to that of West Yorkshire, where the county council was deeply conscious that Leeds, Bradford and Huddersfield were far from the centres of power. To counteract the deficiency, the county council went to great lengths – with some success – to make its mark with Westminster and Brussels. Since Westminster was the centre of the capital, I assumed that Westminster council would have an even wider *weltanschauung*. The opposite was the case: the council was parochial in its attitudes. Fundamental to the thinking of the West Yorkshire County Council was the county's economy, as the indigenous textile, clothing and mining industries disappeared. The success of the local economy was not a concern of the Westminster Council. There was a great resentment of tourism and the problems tourists inflicted on the city's residents. Councillors represented the residents and their concerns, not those of employers. Westminster's location at the centre of the country was a nuisance exemplified by the problems of public order, traffic, tourists, litter, rough sleepers and immigrants. At that time Westminster Council doggedly resisted pressure to convert residential property into commercial use. Councillors were determined that Westminster should not become a ghost city at night, like the City of London. Unlike the City of London, their objective was not to further commercial activity, but to safeguard residents. [Thirty years later the policy had to be reversed, as residential property in Westminster was increasingly acquired by non-resident foreigners and left empty.]

West Yorkshire councillors acquired prestige from their service on the county council. The opposite was the case in Westminster, whose patrician leaders had been prominent figures in their own right. They saw service on the council as a public duty, not as a pathway to distinction. Shirley Porter's attitude was very different to her predecessors: at last she had found a job which conferred importance on her, rather than on her father or husband. She took on the role of leader at a time when it was still relatively unusual to find women in positions of authority, Mrs Thatcher being her precedent. Shirley's plebeian background was very different to the traditional Westminster Conservative councillors. Though conscious of her lack of formal education, she attributed personal set-backs to anti-Semitism. She alleged that her school in Worthing had refused to make her Head Girl because she was Jewish. An indignant Headteacher responded that they had appointed several Jewish Head Girls. In any case Shirley had left school when she was aged only 16, too young to be Head Girl. Moreover, in appointing a Head Girl the School looked for some sort of academic distinction and Shirley had left school without taking a single GCE O level.

Shirley had been denied an opportunity to run Tesco, as her father handed successive control to his sons-in-law – first to the cultured Hyman Kreitman, husband of Jack Cohen's elder daughter; then to Shirley's husband, Sir Leslie Porter, already a successful businessman. When Leslie retired, Shirley organised a claque to press for her appointment to the Tesco Board, pointing out the absence of a woman on the Board. Leslie's successor as Tesco boss was Lord (Ian) MacLaurin. Faced with the demand for a woman on the Board, he hastily appointed Detta O'Cathain, later Baroness O'Cathain. In his memoirs Ian MacLaurin described Shirley as 'a sorcerer's apprentice, obsessed with power'.

Excluded from Tesco, Shirley looked for an opportunity to acquire importance in her own right and hit on local government. She was a member of the Liberal party until, in 1974, it was suggested that she might stand as a Conservative candidate in the city council's election for the Hyde Park ward. She was duly chosen, the local party hoping thereby to attract funding from such a wealthy source. After the selection process it was discovered that Shirley was not even a member of the Conservative party: her membership was hastily arranged.

Shirley Porter on the Council

The *Paddington Mercury* described Shirley as 'Paddington's Mrs Mop' when she was elected to the council and decided to concentrate on litter. She joined the Clean Up London campaign, mobilised schoolchildren in the campaign and was appointed successively as vice-chairman then chairman of the Council's Highways and Works Committee. During the 1979 Winter of

The Winding Stair

Discontent, waste mounted in the streets, a golden opportunity for Shirley. She organised 33 emergency rubbish dumps across the City. Anticipating Mrs Thatcher, she told the press that she would privatise rubbish collection if the dustbinmen did not return to work. Her successive litter campaigns included the 'Cleaner London Campaign', followed by the 'Cleaner City Initiative' in 1980. When boundary reorganisation reduced the number of Hyde Park councillors, Shirley pipped the long-serving Conservative councillor, Trixie Gardner, an Australian dentist by origin, for the Conservative nomination. The deselection did Trixie a favour: she was elevated to the House of Lords as Baroness Gardner of Parkes. [Parkes was Trixie's birthplace in New South Wales.] She became the Conservative spokesperson in the House of Lords on women's rights.

Shirley's public profile soared, thanks to a series of publicity stunts. She dressed up as a Sioux warrior to clear litter. In response the Council leader, David Cobbold, made her chairman of the General Purposes Committee. She had the specific remit of cleaning up Soho, a haunt of depravity for over a century. When David Cobbold stood down as leader it was expected that he would be succeeded by his deputy, Jonah Walker-Smith. Jonah was a barrister with an appropriate pedigree: Westminster School, Christ Church and (later) second baronet. But the demography of members of the city council had changed, following the trend in the Conservative party nationally. *Garagistes* had replaced gentry. Shirley contested the election with her usual determination. She vanquished Walker-Smith, who believed it ungentlemanly to canvass support. Members of the old guard were dismissed and a more raucous regime installed.

The former patrician leaders of Westminster Council had a noble commitment to the under-privileged. The council's finances were unconstrained by the financial pressures faced by other local authorities: Westminster council had the benefit of the business rate, the proceeds of which dwarfed the domestic rate. Seven and a half per cent of the entire country's business rates are in Westminster. A penny rate in Westminster then produced over £3m, though nearly three-quarters of the money was siphoned off to the Greater London Council and the Inner London Education Authority. The Council then spent more per head on social services than any other local authority. Its opulence extended to its staff: every chief officer had a car and driver.

The change of leadership from patrician to grocer's daughter replicated the revolution in Downing Street and had the same cataclysmic effect. First to go under Shirley's leadership was the chief executive, David Witty. A Balliol man, David Witty fitted perfectly into the traditional and courteous environment of the city council. But he certainly did not correspond to Shirley Porter's idea of a chief executive. At Tesco her Father's rubric was YCDBSOYA – you can't do business sitting on your arse. Shirley procured a retirement CBE for Witty as part of his exit package and he duly disappeared. She scrapped the chief officers' cars and drivers (retaining only the chief executive's car and driver). Shirley's new broom even cleared the members' room, which Sir Gordon Pirie had continued to use after he left the council. To his enormous umbrage, he was told in no uncertain terms by Shirley to clear out.

Shirley had an unfortunate start as council leader. The BBC consumer programme, *Watchdog*, asked the council's Trading Standards department if its inspectors could be filmed on their rounds. The Chief Inspector of Trading Standards welcomed the chance of publicity: it would be a caution to traders and increase awareness of his department's vigilance in protecting the public from malpractice. When the trading standards inspectors approached a Tesco supermarket in the Portobello Road, the accompanying BBC reporter suggested that they carry out an inspection. As luck would have it, they discovered discrepancies in the weight of vacuum packed meat. The discovery of the discrepancies was duly televised. Both inspectors left the council's employment and the BBC alleged that they had been forced out. Shirley threatened libel proceedings but the BBC refused to back down. No proceedings were issued. Another Shirley scandal was the conversion from residential to office of the mews house belonging to her Hyde Park penthouse without planning consent. Retrospective planning consent was hastily secured.

22. 1984-89: Westminster
and a Hot Day in Maidstone

I arrived in Westminster in 1984 when these issues were still simmering. The adverse publicity reinforced Shirley's belief that 'they' were out to get her. After working in West Yorkshire with politicians who were pleasant and clever it came as a shock to work with someone who was both unpleasant and stupid. Shirley had only the vaguest idea of politics and current affairs. As a leader she had major drawbacks: Shirley had no ability to think on her feet, nor any concept of the governance of local authorities, then founded on the principle that decisions were taken by a multi-party committee. The formal structure of local authorities did not recognise the reality of political power. The 1972 Bains Committee report on local government management had conceded that discussion would take place in the party group but said, unrealistically, that 'it is, however, at the actual committee meeting that the officer's professional knowledge and experience should play their part in advising members'. This was manifest nonsense when the party group had already taken the decision. It was also directly contrary to the view of such an eminent local government figure as Lord Morrison of Lambeth, who said that 'officers should rarely, if at all, speak in committee, placing responsibility where it should lie – with the elected member'. But the formal position was clear: members of the opposition parties had the same rights to information as members of the majority party. The staff of the local authority owed allegiance to the council as a whole though, *de facto*, policy was settled by the majority party. Shirley could not grasp this institutionalised ambiguity, behaving as though the organisation were an autocracy responsible only to her.

Unfortunately for Shirley, the Labour opposition in Westminster was of exceptional ability. It included Neale Coleman. Neale had taken a starred first in greats at Balliol, and became a key member of the City Hall team under Ken Livingstone. Uniquely he survived into Boris Johnson's rule, the two Balliol alumni quoting Ovid couplets to each other. Later he briefly took the job as head of policy for Jeremy Corbyn (when the latter was leader of the Parliamentary Labour Party) and in 2020 was appointed as a member of the National Infrastructure Commission. Other Labour Group members were David Pitt-Watson (ex-McKinsey and later Assistant General Secretary of the Labour Party), Paul Dimoldenberg (who worked for Lowe Bell), Gavin Miller QC of Doughty Street Chambers (famous for their work in human rights and civil liberties), Andrew Dismore, later an MP, and the imperious Diane Abbott, later shadow Home Secretary. Leader of the Labour Group was Joe Hegarty (with whom I established cordial relationships when, much later, I became a director of the Westminster Primary Care Trust when Joe was chairman). Some goodwill between the parties had survived from the David Cobbold era. At the annual meeting Paul Dimoldenberg would make a witty speech in which, for example, he would ask if the glamorous councillor Elizabeth Flach had received planning permission for the elaborate hat which perched on her head.

Shirley herself had initial support from able councillors like Patricia Kirwan, Angela Killick, Rachel Whitaker and Graham

Mather (later Director of the Institute of Economic Affairs and President of the European Policy Forum). They had supported Shirley because they felt that the old patrician style needed a kick in the pants but they abandoned Shirley as her incompetence was augmented by her dictatorial mode of operation. My friendly relations with them survived my departure from Westminster. They were replaced by Shirley's cronies, David Weeks who became deputy leader; and Barry Legg, Chief Whip, later an MP and, briefly, chairman of the Conservative Party.

Mrs Thatcher's radical agenda prompted defiance from Labour-controlled local authorities. Their chief executives were expected to take the lead in driving forward the majority group's programme of resistance, thus making them centre forward as well as referee. Where officers were inflexible in recognising the reality of political power, Labour-controlled councils employed Labour councillors from other local authorities, who were allowed generous time off to discharge their municipal duties. The tension between Labour local government and Mrs Thatcher's Conservative Government intensified.

Alerted to what it saw as an abuse, the Government stepped in and established a *Committee of Inquiry into the Conduct of Local Authority Business*. Its conclusions were known as the Widdicombe report, after its chairman, David Widdicombe QC. Despite being a member of the Labour party, David was appointed by Michael Heseltine, who had been a contemporary at Cambridge. [David himself thought that Heseltine did not know of his political allegiance; though some years later Heseltine told me that he was well aware of David's Labour party membership.] The review, which reported in 1986, recommended an overhaul of the political structures of local government, mainly around the workings of council committees. It also recommended a ban on council officers serving as members of other local authorities. The result was the creation of specifically political units. Copying the installation of political advisers to Cabinet ministers, Shirley decreed that all committee chairmen should have a political assistant. The Chairmen's office on the 17th floor of City Hall developed into a rival power base to that of the council's chief officers.

Within the council, Shirley relied on the support of David Weeks and Barry Legg. Though Weeks and Legg backed her up in the council, Shirley also needed outside advice to prop up her leadership. She enlisted the help of Sir Alfred Sherman and Michael Ivens, right wing idealogues influential with Sir Keith Joseph and, through him, Mrs Thatcher, as she rose to power. Sherman had been local government reporter for the *Daily Telegraph* and drafted some of Sir Keith's speeches. Ivens ran the organisation *Foundation for Business Responsibilities*. The belligerent policies of Ken Livingstone in county hall were a natural target. With the advice of Ivens, and money from the property magnate Gerald Ronson, Shirley set up an organisation called WARS – *Westminster Against Reckless Spending*. This developed into a battle against Livingstone's Greater London Council. Shirley led a camel over Westminster Bridge to county hall to demonstrate 'the straw that broke the camel's back'.

Shirley's most immediate adviser was David McDonough, a *protégé* of Lord Feldman (later Chairman of the Conservative Party). David ran a public relations firm which later amalgamated with Lowe Bell. David's political views were of (what seemed to me) the extreme right, but he was manifestly able and entirely practical. We got on well and were able to steer Shirley into sensible and productive avenues. Customer care was beginning to occupy the minds of local authorities. If councils are to compete with alternative sources of service delivery then its own services must be user-friendly. This was brought home to me when I was phoned by a persistent woman who had managed to break through the barriers between members of the public and the chief executive. She told me that her aunt had a problem. Different elements of the problem were handled by three different departments in City Hall. Yet to the aunt there was only one problem. The complexities of dealing with three different departments had defeated her.

David McDonough and I sold Shirley the idea of a single interface between members of the public and the council. It would, we said, be like Tesco, the one-stop shop. An office on the ground floor of City Hall was dedicated to members of the public. Chief officers (including me) would each spend some time there to meet members of the public and encounter grass roots experience direct. The idea gained national fame and I was careful that Shirley gained the kudos. The council's own publicity was unctuous in its flattery: 'Lady Porter's vision of providing a fast, effective and friendly service has been turned into reality with the introduction of One Stop. Leading the council in breaking away from the traditional Town Hall image, Lady Porter, the leader of Westminster City Council is, by introducing such concepts, cutting through red tape and forging closer links with the public we serve'. Dr Goebbels could not have been more effusive.

Shirley Porter and Ken Livingstone

David McDonough, however, proved insufficiently audacious for Shirley. Common sense inhibited his advice. Shirley's ambition to be someone of importance in her own right prompted her to hire Roger Rosewell, a former Trotskyite, who devised a three year strategy for Shirley's elevation to the House of Lords. Rosewell's participation in council affairs was rigorously concealed: he even used the goods lift to ascend to Shirley's office on the eighteenth floor of City Hall. Knowing Mrs Thatcher's antipathy to Ken Livingstone, Rosewell urged a vendetta against Livingstone and the GLC. Shirley secured council authority to bring a court action to stop the GLC's campaign against the Conservative Government's policy. The court declared 'Publicity on the rates' to be illegal. After hearing the court's decision against the GLC I returned to City Hall. Piled in the corridor was a stack of Westminster Council leaflets attacking the GLC – publicity on the rates with a vengeance. I gave a hasty order for the leaflets to be incinerated.

The campaign eventually faced a motion in the House of Commons, moved by Ken Livingstone, by then an MP:

That this House calls for a full inquiry into the Foundation for Business Responsibilities, a bogus charity run by the right-wing pressure group, the Aims of Industry, and to investigate the roles of Sir Nigel Mobbs and Michael Ivens, who have been respectively the Chairman and Director of both organisations, into the slush-fund which laundered money through the Foundation for Business Responsibilities to pay for a political campaign managed by the public relations firm Marketforce Communications before the 1990 local elections; notes that Sir Nigel Mobbs is the chief executive of the property company Slough Estates which has donated handsomely to the Tory Party, the Aims of Industry and the Economic League; notes that Dame Shirley Porter used the Foundation for Business Responsibilities to launder cash, firstly from Gerald Ronson and other businessmen for a campaign against the Greater London Council in the mid-1980s, and secondly, from the slush-fund she and her advisers had set up for the Marketforce campaign before the 1990 local elections; and calls on Westminster Council Tories to reveal who donated to this £98,000 election slush-fund.

The Tory vendetta against the GLC became personalised as a struggle between Shirley and Ken Livingstone. In 1986 the annual conference of the Society of Local Authority Chief Executives took place in Maidstone. The highlight of the conference was to be a debate between Shirley and Livingstone. I travelled down with Shirley. On the train I bumped into Ken

Livingstone and introduced him to Shirley. The three of us shared a taxi to the conference venue. It was a suffocatingly hot day and the conference venue had no air conditioning. Unsurprisingly the assembled chief executives had removed their jackets. Having kept company with Shirley and Ken before the debate, I entered the hall as they took the stage. Shirley began by complaining that the assembled chief executives had removed their jackets without seeking her consent 'as a lady'. 'I notice', she said, 'that *my* chief executive has not removed his jacket.' [True: I was still making my way to my seat.] No more effective way could have been devised to alienate the audience. When Ken Livingstone said that every local authority should have a foreign policy, the assembled chief executives cheered lustily. At the end of the debate, they were asked to vote for Shirley or Ken. Livingstone received virtually unanimous endorsement from an audience which almost certainly did not share many of the views which he had promulgated.

Shirley Porter and the pooper-scooter

Shirley remained determined to have her photograph in the press, believing that to be a necessary prologue to her elevation to the scarlet benches of the House of Lords. One press triumph was the marriage of Prince Andrew, Duke of York, to Sarah Ferguson in 1986. Despite my urging, Shirley had consistently refused to authorise any special celebration, like flower planting on the route of the royal procession. But two days before the wedding she summoned me to insist that she must be on national television to mark the occasion. I went to the then Head of Public Relations, John Eames, who was a creative genius. On the evening before the wedding he arranged for Shirley to be photographed outside Westminster Abbey sharing a glass of champagne with the street sweepers as they set off to cleanse the route of the royal procession. Desperate for a story about the wedding, the national TV news channels all featured the event. Next day John Eames arranged for Shirley to be photographed in the meals on wheels canteen, putting a white rose of York on the lunch trays as they were about to be distributed. Once again she hit the national TV news.

Thanks to these initiatives Shirley became a public figure. In the Strand was a vacant site. The *Evening Standard* said that they had been informed by a reliable taxi driver that the site had been reserved for a statue of Lady Porter. Shirley's national profile prompted an invitation to appear on BBC radio's Any Questions, where her briefing filled three ring binders, its bulk completely counter-productive. The invitation was not repeated. She and I also appeared on a TV discussion programme where I was embarrassed by the manipulation of images. After the discussion had ended we were asked to be filmed in various attitudes, for example laughing. The resulting images were spliced into the programme, so that viewers received an image of Shirley and me roaring with laughter as lugubrious tales were told of deprivation in Glasgow.

Sadly Public Relations Head John Eames was too independently-minded for Shirley and joined several predecessors in the exit queue. Successive Directors of Public Relations arrived and disappeared with startling regularity: at least half a dozen during my time in Westminster. After Shirley stood down from the leadership her successor, the odious Weeks, hired Sir Bernard Ingham to improve the council's image. Bernard had left the civil service after the downfall of Mrs Thatcher. He was startled to find that his instructions included getting Weeks's profile in *Hello!* magazine. Bernard soon severed his link with the council.

During a weekend in Paris Shirley came across the pooper-scooter – a scooter with a vacuum-cleaner attachment which the Parisians used to hoover up dog excrement. Having hoovered up the mess, the machine purged the site with a disinfectant spray. Shirley decided to try it out in London. The national press was summoned to Trafalgar Square, together with twelve dogs. Shirley, the relevant officers and I joined the assembled reporters. Unsurprisingly the dogs were overcome by embarrassment and declined to perform. Shirley's brow darkened. The self-conscious dogs looked the other way. The Director of Street Cleansing had, however, foreseen this possibility. Opening his briefcase, he extracted several gobbets of dog excrement. Shirley barked an imperious command into her mobile telephone. A two-stroke engine throbbed and out of Whitehall roared the pooper-scooter, piloted by an histrionic Parisian. As he arrived at the site of the offence, the Gallic driver unbridled his vacuum with a flourish, sucked up the aberrant turds, disinfected the site and roared away. Sadly the financial consequences of the pooper-scooter prevented its adoption in Westminster.

Shirley's other import from the Continent was the public toilet kiosk. This was a ready-made cubicle with accommodation for one person. The door opened on insertion of the appropriate coin. After fifteen minutes precisely the door automatically re-opened. The interior and any remaining occupant were sprayed with disinfectant. The kiosks proved very popular, especially with ladies of the night, since they ensured a regular turnover of clients. Identifying the problem of immorality, the *Evening Standard* touted the suggestion that the kiosks should be fitted with transparent panels so that passers-by could see that nothing untoward was taking place inside.

Disabled toilets also became a preoccupation. In the IRA bombing of the Conservative party conference in 1984, Norman Tebbitt's wife Margaret was severely injured and left paralysed. She took up the cudgels to campaign for toilets for disabled people. Every time she needed a loo and couldn't find one, she phoned me. Thanks to Lady Tebbitt's campaigning Westminster became better provided with wheelchair accessible toilets.

The Winding Stair

Shirley introduced an innovation to the administrative workings of City Hall staff. To keep staff on their toes she issued an edict that staff should carry with them at all times a Filofax. At each meeting Shirley would demand to see their plan for the day as recorded in the Filofax. Compulsive recording resulted. One day calm broke out: Shirley had boarded an El-Al jet to Israel. I was (metaphorically) putting my feet up when the phone rang. It was the pilot of the plane. Shirley had commandeered the radio telephone for an urgent instruction to her chief executive. The pilot handed her the phone. 'Everyone', she instructed, 'who pulls their weight, must be given a leather-bound Filofax to replace the plastic version.' Other officers would then see clearly the rewards of loyalty. Sadly the call was counter-productive: plastic Filofaxes became a symbol of defiance. Only creeps attained the leather-bound version. Soon all Filofaxes were banned from City Hall.

Shirley was exhilarated by humiliating staff. Senior officers were reduced to tears by her. She seemed to have a nose for weakness. I thought that a new Director of Administration, Paul Glicker, might escape censure: he was very competent. Unfortunately Paul suffered from Crohn's disease and was vulnerable to pressure. He was quickly destroyed and left. One of the chief officers lay down in front of Shirley at his leaving party. 'Walk all over me, Shirley', he begged. 'That's what you've been doing for the last eight years'.

It was forbidden to open the windows in Westminster City Hall: the building had a slightly pressurised internal air system. To Shirley a direction of that sort was red rag to a bull: she immediately insisted that the window in her office should be opened. Craftsmen were hired for the job. As the window was prized open there was a faint hope that the pressure would suck her out, like Goldfinger from the aeroplane in the James Bond film.

Humbugs consistently fooled Shirley. They condemned the

council's traditional officers and pretended to superior knowledge. A self-proclaimed expert in central purchasing managed to devastate the council's purchasing systems until he was exposed. A *soi-disant* O&M expert fooled Shirley by imposing his so-called systems on the organisation before being sent on his way. Shortly after I arrived a dispute with the British Waterways Board was about to go to court: the council stood to lose over £1.5m if it lost. Given the size of the dispute I took the file home. I retained confidence in my previous expertise in litigation: it was absolutely clear to me that the council would lose. As it happened I knew the British Waterways top brass well from my time in West Yorkshire, which is riddled with their canals. With the knowledge and approval of Shirley I deployed my relationship with the Waterways people to agree a settlement at less than £500k. Coincidentally I then went on holiday believing that I had saved the Council £1m. Returning two weeks later I found that Shirley had rescinded the decision and given an instruction to fight the case. Of course the council lost and was held liable for the full £1.5m. When I returned from holiday, Shirley's only allusion to the *débâcle* was 'I suppose you'll say I told you so'.

23. Pomp, Circumstance and a Piano

Shirley could make life in City Hall uncomfortable at best and, at worst, impossible. But civic life in Westminster still carried a certain *cachet*. At one civic dinner my wife Clare asked her neighbour about the medal round his neck. That, he said, was the Order of Merit. He was the Nobel prize-winner Sir Aaron Klug. A typical resident was Yehudi Menuhin, ennobled as Baron Menuhin. A sensitive man, he lived in Belgravia and was plagued by traffic noise. He telephoned me regularly in the unavailing hope that I could abate it.

Westminster Abbey was a source of kudos: the council was very much part of the Abbey's community. The Lord Mayor of Westminster is *ex officio* High Steward of the Abbey, which itself is that anomaly, a royal peculiar. As such it is subject to the direct authority of the monarch and outside the jurisdiction of the diocese. In the Abbey's order of precedence the chief executive of Westminster City Council ranked before the Prime Minister, something which Mrs Thatcher gave every impression of resenting as I followed her in the procession up the aisle of the Abbey. The Queen, of course, took the position of honour at the rear.

Every year Norway donates a Christmas tree to the City of Westminster to commemorate the British role in freeing the country from wartime Nazi oppression. The Lord Mayor and I would make an annual civic visit to Norway to choose the tree – our choice heavily influenced by the local arboriculturalists who indicated the preferred specimen. The chosen pine is then felled, transshipped to London and erected in Trafalgar Square, bedecked in white lights. The opening ceremony – performed by the Norwegian Ambassador – is followed by a party at the Norwegian Embassy where Norwegian potato aquavit flows freely. The journey of the Lord Mayor and me to the Embassy was dramatic: our police escort, klaxons blaring, by-passed the traffic by escorting the civic limousine through the Wellington Arch at Hyde Park Corner.

Other public events involved me as Westminster chief executive. Switching on the Oxford Street Christmas lights is a significant event in the London calendar. Every year a celebrity is engaged for the occasion. On one occasion the celebrity was Dame Edna Everage (aka Barry Humphries). S/he emerged from the changing room having donned the appropriate regalia. Nominated to chaperone her, I was cowed by the apparition. 'Don't let me intimidate you', she jeered as I greeted her nervously.

The shades of *Macbeth* made a vicarious appearance in 1985, the year after I arrived in Westminster. The Lord Mayor was Roger Bramble. Roger, an unmarried Old Etonian, had previously been Deputy Lord Mayor, when his consort was Caroline, Duchess of Fife. When he became Lord Mayor his Lady Mayoress was the extraordinarily glamorous Cathryn, Countess Cawdor. Roger hit on a number of wheezes to make his year of office particularly memorable. His Lord Mayoral soirées were attended by leading figures from the arts, including the redoubtable nonagenarian Dame Eva Turner, in her day a famous *Turandot*. Roger founded the New Year's Day Parade, when American marching bands process through central London. Now a regular feature of London life, the Parade attracts a million spectators and was regularly led by Roger on horseback.

Roger elevated his Lord Mayoralty by imbuing it with the prestige of the 400th anniversary of the council. He argued that the creation of the Court of Burgesses in 1585 (after the end of monastic governance from Westminster Abbey) meant that 1985 was the council's quatercentenary. On the strength of this dubious association Roger organised a glittering succession of events, culminating in a garden party in the grounds of the Abbey attended by the Queen, the Duke of Edinburgh and a bevy of prominent people.

The creation of the Court of Burgesses was not the only institution required by the abolition of the monasteries. The monks had looked after the poor. To fill the void, each year an Overseer was appointed for the Parish of St Margaret's in Westminster. The Overseer's duties were to collect the Poor Rate levied on all householders and spend it on the poor of the Parish, who included the workless able-bodied males, the homeless family, the indigent females with children, the sick, the infectious, the insane, the feckless and the vagrant. The relief might be money but could include housing, skill training, medical advice and restraint for the insane. The Overseer also had to return drifters from other parishes to their birthplace – which might involve the Overseer in extensive travelling with unwilling companions.

The Overseers left one enduring legacy to the City: once released from their duties, they formed a society and met regularly. The custom was for the current Overseer to preside over the meeting and provide tobacco for the past Overseers' clay pipes. In 1713, the then President presented the Society with a horn tobacco box which his successors had a duty to fill with tobacco. It became the custom for each successive President not only to fill but also to ornament the tobacco box. As the years went by the tobacco box became encrusted by inscriptions until there was no room for more. The original horn box was then encased in a silver box. Over the centuries the silver box itself became encased in successive silver boxes. Each would be engraved with a memorial of the year of the President. In 1746, for example, the engraving by William Hogarth commemorated the victory of the Duke of Cumberland at Culloden over Bonnie Prince Charlie, the Young Pretender. Over the centuries the Past Overseers' Society had accumulated an extremely valuable collection of silver, with considerable artistic and historical significance.

The Society's annual dinners had become as encrusted with tradition as the silver caskets which encased the tobacco box. In 1805, the members were enjoying a whitebait supper at Greenwich when a sloop in the river brought news of Lord Nelson's victory at Trafalgar. Without a word uttered, the Past Overseers rose to their feet and drank a toast to celebrate the victory and to mark Lord Nelson's death. At every annual dinner thereafter, the Past Overseers would rise to their feet in silence and drink a toast to the immortal memory of Lord Nelson. Clay pipes would then be provided and filled with tobacco provided by the president for the year. When smoking in public places was banned in 2007, the Society's stock of clay pipes was ceremonially smashed after the dinner. The Society's collection of silver was kept in the Westminster Lord Mayor's strongroom and brought with the Lord Mayor to the annual dinner.

Attendance at such events was not the only duty of the Lord Mayor. Every year the incumbent would organise a charitable appeal. In the year of his lord mayoralty, the object of Roger Bramble's appeal was the acquisition of a new piano for St John's, Smith Square. Procuring the piano for an important concert venue is, I discovered, a major exercise. You don't pop

The Winding Stair

into the Steinway showroom in Marylebone Lane and say 'I'll have one of those': Steinway sent to St John's six of their finest instruments. Alfred Brendel agreed to try them out. Three were dismissed quickly and the others given various trials until Herr Brendel pronounced his choice of the piano which best accommodated St John's acoustics. Selected for the opening concert to feature the new instrument was Tamas Vasary, the famous Hungarian virtuoso. Alfred Brendel was unimpressed by Vasary's failure during his performance to take into account the acoustics of the former church.

Around the world are a number of Westminsters. The name is derived not from the City itself, but from the Westminster Conference, an annual evangelical gathering named after the Elizabethan disputation of 1559. In 1986, the Westminster in Colorado built a 130-foot bell tower and invited the Lord Mayor and me to the opening ceremony. As we arrived the local brass band struck up a jazzy tune. Noting that the locals were standing to attention, the Lord Mayor belatedly recognised a hot version of *God Save the Queen*. We hastily adjusted our deportment. Near the bell tower we planted an English oak and satisfied our hosts' curiosity as to whether Westminster UK was near London.

The visit was memorable for our trip to Colorado Springs, site of the American Combat Operations Center. Its ballistic missile early warning system was constructed underneath the mile-high Cheyenne granite mountain. The Center is raised on springs so that a nuclear bomb will not disturb its delicate machinery – they are, allegedly, the only springs in Colorado Springs. Inside the mountain are video screens with transmissions from, *inter alia*, Yorkshire venues like Fylingdales and Menwith Hill. Before our visit we had to complete a security check, including a question on which political party we supported. Surprisingly the guest book showed that in the previous week the military attachés of the Warsaw Pact

252

countries had visited the centre. When I enquired I was told, reassuringly, that the US Government had realised that there was no point in having access to all this information if the Soviets didn't realise that they had it.

The job of Westminster chief executive involved regular contact with the royal family. As chief executive I was invited to the royal garden parties in the grounds of Buckingham Palace. Informality was creeping in: guests often wore suits, whereas morning dress had once been obligatory. On one occasion the Lord Mayor's macebearer, Ernie Hodges, a former Sergeant-Major, caught me setting out for the garden party in my office suit. Ernie immediately remonstrated. I told him that many garden party guests now wore suits rather than morning dress. 'Not', expostulated Ernie, 'a gentleman in your position.' He dragged me back into City Hall to change into tail coat and striped trousers. Occasionally the Lord Mayor and I would be invited to lunch at Buckingham Palace. Plates are cleared away when the Queen has finished eating. On one occasion I went with a Lord Mayor who suffered from a stammer. His attempts to converse with his neighbour were so prolonged that his food was confiscated before he had begun its consumption. After we left the Palace in the Lord Mayoral car we stopped to collect a hamburger.

One Ruritanian feature of life in Westminster accompanied a State visit. In morning dress and white gloves, the Lord Mayor and I would go to St James's Palace. There, in an elaborate ceremony of bowing and scraping, we would assure the visiting Heads of State that they were safe from attack from the locals and that the drains had been inspected for subterranean bombs. In return a grateful but slightly bewildered Head of State would pin to our breasts the appropriate national order of chivalry. Thus I have been honoured with the Orders of Merit of France, Germany, Qatar and Senegal and the order of the Aztec Eagle of Mexico. When I went with the Lord Mayor to welcome King

The Winding Stair

Fahd of Saudi Arabia there was a slight problem: the then Lord Mayor was female and was therefore ineligible for an Arab order of chivalry. As a result the Lord Mayor received a splendid bracelet and I was presented with a magnificent pair of platinum and gold cufflinks in the shape of the Saudi coat-of-arms. While pondering whether I should agree to take such a costly gift, I received a letter on behalf of the Queen which commanded me to accept and dictated the form of an appropriate thank-you letter.

The procedure had its hazards: President Mitterand drew blood when he pinned the French Order of Merit to my chest. That evening, following a state dinner, there was a reception at the French Embassy, to which my wife Clare and I were invited. The invitation specified evening dress or *le smoking*, aka black tie, and asked that those who had been presented with medals by the President should wear them. That evening we were to take our children to the National Theatre to see *Animal Farm*. The show was due to end at 9-30pm, so we planned to wear appropriate clothes – in my case dinner jacket - drop the children off at our flat and go on to the French Embassy. I would put the medal in my pocket and pin it on after the theatre.

At that time the Head of Protocol in the Foreign Office was Bryan Burroughs, whom I knew well: he was also President of the Soho Society and worked with the council on our campaign against the sex industry in Soho. *En passant* I mentioned the invitation to Bryan and my plan to combine it with an evening at the National Theatre, which I would attend in a dinner jacket. Bryan immediately demolished the plan: French protocol requires those wearing French decorations to wear full evening dress. In the United Kingdom there had been a temporary utility measure during the War which enabled those sporting British decorations to wear them with black tie. The measure has never been rescinded. But the same was not true in France: rigid protocol applied. French orders of chivalry can only be worn with white tie. The children had already expressed embarrassment at the idea of going to the theatre with me wearing a dinner jacket: white tie and tails would be too much. 'Don't worry – leave it to me', Bryan responded. A telex went from the Foreign Office to the Quai d'Orsay; relayed from the Quai d'Orsay to the Élysée Palace; back from the Élysée Palace to the Quai d'Orsay; and from the Quai d'Orsay to the Foreign Office. It contained the permission of M le President that at the Embassy reception Mr Brooke would be permitted to wear his Order of Merit *avec le smoking* – black tie. The reception was the grandest I have attended: seemingly every member of the royal family was there. We recognised every guest: the great and the good appeared in force. Luckily we bumped into Bernard Ingham, who chaperoned us round.

Bernard also invited me to a cocktail party in No 10 Downing Street, where I made what I thought was an innocuous remark. It prompted Mrs Thatcher to say 'That is exactly the sort of thing which has brought Britain to the pass it's in today'. The other guests hastily raised their glasses and gulped their contents. My relationship with Mrs Thatcher had not improved with propinquity. On one social occasion at No 10, I was chatting to the Duke of Westminster. The council had, unsurprisingly, a close relationship with the Grosvenor Estate whose influence in the city of Westminster was wholly beneficial: the Estate took the hundred year view, not the quick buck. Pausing to talk to the Duke, Mrs Thatcher, studiously ignored me. The Duke courteously introduced me. 'Mr Brooke and I have met,' responded the Prime Minister icily and continued her conversation with the Duke. On one occasion Mrs Thatcher nearly missed a vote in the House of Commons because of traffic congestion. She demanded an underpass under Parliament Square. Accompanied by Nicholas Ridley, then Secretary of State for Transport, I went to No 10 to tell Mrs Thatcher that it couldn't be done: under Parliament Square ran the Bazalgette trunk sewer and the Circle line. Mrs Thatcher famously could not stand those who said that it couldn't be done: the episode confirmed her opinion of me.

The Prince of Wales's Trust registered my move to London: I was appointed as chairman of its East End committee. We were to disburse our budget to increase opportunities for young people and to mitigate deprivation. This required members of my Committee and myself to visit the young applicants. In a special case we could persuade the central committee to augment our budget. Unsurprisingly Prince Charles and Princess Diana had a particular interest in the East End and were frequent visitors. I conducted Princess Diana round the Broadwater Farm Estate in Tottenham. Shortly after our visit in 1985, the estate became notorious when PC Blakelock was stabbed to death in a riot. Before I went to the estate I would telephone my arrival and be escorted by my contact to the place of meeting.

Chairing the Prince's Trust East End Committee brought with it invitations to royal fund-raising occasions. They included first nights at London cinemas. Standing in the reception line at one of the events I enquired of my neighbour what she did for a living. 'My name', she responded politely, 'is Joan Collins. And I am an actor.' A charming companion on the presentation line was Mandy Rice-Davies, a fellow Dolphin Square resident and famous for her role in the Profumo scandal which had damaged the Conservative Government of Harold Macmillan in 1963. She had made a career as a film star and was a lively member of the reception line. On another occasion the Prince of Wales held me in conversation as he enquired about the latest Prince's Trust scheme in the East End. Princess Diana stood mute at his elbow. When the Prince moved on I apologised for keeping her waiting. 'Don't worry', responded the Princess, pointing to her head, 'brain the size of a pea'.

Twinning with Beijing

In a moment of *folie de grandeur* Shirley Porter decided that Westminster should twin with Beijing. Lord King, then chairman of British Airways, was cajoled by Shirley into promising free first class air tickets and the Chinese Ambassador was shanghaied into arranging the visit. The deputation consisted of Shirley, Trixie Gardner (by now Baroness Gardner of Parkes and Conservative spokesman on equal opportunities in the House of Lords) and myself. There was a *contretemps* on our arrival at Heathrow: the first class seats on the plane were full. A fuming Shirley Porter demanded our entry into the First Class lounge and insisted that a buggy take her to the plane. Trixie and I followed on foot, infantry following the cavalry. Shirley swore that she would never travel steerage again 'with her feet tucked up to her chin'.

Once in Beijing we were received in the Town Hall, which mystifyingly seemed to be a replica of Islington Town Hall. There we were granted audience with the Mayor of Beijing, Chen Xitong, who later achieved notoriety during the 1989 conflict when he signed the order which led to the massacre in Tiananmen Square. Over lidded cups of Chinese tea the Mayor courteously explained that the population of Beijing was twice as high as that of the whole of Greater London and that twinning with Westminster would be somewhat unbalanced. However – it might be possible for Westminster to twin with Beijing's central arrondissement. To Shirley that would have been an unacceptable humiliation. The negotiations were discontinued and the rest of our time in Beijing was spent on a tourist itinerary organised by the Beijing Mayor's office.

Meanwhile I was charged by Shirley with ensuring that her return journey from Beijing to London would be in the first class cabin of the aeroplane. In the days before the world-wide web this proved extremely difficult. International telephone calls failed to connect with Lord King's office and produced only Chinese music. I left message after message but with no response. Eventually I had to resort to the British Airways office in Beijing. They told me that to return in first class would cost just over £1500. I broke the news to Shirley, who insisted that the British Airways representative should attend upon her in our hotel. I managed to engineer this by insisting that Lady Porter was a personal friend of Lord King. There was one further problem: the British Airways representative wanted money for the ticket. Shirley did not have £1500, not even a credit card. Trixie Gardner volunteered hers – and when seeking reimbursement had to justify to Shirley the exchange rate which converted yuan into pounds sterling.

Eventually we boarded the plane, Shirley in First Class and Trixie and I in economy. After 90 minutes we were due to change aircraft in Hong Kong. During the short flight Trixie and I, seated in economy class, were visited by Shirley bearing gifts of salted nuts, eye masks and other offerings presented to those in First Class. Lady Bountiful could not have been more unctuous. We disembarked at Hong Kong. While waiting in the Hong Kong airport I heard an appeal on the Tannoy for *Mr Bluk*. Diffidently I went to the British Airways desk. I was indeed the *Mr Bluk* whom they sought. My messages to Lord King had eventually got through: they had received from Lord King a telex commanding that we be upgraded to First Class. So Trixie and I joined Shirley in First Class, enjoying free a journey for which Shirley had just paid £1,500. During the 13 hours of the flight from Hong Kong to London a fuming Shirley exchanged not a word with us.

Shortly after our return China again figured in Shirley's mind. She had visited San Francisco and encountered the city's Chinatown. It stimulated an inspiration: the creation of a Chinatown in London. Shirley decreed that the Chinese *enclave* north of Leicester Square should be embellished with Chinese arches and flags. The Duke of Gloucester was detailed to perform the opening ceremony. At the ensuing formal lunch I sat opposite the Duke. The first dish combined duck feet with fish lips. The Duke and I politely declined the delicacy, whose delight was the contrast between the crispy feet and the rubbery lips. The next course, though clearly another delicacy, seemed to the Duke and me equally unappetising. The third course, however, was a steaming bowl of pasta: hungry by now, the Duke and I heaped the pasta on our plates. Disaster: the 'pasta' was in fact jellyfish. The Duke and I chewed on the rubbery morsels for quite some time before we abandoned the attempt and then, by tacit consent, secreted the undigested marine mouthfuls in our napkins.

The Greater London Lieutenancy and the Ritz Hotel

As chief executive of the county council in West Yorkshire I had been the Clerk to the Lieutenancy, as was traditional. Similarly the Clerk to the Greater London Lieutenancy was the chief executive of the Greater London Council, Maurice Stonefrost. With the abolition of the GLC the Greater London Lieutenancy was homeless: I offered my services and the lord-lieutenant took up residence in Westminster City Hall. The lord-lieutenant was then Field Marshal Lord Bramall of Bushfield. He had chosen his title because, when a young subaltern, he had got very drunk at the Bushfield army base near Winchester. When a bleary-eyed Second Lieutenant Bramall appeared on parade next morning, his Major greeted him derisively: 'How is Field Marshall the Lord Bramall of Bushfield this morning'. Forty years later the Major was still alive and still a Major. When Lord Bramall was elevated to the House of Lords, he wrote a simple letter to the Major: 'Dear Major: I am, Sir, yours sincerely, Field Marshal the Lord Bramall of Bushfield'.

Though major honours are presented at Buckingham Palace,

the lord-lieutenant has the job of presiding over lesser awards, including the Queen's Award for Industry. One year the Award was given to the Trafalgar House Group, which then owned the Cunard line and the Ritz Hotel. Flagship of the Cunard line was the liner Queen Elizabeth II, whose Captain traditionally joined the Trafalgar House Board on retirement. Public Relations Manager of Cunard was my fellow Yorkshireman, Eric Flounders. Coincidentally Eric was also leader of Tower Hamlets Council. He phoned me with a request. When the QE II had been requisitioned as a troop ship during the Falklands War, its captain was Peter Jackson. He was now on the Cunard Board. The requisitioning of the QEII had been made by Lord Bramall, who was chief of general staff during the Falklands War. Would the lord-lieutenant present the award on board the QEII? A helicopter would pick us up in central London and deposit the lord-lieutenant and me on the QEII deck in Southampton.

Sadly I had to say that if the presentation were in Southampton, then it would have to be made by the lord-lieutenant of Hampshire. Of course that would defeat the object of bringing together the Captain of the QEII with the Field Marshal. So instead the presentation was made over lunch in the Ritz. We ate on the Nanking porcelain which had left Canton in 1750 and spent 235 years on the bottom of the South China Sea. Captain Jackson regaled us with his experience of being commandeered by Lord Bramall. He was on the QEII in New York with 3,000 passengers aboard when he received the requisition. Then unaware of the Falklands conflict, he dismissed the request as a practical joke until he switched on the radio to find that the UK was at war with Argentina.

Field Marshal Lord Bramall was the younger brother of Sir Ashley Bramall, Labour MP for Bexley until unseated in 1950 by his Oxford contemporary and friend Edward Heath, who had an initial majority of just 133. After a couple of unsuccessful attempts to regain the seat, Sir Ashley became a Westminster councillor and for 11 years was a distinguished chairman of the Inner London Education Authority. When the Authority faced abolition as part of the Education Reform Act 1988, the Field Marshal told me he was off to the House of Lords to vote against it. I pointed out that Lords-Lieutenant were supposed to be politically impartial. My remonstrations were in vain: 'If I don't go vote, then Ashley will never speak to me again', responded the Field Marshal.

24. Dolphin Square
Sex Scandals

Scandals home in on Dolphin Square, where Sir Ashley Bramall was a director when he was a City of Westminster councillor. With over 1250 flats, Dolphin Square is said to be the largest brick-built block of flats in Europe. It was a self-contained community with a four-star hotel, shopping arcade, garage for 300 cars, tennis courts, croquet lawn, restaurant, gym, squash courts, swimming pool and 3.5 acres of gardens (Grade II listed). Built by Costains in the 1930s, its lease was for sale in the early 1960s. There was a rumour that Pan American Airways, then the world's largest airline company, planned to buy Dolphin Square as lodging for its passengers and air hostesses. Westminster Council then had a passionate commitment to retaining residential accommodation in Westminster in order to prevent it degenerating into a ghost town at night, as had the City of London. It intervened in the sale of Dolphin Square. In 1964 its chief executive, then Sir Alan Dawtry, persuaded Sir Keith Joseph, the relevant Minister, to give consent for the council to borrow the £4.5m necessary to buy the lease on the Square. The council then sub-leased the Square to the Dolphin Square Trust for the length of its own lease (expiring in 2034) less three days, on terms which meant that none of the cost fell on the council or its ratepayers. To protect the tenants, the lease from the council to the Dolphin Square Trust required council approval both to the rents and to the appointment of trustees. When I moved to Westminster a flat in Dolphin Square was made available to me. I became a member of the Dolphin Square Trust Board and I took over as chairman of the board a year or so later when Maurice Stonefrost, the GLC chief executive, stood down.

The Dolphin Square Trust was pledged to rent the flats to people who needed to live and work in central London. There was special provision for peers and Members of Parliament. In 1964 *The Guardian* wrote: 'MPs find Dolphin Square a convenient place to live and get priority on the waiting list provided only that the number of Conservative and Labour MPs are even. The Manager keeps Vachers [the encyclopaedia of UK politics] on his desk to keep the balance.' Since the debt repayments from the trust to the council related to the cost of the Square in 1965, subsequent inflation meant that it was possible to keep the rents at a very affordable level. The rents of the flats were also subsidised by profits from the four-star hotel and restaurant (to which we recruited as head chef Gary Rhodes). As a result the Square could provide accommodation which enabled people on modest incomes to live in central London at no cost to the public purse. If it had been copied elsewhere, the model would have provided an admirable solution to the problems of accommodation in central London, where the cost of housing is now beyond the reach of key workers, including doctors, nurses and social workers.

Dolphin Square has a colourful history and a louche reputation. Before the 1939-45 War postmen were required to go to the basement to be supplied with red overshoes so they didn't walk on the carpets. In his wartime broadcasts from Germany Lord Haw-Haw claimed that it had been razed to the ground. General de Gaulle and the Free French occupied part of Dolphin

Square during the war. Sir Oswald Mosley lived there before his internment. Winston Churchill's daughter Sarah was ejected from the Square for drunken behaviour. Other residents included the entertainer Bud Flanagan, lesbian writers Radclyffe Hall and Bryher, Chief Justice Lord Goddard, Christine Keeler, Harold Wilson, David Steel, William Hague, Patrick Jenkin and HRH Anne, Princess Royal. Mandy Rice-Davies, also a resident, said that the good thing about living in Dolphin Square was that 'you could send the porter for your breakfast – two Mars bars if you like'.

Outside every flat in Dolphin Square is a cupboard for refuse, which is emptied daily. Its contents are then compacted and carted off to the council tip. After the Falklands War in 1982 Lord Shackleton, a Dolphin Square resident, was asked by the Government to review the future of the Falklands Islands. He carried his briefcase containing the highly sensitive Falklands Islands papers back to his flat. Arriving there, he realised that he had forgotten his flat key. He popped his briefcase in the refuse cupboard during the few minutes required to descend to the Dolphin Square office and procure a duplicate key. Unfortunately it was during those few minutes that his briefcase was collected and sent to the council tip. The security services had to grub through the council tip to unearth the briefcase, reduced after its compaction to the size of a box of matches.

Lord Shackleton's sensitive papers were not the only secrets concealed in Dolphin Square. Its proximity to MI5 and MI6 gave Dolphin Square a special relationship with the security services. From his flat, no 308 Hood House, Maxwell Knight established Unit B5(b), responsible for infiltrating agents into potentially subversive groups. It became well known that Dolphin Square provided a safe house for refugees from the Iron Curtain. Interestingly a lowly Admiralty Clerk, John Vassall, lived there in some luxury thanks to his income from the KGB. After he had been sentenced to 18 years in prison for espionage, his flat was taken over by Vice-Admiral Sir Louis le Bailly, who was Director-General of Intelligence. Princess Anne and her husband, Commander Timothy Laurence (now Vice-Admiral Sir Timothy Laurence), came to live in Dolphin Square when he was posted to the Admiralty in Whitehall. The Princess played a significant part in the life of the Square.

The Scottish writer D L Kennedy described the Square as the 'nest of scrimping aristos, MPs, and spiers and shaggers, singles and nutters and incognitos.' When going to the restaurant in 1976, John Betjeman remarked 'Oh dear, is this what purgatory is going to be like?' George Bernard Shaw complained of seeing semi-naked women in the swimming pool while he was eating. When we persuaded Gary Rhodes to take over the Square's restaurant in 1988, the restaurant critic A A Gill wrote that he 'couldn't be more surprised if you had told me that they were putting a grill in Putney crematorium. I'd have thought Dolphin Square was best left to secretaries with a long shelf life.'

Dolphin Square had a reputation for immorality. As *Vanity Fair* proclaimed: 'There's a bleak certainty in British public life that whenever the words 'sex scandal,' 'M.P.s,' 'establishment', and 'cover-up' appear in pretty much any order, the name of a vast central London apartment block, Dolphin Square, follows soon afterwards.' The most outlandish accusation came from a serial fantasist called Carl Beech. He alleged that Conservative Members of Parliament belonged to a paedophile ring that operated in the Square between 1975 and 1984 and was responsible for the murder of at least one young boy. The names of Prime Minister Edward Heath, Home Secretary Leon Brittan and Field-Marshal Lord Bramall were linked with what the Metropolitan Police implausibly described as 'credible' allegations. They were, of course, completely false, as was the strange allegation that I was linked to the Israeli Security Agency. The internet still carries the following rhetorical questions:

The Winding Stair

What could Field Marshall Bramall possibly know about Dolphin Square's connection via Sir Rodney Brooke, former Chairman of the Dolphin Square Trust, to the creepy Tavistock Institute with its links to Zionism and clinical obsession with the effects of sexual abuse on children's minds and personality development? Or, indeed, Dolphin's Square connection, again via Sir Rodney Brooke, to the former regulatory body for UK social workers, the General Social Care Council?

And what might Field Marshall Bramall know about Dolphin Square's apparent link, via Zionist Tory operative Shirley Porter and her influential Zionist offspring, to the "national security" of Israel... and indeed to the Secret Security Agencies of Israel, the U.S., and the U.K.?

I also read on the internet that a lady named Miss Holly Wood had fellated me in Dolphin Square, an episode of which I have no memory. My then chief executive, Lynne Berry, commented that if Miss Wood had done that, then I would surely have noticed.

One sadly accurate report of a Dolphin Square scandal concerned Lord Sewel. John Sewel was a Grammar School boy from Bradford, who had risen in the world of academia. He had also become President of the Convention of Scottish Local Authorities in which capacity I came to know him well. We found each other congenial company and often sat together at the dinners which followed local authority meetings spanning England and Scotland. Translated to the House of Lords, his ability prompted his appointment as chairman of Committees and Senior Deputy Speaker. In the absence of the Lord Speaker, John presided over the Lords' meetings. John was the eponymous originator of the famous Sewel convention, which provides that the Westminster Parliament should not legislate for devolved matters without the consent of the devolved legislature affected. His distinguished career ended when he was filmed in his Dolphin Square flat wearing an orange *brassière* and snorting cocaine off the breasts of two prostitutes.

As the tradition of high-minded Conservatives on the city council dwindled, the council realised that that it owned a valuable asset in Dolphin Square, albeit that its legal interest was confined to a three-day reversion in 2034. It sought to realise the asset. Provisions in the lease from the council to the Dolphin Square Trust had been designed to protect the tenants. They were used by the council to eject the Trust. The council told the Trust that while council consent had (in accordance with the lease) been given to the rent levels, that consent no longer held good. This may or may not have been a valid interpretation of the lease to the Trust, but it was clear that the council would block any future rent increases – which made the financial future of the Square unviable. Moreover the council had to approve the appointment of trustees, whose decisions would be quorate only if seven trustees were present. Clearly the council would not approve future appointments and the age of the trustees made it certain that the Board would become inquorate long before the Trust's lease expired in 2034.

The council's threats meant that the Trust had no realistic option but to agree to a sale. An obvious purchaser was the freeholder, Friends Provident, with whom the Trust had previously enjoyed very friendly relations – no doubt because its former chairman, Patrick Jenkin (Lord Jenkin of Roding), lived in the Square. My personal phone calls to the Friends Provident chief executive were unanswered. Inexplicably Friends Provident refused to talk to the Trust, but won over the tenants by offering substantial sums in exchange for support for a Friends Provident takeover. Of course the objective of the Trust was to provide accommodation for key workers, not to enrich the tenants. Denied the possibility of a deal with Friends Provident, instead the Trust invited other offers. We agreed terms with a North American Investment Company, Westbrook, with safeguards for the then current tenants, whose security and rents were protected. Nevertheless the sale infuriated the tenants – both those who had hoped to benefit financially from the sale and those who wished to remain under the Trust's benevolent rule. The tenants found it difficult to appreciate that the trustees had no option. I had to preside over several fractious meetings with tenants at the Queen Elizabeth II conference centre. Death threats were issued. At the meetings a helpful voice always came from a tenant, Axel Rüger, at that time curator of Dutch paintings at the National Gallery and now chief executive of the Royal Academy after a spell as director of the Van Gogh Museum in Amsterdam. Axel was a friend of my son and became godfather to my eldest granddaughter.

Overall the deal was advantageous to the Trust and its tenants: its bargaining power would decline as the outstanding term of its lease contracted. The deal was completed in 2005. The council received £50m for its three-day reversion and from its own share the Trust transferred £124m to the Dolphin Square Charitable Foundation. The Foundation is to replicate as far as possible the objectives of the Trust by providing middle-income housing in central London. Its target customers are the people who make the City work – doctors, nurses, social workers, police, restaurateurs, chefs – all the people who need to live or work in central London but who are excluded financially from the traditional property market. Fifteen years later the Trust had a portfolio of almost 1,000 dwellings in central London.

Pimlico School and danger

Across the road from Dolphin Square is Pimlico School. In 1998 it attracted national notoriety. The chairman of the Governors was Jack Straw, the only ever-present in the cabinets of Tony Blair and Gordon Brown. Jack was then Home Secretary. His son

Will, a pupil at the School, was induced by a *Daily Mirror* reporter to offer her cannabis in the local pub. Will was marched off to a police station by his father: front page news in every national paper.

In 1999 I joined Pimlico School's Governing Body, which must have been the most illustrious in the country. It included Matthew Taylor (then Tony Blair's Head of Policy and later chief executive successively of the Royal Society of Arts and the NHS Confederation), Anthea Masey (Evening Standard property correspondent), Deborah Arnott (Director of Action on Smoking and Health (ASH) and responsible for securing the legislation banning smoking in public places), Michael Ball (Director of the celebrated Coin Street Neighbourhood Project), Mair Garside (who had been Ashley Bramall's deputy at the Inner London Education Authority, ILEA), together with a QC and a trustee of the Grosvenor Estate. After a couple of years I became chairman of the Board of Governors.

An immediate problem was the school building. A brutalist masterpiece designed by a leading architect of the ILEA, it was listed as of special architectural interest. It suffered from a legion of problems. I noticed when I attended my first Governors' meeting that some seats in the room were unpopular. I discovered why when it began to rain. In summer its glass frontage made it unbearably hot. Its maintenance required constant attention.

One Saturday afternoon I was on top of Whernside, half way through my annual circumnavigation of Yorkshire's Three Peaks. On the summit my mobile phone rang. It was Phil Barnard, the Headteacher of Pimlico School. He had just been told by the maintenance contractors that the enormous glass panes which constituted most of the frontage of the school were unsafe and could drop out at any moment. If they did they could certainly cause serious injury or worse. 'What should I do?' asked the Headteacher. 'Ask Westminster Council', I replied. 'I have', he said. 'They say it's up to the governors'. I clearly could not risk the decapitation of our pupils and ordered the school to be closed until safety measures could be taken. Volunteers were summoned to the school on the following day (Sunday) to tell parents of the school's closure. A posse was stationed outside the school the following morning to divert pupils whose parents had not been contacted.

Replacement of the school was clearly necessary on practical grounds. Since it was a listed building, demolition of the school required the consent of the Planning Minister. A ministerial visit was arranged. The relevant minister was Lord (Andrew) Mackintosh, the former GLC leader deposed by Ken Livingstone and now elevated to the House of Lords and a ministerial post. I knew Andrew well. When I welcomed him to the school on his ministerial inspection he hissed 'Rodney – I cannot talk to you.' (Private communication would have invalidated his decision.) His consent to demolition was forthcoming.

Most of the Pimlico pupils came from working class areas across the river. But Pimlico was the ILEA's specialist music school. Because of that it attracted a leavening of middle class pupils whose parents sought the special musical tuition – the most famous being Sir Antonio Pappano, who became Music Director of the Royal Opera House and Chief Conductor of the London Symphony Orchestra. Because of the middle class musical element, the school's A level results were usually excellent: the middle class children stayed on and did well at A levels. Its O level results were much more precarious. As a result its Ofsted classification hovered uneasily between 'requires improvement' and 'failing'. One challenge was the number of pupils from immigrant families who would disappear for weeks of unauthorised absence in Pakistan.

Key to improvement in Ofsted's classification was to move pupils taking the GCE O-levels up from Grade D to Grade C. In common with other governors I spent some time coaching pupils on the brink between the two grades. A charming lad of Afro-Caribbean heritage told me how bitterly his uncle, a plumber, resented being undercut by Polish immigrants. But the school's performance was given a body blow when the new headteacher at another local secondary school boosted her school's performance by permanently excluding 50 pupils, most of whom transferred to Pimlico.

After struggling with all this, I eventually handed over the chair of the board to Mair Garside, shortly before the school was put into special measures. Under the new legislation responsibility for the school was transferred to a trust, created by a fund manager. This decision was bitterly opposed by the school's stakeholders (governing body, teachers, students and parents). They were unanimous in wanting Pimlico to remain as a school run by the community for the community. The Westminster NUT voted in favour of strike action to express their objections to Westminster Council's strategy. Staff, students, parents and former school governors asserted that the school's underperformance was due to long-term neglect by Westminster Council. But the protests proved ineffective: responsibility for the school was transferred to the trust run by the fund manager. The resulting unrest still simmers. In 2021 the school became the focus of further protests about the school's management. NEU, the teachers' union, passed a motion of no confidence in the school's leadership. Sir Michael Wilshaw, a controversial head of Ofsted, was brought in by the trust to restore order. I find it very difficult to accept that a community school should be run by people appointed by a private sector financier.

One big scandal did follow the change. Before becoming chairman of the Governing Body, I had chaired the Finance Committee. Both then and when I was chairman, I had, despite pressures, always taken a conservative view of the budget and built up prudent reserves. Jo Shuter, the new Headteacher appointed by the Trust, dissipated the reserves within six months of her appointment and was sacked when she used school funds to pay for a £7,000 party to celebrate her 50th birthday.

25. Protests, Cemeteries and the Arts

The Thatcher Government imposed a climate of public belt-tightening. Shirley Porter felt that Westminster Council – despite its cushion of the business rate – should set an example. She appointed Robert Davis, a young solicitor, as chairman of the committee responsible for libraries. He masterminded the closure of the library in Portland Street, with an annual saving of £30,000 – a fleabite when a penny rate raised £3m. The decision gave the Labour opposition the opportunity they needed to attack Shirley and her colleagues as local manifestations of the Thatcherism they despised. Protestors surrounded City Hall. Every council meeting – held in the old Marylebone Town Hall – became a showground of opposition to Mrs Thatcher through her local government doppelgänger, Shirley Porter. Councillors required a police escort to jostle them through the crowds into the Town Hall.

The council meetings turned into raucous protests. The public gallery was crowded and often had to be cleared to enable councillors to make themselves heard. Councillor Diane Abbott (later Jeremy Corbyn's shadow Home Secretary) was prominent among the councillors who ignored standing orders.

The Winding Stair

Lord Mayors declined to eject her, anxious to avoid photographs on the front page of the national press showing Diane being carried out by three or four policemen. For a similar reason I took no action when I found Diane using the councillors' retiring room for a private meeting. 'Aren't you surprised', she jeered, 'to find all these black people here?'

Shirley thrived on the controversy. The publicity from the council's quest for savings incentivised Shirley to seek further economies. She hit on the council's three cemeteries. Because of their legal duty to bury the dead, each of the three former constituent local authorities – Westminster, Paddington and Marylebone – had owned a cemetery. Westminster City Council inherited them. All three were in the London suburbs – Ealing, Mill Hill, and Finchley – and in the late twentieth century Westminster residents were unlikely to be buried there. The cemeteries were a substantial financial liability. Their maintenance then cost the council over £400,000 annually. The obvious solution, widely adopted in graveyards elsewhere, would be to reduce the maintenance costs by relocating the gravestones; they would then become lawn cemeteries. Instead Shirley proposed to sell them. I submitted a report couched in the strongest possible terms, pointing out that sale of the cemeteries would inevitably result in their neglect: the council had accepted responsibility for their maintenance and had a moral obligation to the relatives of those buried in them. Privately I also pointed out that the Finchley cemetery was in the constituency of Mrs Thatcher. Shirley was obdurate and insisted on sale at all costs. Despite advertisement, only one purchaser could be found. After much negotiation and bullying by Shirley, they were eventually sold for 5p per cemetery. The Director of Property Services had been led to believe that they were to be sold to a representative of the Western Synagogue, for whom the acquisition might have made some sense.

But the reason for the acquisition, by a sharp property man, was very simple: the cemeteries included three lodges, one flat, a crematorium and over 12 acres of development land. The purchaser kept the valuable assets and passed the worthless cemeteries to a shell company. A series of complicated deals followed when the graveyards were traded for over £1m in the West Indies. A representative from the Inland Revenue quizzed me about the transactions. Eventually, in 1992, moral pressure compelled the council to buy back the cemeteries (minus the assets) for over £4m. Sale of the cemeteries became a national scandal. A music hall joke was: 'Do you remember the eighties when you could buy a packet of cigarettes and three cemeteries and still have change from a pound?'

There were inquests by both the District Auditor and the Ombudsman. Unsurprisingly both were critical. My own role was in the spotlight. I was cleared of impropriety by the District Auditor. The Ombudsman found maladministration and decreed that I should have refused to carry out the decision of the council to sell the cemeteries. I was certainly convinced that the council should not have taken that decision – as my report had made clear – but it was perfectly lawful. The councillors had been made fully aware of the likely consequences. I remembered the two decisions by Stockport Council, which at the time I was convinced were bad – but came to believe were absolutely right. It would be a bad day for democracy if officials were to substitute their own decisions for those who are elected.

Sale of the cemeteries reinforced the protests outside the Marylebone Town Hall. The protestations inside became equally vociferous as the highly articulate Labour opposition exposed Shirley's lack of grasp of affairs. Before each council meeting many hours of effort were spent in preparing briefing material for Shirley and answers to hypothetical questions. The effort was counter-productive: Shirley became lost in the briefing material as the Opposition consistently exposed her ignorance and inability to think on her feet. The Labour councillors raised countless points of order. On one memorable occasion the points of order lasted for 4½ hours and consumed the entire length of the council meeting. We never reached the first item on the agenda, confirmation of the minutes of the previous meeting. Under standing orders a guillotine motion was deemed to be put at 10.30pm. The recommended actions were then automatically authorised without debate. The Labour councillors jeered as they stalked out of the Council Chamber.

From time to time attempts were made within the Conservative Group to depose Shirley as leader. Shirley's original allies, Patricia Kirwan, Rachel Whitaker and Angela Killick had long been jettisoned, being far too sensible. Tony Prendergast led one abortive attempt, but he represented the old guard. A more serious attempt was masterminded by a senior councillor, Alan Bradley, with support from a popular member of the Group. On the day when the coup was planned a despondent Bradley phoned me: his main supporter had backed out. Shirley had managed to find a prestigious job for her. Other supporters had been similarly nobbled. The planned putsch fizzled out.

The old guard's remaining ploy to eject Shirley from the council was to engineer her entry into the House of Lords. Shirley had often boasted of her friendship with Mrs Thatcher. As it happened I knew Mrs Thatcher's PPS, Michael Alison: he was a Yorkshire MP. With Roger Bramble, the former Lord Mayor, I arranged to see Michael to engineer Shirley's admission to the scarlet benches. I explained to Michael how friendly Shirley was with Mrs Thatcher. Michael exploded: 'Margaret can't stand the woman'. The plot failed.

The Arts after the Greater London Council

Abolition of the Greater London Council (GLC) caused unforeseen problems for the Government. Especially in its latter days, the GLC had sprayed money at good causes, as well as more dubious enterprises. It became clear that there would be much bad publicity if many worthy London organisations went to the wall after the elimination of the GLC. The London Boroughs Association (LBA) was expected to pick up some of the responsibility. Freed from the financial demands of the GLC, a substantial sum of money was set aside for this purpose in the LBA budget. David Cobbold, former leader of the Westminster Council, chaired the LBA Grants Committee and was responsible for distributing the largesse. I was puzzled by the needs of some of the recipients. £25,000, for example, was given to the Gay Bereavement Society, not a cause which I should have thought would commend itself to a Conservative-controlled LBA. I asked David why he had supported the gift of £25,000 to such an unconventional cause. 'Ah', he responded, 'but you should have seen the others. And we had to spend the budget.'

More fundamental was the loss of funding for many of the capital's famous cultural organisations – English National Opera, London Festival Ballet, Wigmore Hall, the Institute for Contemporary Arts, Serpentine Gallery – all of which depended on financial support from the Greater London Council. Its abolition would rob them of a substantial part of their budget and cripple them financially. It was also mean a substantial loss of jobs: 43 per cent of jobs in the creative industries are in London and the South-East. The Director of English National Opera was Lord Harewood, who knew me well from my help in his foundation of English National Opera North (now Opera North) back in West Yorkshire. He sought my advice over lunch at J. Sheekey's restaurant, just across the road from the Coliseum, English National Opera's home.

I hit on a solution. The institutions in question were all in the City of Westminster. Abolition of the GLC would relieve the Westminster City Council of the levy imposed by the GLC on Westminster's business rates. The City Council would not be allowed to keep such an unjustified bonanza. The financial equivalent of the levy was destined to be confiscated and placed into a national pool. I went to see the relevant Secretary of State, Kenneth Baker, who had a strong commitment to the arts. I proposed that the Westminster Council be allowed to keep that part of the GLC levy which supported these leading cultural institutions, including English National Opera, on condition, of course, that the council transferred the cash to the organisations involved. Kenneth Baker was well aware of the problem and welcomed my solution with open arms. If I could procure an amendment to the legislation going through Parliament then the Government would not oppose it.

I briefed Roger Bramble, the Old Etonian chairman of the Westminster Council's Recreation & Arts Committee. Roger was enthusiastic in support, relishing the idea that the Council should rescue such famous organisations and incidentally become a major patron of the arts in London. By this stage the Government's Local Government Bill was in the House of Lords. Armed with an appropriate amendment we set to procuring support from their lordships. Roger wrote to solicit support from those of his Old Etonian chums who happened to be peers, using their Etonian nicknames: 'Dear Brookie', for example, was the Earl of Warwick, whose premier title was Earl Brooke. The Government welcomed our amendment, which sailed through the House of Lords with Government support.

Suddenly Westminster Council was catapulted into being a leading patron of the arts. Lord Harewood put me on the Board of English National Opera (and its General Director, Sir Peter Jonas, supported my membership of the Athenaeum). Shirley Porter was suddenly seen as a sponsor of the arts in London. One evening Sir William Rees-Mogg, chairman of the Arts Council (and father of Jacob Rees-Mogg), called on her on his way to the Royal Opera House. Unfortunately – the time approaching 7pm – Shirley's office was locked while we were inside, leaving Sir William, Shirley and me immured. Shirley's insistence on security meant that the key was in the possession of her PA, who had already gone home. The delay before our release meant that Sir William missed the first Act at Covent Garden and cultural relations became temporarily strained.

Shirley had no affinity for culture other than the social prestige offered at Covent Garden and Glyndebourne. To persuade her of the desirability of putting arts institutions on the council's payroll I proposed the Rescard – a card for residents which would confer free or preferential terms when they patronised the institutions supported by the council – and others in the City, like the Regent's Park Open Air Theatre (a favourite of mine). The scheme mushroomed. It is still a popular bonus for Westminster council tax payers and is now copied elsewhere.

The council's financial responsibilities were not without problems. The Wigmore Hall had been put on the international map by its charismatic director William Lyne. His relationship with the council required careful handling: William could not understand the reluctance of the council to finance improvements to the Hall's Green Room. The Institute for Contemporary Arts (ICA) on the Mall was often a thorn in Shirley's side. The ICA presented a radical artistic programme, dedicated to exploring the taboos of Western society: it was there that Genesis P Orridge and Cosey Fanni Tutti staged their notorious pornographic performances and where Cosey Fanni Tutti's used tampons were exhibited. An exhibition presenting a pro-Palestine and anti-Israel viewpoint infuriated Shirley Porter. With difficulty I dissuaded her from withdrawing the Institute's grant: such an action would have threatened the financial settlement which I had negotiated. A further problem came when the Institute featured a female performance artist whose contribution to culture was the insertion of a mango into her vagina. Shirley took some persuasion that this was art.

Finally, when the poll tax was introduced in 1990 (and after I had resigned), Shirley welshed on the financial deal I had arranged with Kenneth Baker. She cut the Westminster Council grants to the arts companies by 90 per cent. Money destined for the arts was plundered to keep the newly introduced poll tax in Westminster artificially low, a move described as 'scandalous' by the new chairman of the Arts Council, Lord [Peter] Palumbo. The Government connived in the cut, which allowed its 'flagship Tory council' to set the spectacularly low poll tax of £195. More typically, next door Labour-controlled Camden council had to set its poll tax at £534. Gates were erected at the entrance to Downing Street to protect No 10 from the poll tax riots which eventually brought down Mrs Thatcher.

Across the city from the Coliseum, I made the acquaintance of Sir John Tooley, Director of the Royal Opera House in Covent Garden, at that time contemplating a major redevelopment of the Opera House. John felt it politic to have a good relationship with the chief executive of his local authority and took me to lunch. His hospitality paid off: soon afterwards he phoned to solicit my assistance: *Tosca* was on the stage. When Tosca stabs Scarpia at the end of Act II, then, according to the stage directions, she enacts a little ritual around his corpse. She lights two candles, places them by his side and plants a crucifix on his chest. Puccini wrote an extended orchestral postlude – 30 bars, in slow tempo – to accompany these gestures and other mopping-up activities by the heroine. Entertainments licensing was quite a major function in Westminster. Within its boundaries were the West End theatres. The council's inspectors had refused consent for the candles in *Tosca*, citing the fire risk. John Tooley appealed for my help. Marshalling my knowledge of the opera, I instructed the inspectors that lighted candles were essential to the plot. They sanctioned the flames provided that a fire extinguisher was manned off-stage.

When the Opera House re-opened after its redevelopment, I attended the opening night to hear the first performance of

Harrison Birtwistle's Wagnerian *Green Knight*. Sadly the new high-tech mechanics malfunctioned and the fearsome Knight on his green horse failed to arrive on cue. The audience sat patiently for 45 minutes until the problem was rectified. When the terrifying figure of the Green Knight finally appeared, the first words spoken were 'This is the moment we have all been waiting for'. The tension disappeared as the audience erupted into laughter. When Sir John finally relinquished his role at Covent Garden there was a great ceremony, with red balloons descending on the stage in his honour. The following evening I went to hear *Lohengrin*. In the middle of the sinister plotting between Ortrud and Telramund a solitary red balloon descended, almost exactly 24 hours too late. At Covent Garden I also witnessed the *Eugene Onegin* when Onegin's pistol failed to explode in order to despatch Lensky. After a fruitless wait, Lensky finally fell to the floor without an accompanying bang. As soon as he was recumbent there was an immediate explosion. John Tooley told me that it was, in fact, a startling coincidence: a light bulb had exploded.

Below the Royal Opera House at the bottom of Bow Street is the Lyceum Theatre, one of the largest theatres in London. It had been bought by the London County Council in 1939. The County Council had planned to demolish the theatre to widen the road. When the road-widening scheme was abandoned the Lyceum became a dancehall and the seating was removed. Its ownership transferred to the GLC in 1986. The Royal National Theatre had staged Tony Harrison's version of the Wakefield Mystery Plays in the theatre, seats not being required for an ambient audience. Since then the theatre had been disused and it became semi-derelict. On abolition of the GLC its ownership transferred to the London Residuary Body.

One day a well-known theatrical agent called Hemingway came to see me with a proposition to take over the Lyceum. He was acting for a principal of immense wealth whose wife had been a ballet dancer. Because of his enthusiasm for ballet, Hemingway's principal was willing to buy the theatre from the London Residuary Body and convert it into a receiving house for dance. That was a facility which London notoriously lacked: visiting ballet companies had to fit into holidays at the Royal Opera House or the Coliseum, where there was no sprung stage. Hemingway's principal was prepared to put £20m into the project – more if necessary. He would see the theatre transferred to a charitable trust and would seek no influence himself over the enterprise.

Hemingway had recruited a distinguished company who were prepared to become trustees of the charity. They included Sir Robert Armstrong (later Lord Armstrong of Ilminster), then just coming to the end of his service as Cabinet Secretary but still a member of the Board of the Royal Opera House. Hemingway wanted me to arm myself with the support of the Westminster City Council and to approach Sir Godfrey Taylor (known to all as Tag), chairman of the London Residuary Body to persuade him to transfer the Lyceum to the charitable trust. The support of Roger Bramble, chairman of the Westminster Culture Committee, was straightforward. Armed with his enthusiastic consent I went to see Tag Taylor. Tag insisted on knowing the name of Hemingway's principal, whose identity had been kept confidential. I relayed the request to Hemingway, who arranged for me to meet his principal over breakfast at Claridge's. There I learnt that the balletomane was the Deputy to the 'Reverend' Sun Myung Moon, leader of the Unification Church, commonly called the Moonies.

The Moonies were Korean in origin, but had moved the headquarters of their operation to the United States. Their founder was born in what is now North Korea. He had been imprisoned by the North Korean communist government during the Korean War, and believed that the defeat of communism by democracy was a necessary step in the Divine

Providence to establish the Kingdom of God on earth. The Reverend Moon was famous for collecting Rolls Royces, of which he was reputed to have a dozen. His theology may have been unconventional. However he had no criminal record, though he and his colleagues were extremely good at parting Moonie followers from their money. But, as my Westminster chairman Roger Bramble, pointed out, that was an occupation common to all religions. Roger was an enthusiastic supporter of the scheme for the ballet theatre.

I told Tag Taylor of the source of the funds. He said that he would agree to the transfer of the Lyceum to the new trust if we had the consent of the chairman of the Arts Council, the formidable Lord Goodman. As it happened I knew Arnold Goodman quite well. As a solicitor he had sought my help on several occasions on behalf of his clients and from time to time took me for lunch at the Oxford & Cambridge Club. Christened by *Private Eye* magazine as *Two Dinners Goodman*, he was extremely corpulent. On his laborious ascent of the Club steps he would be greeted as 'Master' – he then being the Master of University College, Oxford. I tackled Arnold Goodman about the Lyceum over a substantial breakfast in his flat. When I told him of the Moonies' involvement, he gave a resounding 'no' to the proposition and the possibility of a London receiving house for dance disappeared. Tag's London Residuary Body then sold the Lyceum to the Apollo Leisure Group and the building resumed life as a commercial theatre after substantial refurbishment.

The Lyceum Theatre was only one of the GLC assets which Tag Taylor and the London Residuary Body had to sell. The most conspicuous was County Hall, whose location across the Thames from the Houses of Parliament had so provoked Mrs Thatcher. Its imposing curved frontage, Ionic columns, porthole windows and flagpoles made an emphatic statement. Tag had firm instructions from Mrs Thatcher that County Hall should never again be allowed to become a competing centre of power to the Government. Sold to the private sector, the grand former symbol of the importance of London government now houses two hotels, the London Aquarium, London Dungeon and an amusement arcade. Beyond them, in the heart of the building, is the council chamber, once the epicentre of political debate about London and the power base of Herbert Morrison. Behind a locked door its leather benches gather dust.

26. The Rot Sets In: The Mortuary, the Sex Trade, the Election and Lies

West Yorkshire was a long way from the centre of national attention. Westminster was right in the middle. A minor scandal in Leeds or Bradford could be brushed aside. In Westminster it would attract national publicity. One day Giles Shepard, managing director of the Savoy Hotel, phoned me. Giles was a deputy lieutenant and a former High Sheriff. I knew him well. The council's trading standards inspectors had detected short measure in the gin served in the Savoy's American Bar and planned to prosecute. Of course there was no suggestion that the management had authorised the inadequate measure. The barman had been sacked. Because of that Giles pleaded with me to halt the prosecution of the Savoy. The Council's Director of Public Protection told me that the hotel had received a previous warning of short measure drinks. He felt strongly that the management should have taken effective preventive action – especially given the price the Savoy would charge for the gin. It was the policy to prosecute after one warning. I agreed that the Savoy should be treated no differently to the Dog and Duck. The prosecution went ahead. *Savoy fined for short measure* attracted national headlines.

The Winding Stair

The chairman of the board of another world-famous hotel pleaded with me to halt 32 charges of inadequate hygiene in the hotel kitchens, which were supervised by an equally world-famous chef. The chairman contended that the hotel and its kitchens were shortly to close for a complete modernisation; the hotel management realised that standards were inadequate; they would soon be improved. It was quite unnecessary to prosecute, he argued. I showed the chairman photographs of cracked dishes and clogged drains – all due to poor management and nothing to do with the antiquated layout of the kitchens. The hotel pleaded guilty to all 32 charges and sacked the chef.

A more humble Westminster hostelry also hit the front page. The Horse and Bower pub was just across the road from the council's public mortuary in Horseferry Road. Pausing in the pub for refreshment at lunchtime towards Christmas 1985, a *Daily Mirror* reporter ordered a turkey sandwich from the helpful barmaid. As they chatted she pointed to the sandwich and said 'You'll never guess where that came from!' Pursuing the enquiry he discovered that the enterprising mortuary manager had franchised the mortuary for storing Christmas turkeys. The *Mirror* published a photograph of a turkey reclining by a label attached to the foot of a shrouded corpse.

Though an entrepreneurial example of privatisation, this was a step too far. But Westminster Council responded enthusiastically to the Thatcherite agenda of privatisation of public services. The first Westminster service to be transferred to the private sector was the maintenance of the council's parks and open spaces. The parks workforce also had the responsibility for decorating the routes of royal parades. When there was to be a royal procession, the council's workforce would skip cutting the grass in the parks that day and instead spend their time planting flowers along the route of the procession. When we prepared for the first royal pageant after privatisation, it came as a shock when the contractors stuck to the terms of their contract and asked a substantial sum for the extra-contractual job of decorating the processional route. When privatisation spread, the Director of Cleansing and his second-in-command put in a successful bid for the refuse collection contract and became wealthy as a result.

Privatisation and the One-Stop Shop were not the only revolutions in service delivery. In my first couple of years in Westminster Shirley went along with a number of exciting ideas. One successful innovation, later copied nationally, was the introduction of capital value accounting. The idea does not sound exciting but it yielded spectacular results. As with most local authorities, the council's revenue budget ignored the capital value of the assets involved: the asset stood in the books at the cost of its acquisition. Incorporation of capital values completely changed the understanding of the budget. The Cleansing department had a depot in Mayfair. Its capital value was many millions of pounds. Selling it for redevelopment and developing a replacement depot in Paddington generated a huge cash sum. Of course the trick doesn't work in Rotherham or Knowsley, where there are no such discrepancies in the value of land. But it has spectacular results in central London.

I introduced performance related pay for the top seventy staff – an idea particularly congenial to Shirley and then unknown in local government. Though performance appraisal is not uncommon in local government, it is not usually linked to pay. To make performance pay effective, budgets were broken down to cost centre level. Zero-based budgeting built up budgets from their cost centre base rather than breaking them down from a departmental total. That dramatically changed the aspect of the budgets. Linking a key task to financial reward concentrated the mind. The extra rewards helped greatly in retaining high-quality staff, always a problem in central London. As part of the new system, staff members were offered four-year contracts: 75 per cent accepted (including me).

The Winding Stair

An issue peculiar to Westminster was the profusion of inspectorates. The council itself employed twenty-nine different inspectorates, responsible for everything from sex licensing to cracks in the pavement. If you ran a late-night topless café in Soho you could be visited by twenty different inspectorates. I hired the Institute for Local Government Studies at Birmingham University to look at the problem. On their recommendation we created three multi-purpose inspectorates – one based on premises, one on highways and one on development. They made a real difference by taking an integrated approach to a neighbourhood.

The sex trade was a substantial feature of life in Westminster. The Metropolitan Police Vice Squad was then notoriously corrupt, on occasion selling back to the sex shop owners the pornographic material which had been confiscated in the police raids. Since 1982 the sex trade had been subject to licensing by the city council. On my arrival there were 65 licensed sex establishments in Soho. The multi-purpose inspectorate established an integrated approach to wiping out illegal establishments by working with other agencies. It was often simpler to close a sex establishment down on grounds of fire safety than go to court to prove the defrauding of embarrassed customers. The ultimate solution was the discovery by the Soho landlords that they could make more money out of property development than from sex. Soho lost some of its raffish character as a result.

These innovations attracted a great deal of publicity, especially in local government circles. Westminster became known as an exhilarating and innovative local authority. Shirley enjoyed the publicity which resulted.

After two years it all went sour.

The Rot Sets In: The Mortuary, Sex Trade, Election and Lies

The 1986 Westminster election

On 8th May 1986 arrived the quadrennial council elections. By then the Falklands effect had worn off. Abolition of the Greater London Council was very unpopular: Ken Livingstone remained a talismanic figure. The miners' strike had petered out but the Government's inflexibility had damaged its popularity. Neil Kinnock was an engaging leader of a resurgent Labour Party. Moreover the demography of Westminster was beginning to change: overseas magnates were buying flats as investments and leaving them empty or staying only occasionally. In either case they had no vote. The election was expected to generate a close result.

The count after an election is always stressful. As presiding officer on the day of the poll I would be out at crack of dawn to make sure the polling stations were open and operational. During the day I toured the polling stations concentrating on those where trouble was reported. Westminster, being Westminster, meant that any difficulties would hit the national press. A typical problem arose when one of the most eminent politicians in the country complained to the *Evening Standard* that he had been disenfranchised by an incompetent Westminster Council: his name had been omitted from the electoral register. His photograph was on the front page of the *Standard*, taken as he left the polling station after being refused his vote. The simple reason for the omission of his name from the electoral register was that he had left his wife; unsurprisingly she had removed his name from the electoral registration form. His mistress had failed to register him at her address. But that was not an explanation which you can tactfully relay to the press.

As the ballot boxes were opened on 9th May 1986 it became clear that the result would be close. Conservative strongholds like Bayswater, Little Venice and Millbank fell to Labour. The outcome would depend on the Cavendish ward in Fitzrovia. If Labour took Cavendish then they would control the council, something hardly believable in a city regarded as a bastion of the Conservative party. Dramatic changes would have followed a Labour-controlled Westminster. The Westminster Labour Party was pledged to rename Trafalgar Square: Nelson's column would have found itself in Nelson Mandela Square. The GLC might have been a thorn in the Government's flesh: a Labour-controlled Westminster Council would have been a dagger to the heart. Many comfortable arrangements with police and the security services would have been challenged.

As the votes were counted and recounted in the marginal seats, an enraged Shirley jabbed me in the chest: 'If we have lost this election it's your fault', she hissed. The exciting things I engineered had enhanced Westminster's reputation in local government and put Shirley on the national stage. They cut no ice with an electorate disaffected with Margaret Thatcher and sympathetic to Ken Livingstone. In the event, Shirley's Conservative majority narrowly survived. But if 106 more voters in the Cavendish ward had cast their votes for Labour, then the council would have had a Labour majority for the first and only time.

The narrowness of the result had two effects. It destroyed any remaining trust which Shirley might have had in me. And it set her on a course of gerrymandering which resulted in a twenty-one year saga of investigation and court proceedings, and which ended with her being surcharged £42m. In her unpublished ghosted autobiography, Shirley complained that I kept telling her what she couldn't do – annoying given my own view of my job as the Geographer of Policy Space. But had Shirley taken my advice, she would have been many millions of pounds better off.

The Rot Sets In: The Mortuary, Sex Trade, Election and Lies

Gerrymandering and bugs

A week after the nail-biting 1986 elections Shirley convened a meeting of chief officers. At the meeting Shirley, flanked by Weeks and Legg, told the meeting that the close election result was the fault of the chief officers and myself. There would be a change of direction. The key objective was to win the 1990 election. Thus began the saga which continued for twenty-one years.

Pork-barrel politics are far from unusual: in Britain the most famous example is the construction of the Humber Bridge, a magnificent edifice of dubious economic value to which is credited the Labour Party's victory in the 1966 bye-election in the marginal seat of Hull North. I once asked Richard Wilson, then Cabinet Secretary, and another Permanent Secretary what they would have done had they been asked to arrange the building of the Humber Bridge 'in order that the Labour Party could win the Hull North bye-election'. They had no hesitation in replying: 'We would say, Prime Minister, that you cannot build the Humber Bridge for that reason – but you can, of course, build it for reasons a, b and c.'

Shirley Porter, Weeks and Legg announced the selection of eight wards as 'key wards'. In public it was claimed that these wards were subject to particular 'stress factors' leading to a decline in the population of the City. The eight wards selected had been the most marginal in the 1986 City elections. Three – Bayswater, Maida Vale and Millbank – had been narrowly won by Labour. A further three – St James's, Victoria and Cavendish – had been narrowly retained by the Conservatives. In the West End ward an Independent had shared the two seats with a Conservative, while in Hamilton Terrace the Conservative incumbents were threatened by the Social Democratic Party.

Particular attention, instructed Shirley, must be paid to the eight marginal wards. She set up a working party to roll out good things in these wards. It commissioned a series of environmental projects, admirable in themselves. The eight marginal wards were immersed in hanging baskets and flower tubs. Dropped kerbs were installed and environmental improvements made. The John Lennon statue in Carnaby Street was cleaned. The Tachbrook Street market was repaved. 74 schemes, costed at £4.5m, were targeted mainly at the marginal wards – with a sufficient number elsewhere to divert suspicion. As the programme developed, the normal, but unwritten, conventions of local government were eroded. There was increasing divergence between the formal structure of the council and its actual procedure. Shirley's acolytes ignored the need for a committee decision. They began to give orders directly to officers and to issue press statements without formal authority. In October 1986, I documented and circulated to chief officers the conventions which should operate. Shirley refused to sanction their adoption by the council. Bullied chief officers were by-passed.

Improving services and commissioning environmental projects in marginal wards were not enough for Shirley. She espoused the idea of social engineering, believing that Westminster could learn from Wandsworth across the river. There a Conservative council had sold off council dwellings, whose grateful new owners secured a safe Conservative majority. The former leader of Wandsworth Council, Chris Chope, became a regular visitor to Westminster City Hall. By then an MP, he became a Minister in the Department of the Environment. However, Westminster had only half as many council dwellings – 24,000 compared to Wandsworth's 42,000.

Westminster had a major problem of homelessness – the biggest in the country – and a demand for tenancies which far exceeded supply. The Local Government Minister, Sir George Young, became famous for saying that 'the homeless are what you step over when you come out of Covent Garden'. That was a social comment from George, misinterpreted by the press: he was a benevolent old-style Etonian Tory. Rehousing homeless people was a major issue in Westminster.

Nevertheless, Shirley determined to sell council dwellings and to target sales in the marginal wards. Giving me the credit for having nothing to do with it, Shirley approached Sir Terry Heiser, Permanent Secretary of the Ministry of Housing and Local Government (who famously claimed that he was awarded the CB for scrapping the rates; the KCB for introducing the Poll Tax; and the GCB for scrapping it) and asked for the loan of a pliable civil servant. Though Terry was, of course, completely unaware of Shirley's plan, he seconded an Assistant Secretary, Bill Phillips, who was seen by the Department as having reached the limit of his competence. Phillips was appointed as Westminster Council's 'Managing Director' a post unique in local government.

My remit as chief executive continued to encompass all the council's normal services. Nominally subordinate to me, Phillips's jurisdiction was confined to a mysterious and confidential project code-named *Building Stable Communities*. At a secret meeting at Shirley's Oxfordshire house, Phillips received his instructions to 'stop rehousing in marginal wards' and 'to introduce political control over housing allocations'. The planning system was to be used for 'social engineering'. PA Cambridge Economic Consultants were hired to examine the problem. Their report was kept absolutely confidential within the Chairmen's Group and not released to the Opposition. I obtained a copy. To my surprise it was – as might be expected from extremely reputable consultants – entirely sensible. I could not then understand why it had therefore to be kept confidential. Of course the reason was precisely because it was sensible: it did not in any way support the policy which Shirley wanted to develop and of which I was then unaware. An important part of this policy was the designation of much of Westminster's council housing for sale, rather than reletting them when the properties became vacant. The grateful new owners would then vote Conservative, unlike Council tenants. The council housing earmarked for sale was concentrated in the key wards. Many of these dwellings lay vacant for months or even years before they could be sold. To prevent their occupation by squatters or drug dealers the flats were fitted with security doors at a cost of £50 per week per door. A refuge for the homeless was sold off to private developers and converted to private flats for young professional people.

The other vital part of *Building Stable Communities* was the relocation outside Westminster of homeless voters and hostel dwellers so that they would not occupy flats in the marginal wards. Unsurprisingly this policy met with considerable resentment from the recipient local authorities who had to provide social services to these vulnerable people. It became more and more difficult to move homeless people outside Westminster. The connivance of the Director of Housing, Graham England, was clearly necessary. By-passing me, Phillips secretly suborned England into Shirley's plot. At England's request, the advice of leading counsel was sought. The silk advised that it would be unlawful to target wards for electoral advantage. To camouflage the motive Phillips put together an authority-wide strategy. This kept the target figures for gentrification in the marginal wards but added extra sales in non-key wards as a disguise. Tenants were moved and their flats boarded up pending 'gentrification'. In all, 4,401 out of 6,213 properties (71 per cent) were designated for sale in the eight marginal wards, while only 3,807 (22 per cent) of the 17,373 properties in the 15 other wards were designated for sale. The policy to win the 1990 election was under way. To reinforce his influence, Phillips recruited as Head of Policy a colleague from the Department of the Environment, Nick Reiter. The gentrification policy was extended: a relaxed planning regime would encourage luxury flats. The council's Chief Planning Officer, James Thomas, declined to subvert the planning system for social engineering purposes and was removed by Shirley.

It is difficult to exaggerate the rancid atmosphere in City Hall. Shirley had her room swept weekly for bugs. I was informed by one of the political advisers that my City Hall telephone was bugged. Fortunately I retained the confidence of the Chief Officers who were, of course, well aware of the alternative power structure headed by Phillips. Phillips's *modus operandi* was simple. Shirley would demand that he produce green cheese from the moon by next Tuesday. When asked on Tuesday to produce the green cheese, he would explain that he had instructed the relevant officer to produce the cheese. The officer would be summoned, asked to produce the lunar cheese and be castigated for its absence.

The Chief Officer meetings which I chaired began to resemble the garrison of a citadel surrounded by enemy forces. Unsurprisingly the vigilant Labour opposition smelt a rat and began to demand answers. In October 1988 they engineered an article in *Time Out* magazine which alleged gerrymandering. The following day Shirley wrote to me enclosing a letter from 'a local resident' alleging that Labour councillors Dimoldenberg and Bradley had used their status as Westminster councillors to procure work for their employer, the public relations consultancy Good Relations. 'Do you', asked Shirley rhetorically, 'think I should contact the Fraud Squad?' I responded with a straight bat: 'There is no evidence from the papers sent to me that either Councillor Dimoldenberg or Councillor Bradley has misused his membership of the council...There is no offence in stating that a person is a councillor as part of his curriculum vitae'. The following week she procured the council's Policy and Resources Committee to instruct me to conduct 'an enquiry' into the allegations. I repeated my previous conclusion.

The Winding Stair

Asbestos and my departure

The most disgraceful element of Shirley's strategy related to Hermes and Chantry Point, two multi-storey blocks of council flats off Elgin Avenue in North Paddington. The two blocks were riddled with asbestos, the danger of which had been identified shortly before I arrived in Westminster. The asbestos could not be safely removed while tenants were there. Given the danger, highlighted in Government guidance, it was clearly essential that tenants be rehoused as quickly as possible so that the asbestos could be removed. Despite Shirley's reluctance, I had insisted that this be done. The tenants were progressively rehoused as soon as replacement flats became available.

Because of the cost of removing the asbestos to make the flats fit for habitation, Patricia Kirwan, chairman of the Housing Committee, pushed for a sale of Hermes and Chantry Point. But the two blocks – by now almost empty – came to be seen by Shirley as a crucial part of her social engineering policy. Despite the dangerous asbestos, they could be used to rehouse the homeless. They were in a safe Labour ward where their votes could do no harm. That would allow flats in the marginal wards to be sold and occupied by Conservative-voting lessees. There were two obstacles to this policy: Patricia Kirwan (as chairman of the Housing Committee) and me. Patricia was deposed as Housing chairman. And on 8th February 1988, to my surprise, I was summoned to Shirley's office where Shirley, Barry Legg and David Weeks told me that my contract would be terminated immediately. I was, of course, completely unaware of their intentions for Hermes and Chantry Points. My contract was due to end on 31st December 1988, when it clearly would not be renewed. I had expected to soldier on until then and was puzzled at the urgency of my removal. I now realise, of course, that I was seen – correctly – as an insuperable obstacle to rehousing the homeless in the asbestos-ridden blocks of flats.

The Rot Sets In: The Mortuary, Sex Trade, Election and Lies

Shirley introduced me to Michael Silverman of Merton Associates who would, she told me, be conducting the negotiations for my departure. He had conducted similar tasks for Tesco. Silverman was obsequious in his sympathy, unaware that every fibre of my being was rejoicing in my prospective liberation. Of course the terms of my contract would be honoured, he assured me. In particular I would continue to be paid for the rest of the year and – as provided in my contract – would be entitled to my pension at the end of the year, when I would be aged just over 50. Shirley interrupted his explanation: 'He cannot take the car', she screamed, referring to the rather elderly Rover assigned for my use and whose value was relatively insignificant. The City Solicitor, Mathew Ives, was summoned to Shirley's office and instructed to affix the seal to an agreement for my departure. He refused point blank: 'You can't sack the chief executive without council approval', he insisted. Hectored by Shirley and her cronies for over three hours, 'it was', he told me later, 'the worst day of my life'.

Silverman and I adjourned to my office to discuss the termination agreement. I insisted that it provided that the council should be able to call on my services for the rest of the year (though I should be free to take other employment). I had a strong commitment to preparing the council for taking over education on 1st April 1990 after the abolition of the Inner London Education Authority and was determined that the council made proper preparation for the takeover. For that purpose I had engaged as a consultant Jack Springett, the former Head of Education at the Association of Metropolitan Authorities, who provided valuable doctrinal underpinning. To tackle the nuts and bolts I had appointed an impressive young graduate, Roger Crouch. Roger had left school aged 16 to work in a warehouse before making his way somehow to King's College, Cambridge. He attracted my attention when he imported a carton of fish and chips to a lunchtime meeting in my office, an act of flagrant insubordination. Roger clearly needed guidance in his preparation for the transfer of the education service to the City.[3]

In my discussion with Silverman I insisted that an agreed press statement be prepared to make it clear that my contract had been terminated by mutual agreement. The statement provided that no further statement by either party was to be issued. Silverman made no objection. The agreement for my departure specifically permitted the publication of my book on *The Enabling Authority*, which I had almost completed. The press statement was prepared and agreed, though Silverman insisted that it was quite unnecessary: 'Mr Brooke', he said 'you will simply fade away quietly. You will disappear without trace. No-one will hear of you again'. Nothing, of course, was further from the truth. I left City Hall with a copy of the agreement and the press statement.

The Labour opposition on the council had a field day when my departure was announced. My exodus was featured on the front page of the national press. Newspaper photographers camped out on the lawn in front of my house in Yorkshire (generously pronounced on the front page of the *Daily Express* to be 'a rambling stone-built mansion'): we kept the curtains drawn all weekend. My 14-year-old son (described in the *Daily*

---

[3] Roger Crouch also took up residence with and later married my secretary, Paola. His immersion in the transfer of education to Westminster drew him into the world of education and he became Chief Education Officer for Gloucestershire. Sadly his son Dominic, aged 16, committed suicide and Roger followed suit a couple of years later. I regarded Roger as my *protégé* and, like many in similar situations, feel that in some way I should have prevented the double tragedy.

Express as 'a bespectacled young man') was interviewed on his way to school, an experience which he thoroughly enjoyed. The following week the terms of my departure were announced at the Policy & Resources Committee: the Opposition compounded my pension so that they could talk of a £1.2m payoff. That made the front page once more. When the council press department phoned me to secure my agreement to a press statement: I referred them to the agreed statement which, of course, bound the council as much as me.

The reverberations continued: a Conservative councillor and fellow member of the Athenaeum, Cyril Nemeth, took me to lunch at the Carlton Club to get my version of events. There I had the pleasure of seeing Michael Silverman and his startled expression as I appeared – having signally failed to 'disappear without trace'. When Shirley proposed a reorganisation to plug the gaps after my departure she was defeated in council, when five Conservative councillors joined the Opposition in voting against her proposals. John Ware, an investigative reporter for the BBC's *Panorama* programme got in touch with me. He proposed a meeting in the Green Man and French Horn pub in St Martin's Lane, when I was able to give him the background and appropriate documentation for what became a gripping *Panorama* programme. Screened in July 1989, it gave a picture of 'gerrymandering, corruption and dirty tricks', as Andy Hoskens described it in *Nothing like a Dame*, his account of the Shirley Porter scandals.

Scandal

On 21st February, a fortnight after my departure, when I was not around to protest, Shirley struck. The key policy was 'social engineering'. To keep Labour voters out of marginal wards she gave instructions to rehouse the homeless in the asbestos-ridden tower blocks. This scandalous policy deliberately subjected 122 homeless families to a life-threatening danger. The timing of my departure had been engineered in the knowledge that I would not have countenanced such a decision. Six years later, when the consequences of the decision had become apparent, an enquiry into the policy was commissioned from John Barratt, former chief executive of Cambridgeshire County Council. Published in July 1994, John's 641-page report concluded that 'those acting on behalf of a public body repeatedly took risks...with the health of people who ought to have been entitled to assume that such risks were not being taken'. Since the council was aware of the danger, the council's insurance company made it clear that it would not cover the council for any claims made against it as a result of the rehousing. Since asbestosis may take years to develop the council might still face claims resulting from the callous action.

After I had left the 'social engineering' campaign gathered impetus. Despite its secrecy, the Labour opposition accumulated evidence about the *Building Stable Communities* policy, Shirley's code name for gerrymandering. Later in 1989 they handed it over to John Magill, the District Auditor, who commenced an investigation which was to last for seven years. Despite the active investigation, at John Major's instigation Shirley was honoured as a Dame of the British Empire in 1991.

The District Auditor's investigation hit an immediate obstacle: Phillips had destroyed the relevant papers. However ex-Councillor Simon Mabey had meticulously kept every document relating to *Building Stable Communities*: their bulk had required him to build an extension to his house. The existence of Simon's papers demonstrated that the crucial documents had been removed from the Council's records and had been shredded by Phillips. Magill scoured the underground storerooms of City Hall to uncover further documents. His first report appeared in January 1994, which identified the gerrymandering as 'a disgraceful and improper purpose'. That year public hearings followed. I was duly summoned to give evidence. Unfortunately when I crossed the road to reach the hearing venue I was knocked down by a motor cycle. Though not seriously hurt, I arrived at the public hearing looking rather damaged. On enquiry I explained that I had been knocked down by a motor bike. My interlocutor said: 'Shirley Porter must have taken out a contract on you'. 'Oh no,' I responded. 'If it had been Shirley it would have been a ten-ton truck, not a motor bike.' It was overheard: my response featured in *The Guardian* gossip column next day.

Eventually, in May 1996, the District Auditor issued his final report. He concluded that the council had been 'engaged in gerrymandering, which I have found is a disgraceful and improper purpose'. He determined that as a result the council had suffered a loss of £31.6m, mostly in lost rents. Shirley and the deputy leader, Weeks, were required to reimburse that amount to the council. Ironically Shirley was probably the only councillor in the country who happened to have £31.6m. The same sanction of surcharge had once applied throughout the public sector, but civil servants had secured removal of the requirement as it applied to them, using the argument that reimbursement would be of such large amounts as to be unaffordable and unreasonable. It is difficult to avoid the conclusion that the imposition on Shirley was an unreasonable requirement, however disgraceful her conduct. Had her behaviour constituted a crime, it is difficult to believe that she would have been fined £31m.

Shirley appealed to the courts. There Lord Justice Rose said that Shirley and David Weeks 'lied to us as they have done to the auditor because they had the ulterior purpose of altering the electorate'. There was a tiny crumb of comfort for Shirley when the judges ruled that the original surcharge of £31.6m was too high and reduced it to just over £27m. But by the time the final ruling emerged from the House of Lords in 2001 it had risen to

£42m. In the House of Lords Lord Bingham highlighted 'the evasive, false and misleading evidence given to me by Lady Porter'.

While the proceedings were in process, Shirley decamped to Israel. There the Porter family has some eminence. It funds several charitable projects, including the Porter School of Environmental Studies at Tel Aviv University. Of course by this time Shirley had removed all her assets from the UK except for a forest in Scotland, which she had presumably overlooked. The share register of Tesco showed that her shareholding had disappeared into thin air. Half-hearted Council attempts to find the money got nowhere. In 1998, BBC2 screened a documentary, *Looking for Shirley*, which profiled Westminster City Council's efforts to recover the surcharge and Porter's efforts to move her estimated £70m assets into offshore accounts and overseas investments. As the council purported to search for Shirley's assets, the new Westminster Council leader, Simon Milton (later Sir Simon), and his deputy, Robert Davis, dined with Shirley in Tel Aviv. But there was still no trace of the assets. The search seemed to have hit a dead end.

Then Shirley's son John fell out with his business partner, who disclosed a series of emails which identified the accounts from which Shirley had transferred money to her son. Given this information, the council had to pursue its claim and froze the accounts. The council agreed to settle the debt for £12.3m, having declared that the cost of legal action would be far greater than the amount to be recovered. The Labour members of Westminster Council appealed and another District Audit investigation began. In 2007 the District Auditor agreed that further action would not be cost effective and the saga ended - over 21 years from the launch of the policy. Shirley surrendered the £12.3m, was released from bankruptcy and permitted to return to England. But all this, of course, was many years after I left the City Council's employment.

The Rot Sets In: The Mortuary, Sex Trade, Election and Lies

City Council officers escaped surcharge – surprising in the case of Phillips – but several were heavily criticised. The scandal blighted their lives. Housing Director Graham England lost his job and became a motor cycle dispatch rider. Nick Reiter was appointed as chief executive of the Shetland Isles Council, but removed from the job when his involvement in the Westminster scandal was revealed. The affair ended the local government career of others.

27. 1989: Life after Westminster, Sex and the Poll Tax

My precipitate departure from the Westminster city hall had prevented any farewells. But, touchingly, a couple of months after I left, my colleague chief officers took me to dinner at the Goring Hotel and presented me with a set of lithographs of the Yorkshire Dales. I retained one other connection with the city council. My leaving deal with Westminster required me to advise the council on any matter the council required. The Inner London Education Authority (the ILEA), last fragment of the old London County Council, ran over a thousand schools and colleges in inner London. Uniquely it tested pupils and classified them in three grades – 25 per cent A, 50 per cent B, 25 per cent C – which gave every ILEA school an identical intake – at least in theory. It was thus possible – in theory – to assess the comparative effectiveness of every school. When the ILEA was abolished on 1 April 1990 the inner London borough councils were to take over. Given the lack of any other source of informed knowledge, I believed that my advice on Westminster Council's takeover of education was essential. I took care that my reports on other matters would be as uncongenial as possible. Shirley and her colleagues did their best to conceal them from the

Labour Group, who, of course, took great pleasure in demanding them.

Unexpectedly I maintained one significant presence on the London local government scene: my secretaryship of the London Boroughs Association ('the LBA'). The LBA was the umbrella body then representing London boroughs. Its secretaryship had been an appurtenance of the chief executive of Westminster since it was created. A Deputy Secretary and a small staff discharged its day-to-day functions. I expected my role there to end with the severance of my relationship with the Westminster City Council. The chairman of the LBA, Sir Peter (now Lord) Bowness, did not. Peter was not an admirer of Lady Porter and asked me to stay as Secretary.

An enraged Shirley banished the LBA from City Hall and we relocated to Berwick Street in Soho. The exile to Soho prompted a sea change in our small staff. A raffish aura crept into the organisation: colleagues would pop out during the morning for an espresso. Immediately outside the office was Berwick Street market. Emerging from the office at 6-30pm I would be seduced by the bargains available from the closing stalls and would return to my flat with half-a-dozen persimmons and eight avocados, all over-ripe. The office was encircled by sex establishments. The LBA's solicitor, a girl of fragile, doll-like beauty, doubled up as Westminster Council's sex establishment lawyer. When we emerged from the office a junior colleague would breathe *Hworr* at the images on display. The lady solicitor would dismiss him contemptuously: 'That's nothing', she would say. 'But it's all happening at number 36: we're not going to raid that until Tuesday'. My service at the London Boroughs Association kept me in touch with London local government until the end of the year, when I handed over the reins to a full time paid successor.

The Inner London Education Authority had provided a magnificent though costly service to its schools. Typical was its

Nature Study Service, which, I was proudly told by one Westminster school, had on request supplied 20 woodlice, one carnivorous plant, 12 African snails, a quart of tadpoles and six goldfish. The London boroughs had to plan the future of education (including further education) in central London after the abolition of the ILEA. It is, of course, much easier to merge organisations – as in the 1974 local government reorganisation – than to divide them up – in the case of ILEA, between the twelve inner London local authorities.

The LBA had to devise a plan which ensured the continuity of the cross-borough establishments. Determined to avoid cumbersome joint committees, the LBA assigned responsibility for cross-borough services to lead authorities. The Labour-controlled boroughs were anxious to preserve ILEA services; the Conservative boroughs to eliminate what they saw as ILEA's prodigality. As a result the removal of the ILEA increased the cost of education in Labour boroughs but decreased it in Conservative authorities. Dividing responsibility for further education was a challenging problem, and its solution frustratingly short-lived: the Further and Higher Education Act 1992 removed responsibility for further education from local authorities. A typically short-sighted centralising measure, this prevented local authorities from tailoring their further education provision to the economy of their area.

In the aftermath of the abolition of the Greater London Council, relationships between the political parties were at an all-time low. Faced with rate-capping by the Government, councils like Lambeth refused to set a rate. As a consequence the responsible councillors were surcharged £126,947, the resulting loss. Hostility between the political parties increased. The Labour London boroughs set up an organisation to rival the LBA named the Association of London Authorities (ALA). Its secretary was the able, urbane and articulate John McDonnell, formerly Ken Livingstone's finance chairman at the Greater

London Council and later Jeremy Corbyn's shadow Chancellor. The meetings between members of the LBA and the ALA were without question the most unpleasant I have ever attended. Sir Peter Bowness presided with unflappable politeness but encountered unremitting hostility, a proxy for the hatred felt by the left for Mrs Thatcher. The Government proceeded with its (by now) usual contempt for local government. The Home Secretary announced the appointment of a Police Commissioner for London without mentioning it to Sir Peter Bowness. Peter learnt of it from the press but, as the Conservative local government spokesman for London, was expected to defend it.

Though it was only part of the supporting cast, the LBA joined the national local government associations at the annual ceremonial 'consultations' with the relevant Secretary of State. During my time at the LBA I encountered four Secretaries of State for local government, all, of course, Oxbridge graduates. When I arrived the relevant Secretary of State was Patrick Jenkin, who was consistently wrongfooted by Ken Livingstone. The disgruntled Edward Heath commented that 'the Government had achieved the inconceivable in swinging the population of London behind Livingstone'. The lugubrious Jenkin gave the strong impression of distaste for Government policies. He took pleasure in describing the Treasury as *The Kindly Ones*, a Greek euphemism for the Eumenides, the Furies. Patrick Jenkin was succeeded by Kenneth Baker, who took a much more cavalier approach. In turn he was followed by the patrician Nicholas Ridley, who masterminded the details of the poll tax and was in charge when the resulting riots began. He is credited with remarking on the existence of a Scottish restaurant behind Beijing's Tiananmen Square named McDonald's. Ridley addressed the representatives of local government as if they were the beaters on his grouse moor.

By contrast, his successor, Chris Patten, dazed the local government contingent at his first consultative meeting by walking round the room and shaking hands with everyone. Patten made it clear that he would like to get rid of the poll tax if at all possible. And, of course, it was abandoned – though only after Mrs Thatcher had been ejected. When Labour won the 1997 General Election and Tony Blair took over, local government was absorbed in a jumbo ministry led by Deputy Prime Minister John Prescott. At his first meeting with local government leaders John Prescott, a former ship's steward, appeared with a tray of drinks held elegantly above his head. 'I never forget a skill', he announced.

Patronage and the Secret Service

Across St James's Park from Soho were the offices of the Royal Institute of Public Administration (RIPA). This respected organisation, sadly now defunct, provided a number of useful functions. One of them was the Institute's capacity to arrange for a Permanent Secretary to take informal soundings from knowledgeable individuals on the Minister's latest idea. Armed with ammunition from the experts, the Permanent Secretary could kill the Minister's half-baked wheeze or insist that it be tried out in a limited scale before it was rolled out nationally. The RIPA appointed me as an Honorary Fellow – together with Peter (now Lord) Hennessey. This had the great advantage of giving me a platform – as well as an office overlooking St James's Park, which was invaluable when my term at the London Boroughs Association ended.

I had come into contact with the No 10 Patronage Secretary (as he was informally known). He was then John Holroyd – nephew of my former Morley patron Miss Clara Hepworth. John procured my appointment as an external member of the Final Selection Board for the Senior Civil Service, where an outsider – such as me – joined senior civil servants in deciding which candidates should be admitted to the Fast Stream, which promised hastened promotion. The theoretical objective of an external member was to prevent the civil service from becoming too introverted or, more plausibly, to put an external fig leaf over the process. Candidates were, after a preliminary assessment, required to undertake an exacting course and examination, which involved observing their personality, leadership skills and ability to work in a team, as well as assessing their intelligence. They were placed in seven grades.

Those emerging from the process in grades 1 to 4 were summoned to the Final Selection Board. Only candidates placed by the Board in grades 1, 2 and 3 were recruited and put on the fast track to the higher ranks, so the key test was to differentiate between those on grade 3 and those on grade 4. As part of my induction I attended my first panel, when the chairman of the Panel, a retired Permanent Secretary, began the interview by telling the candidates that on the train to London he had been reading *The Unbearable Lightness of Being* by Milan Kundera. In the book, he said, appeared the assertion that 'Music puffs up the soul'. 'Do you', asked the chairman, 'think that this is as true of Telemann as it is of Tchaikovsky?'

At the end of the interviews I asked the chairman: 'Suppose they hadn't heard of Telemann?' 'I was', he said, 'going to say Bach, but then I thought of the *St Matthew Passion*.' The interview undoubtedly favoured Oxbridge graduates. Eventually the Final Selection Board was abolished by Tony Blair because it continued to prefer Oxbridge candidates, largely WASP, who (unlike red brick graduates) were accustomed to the dialectic expected by the Board.

The 'Secret Services' – GCHQ, MI5 and MI6 – operated their own recruitment system – believed to be a tap on the shoulder at Oxbridge. Notorious defections had proved this to be fallible. They decided to come in out of the cold and submit candidates to inquisition from a Final Selection Board, modelled on that of the Civil Service. I was asked to take part and had a fascinating induction, which I cannot, of course, describe, having signed up to secrecy. The big problem they faced was that the length of time required to undertake both positive and negative vetting meant that many of the most promising candidates had obtained an appointment elsewhere before they could be recruited.

Other jobs flowed in. My book *The Enabling Authority*, published by Longmans, was quite influential. Paradoxically, I argued, the loss of functions by councils enabled them to lift their eyes from service provision, take an holistic view of their community, its environment and its needs and hold to account otherwise unaccountable bodies. Among other ideas, it canvassed the use of purchasing and contracting for policy purposes, including producing specifications which favoured local firms. I should like to think that it is the ultimate source of Preston Council's pioneering work in public procurement as a tool to deliver economic, social and environmental benefits for its locality. The book sold out its print run of 2,000 copies. It prompted the anarchic suggestion that a local authority should have four departments: the Department for Unlimited Strategic Thought (DUST); the Department for Ensuring Satisfaction of Consumers (DESC); the Department for Doing Things (DDT, a small department); and a Business Unit for Stopping Things (BUST), especially DDT.

Sex and the Poll Tax

Encouraged by the success of *The Enabling Authority*, Longmans asked me to take on the job of publishing editor for their local government series. My job was to identify a potential topic; write a synopsis; commission an author; and be rewarded with a percentage of the sales. A typical product would be an encyclopaedia on some element of local government practice and law which would be kept up-to-date by annual supplements. The prime volume would retail at £400 or more and the supplements, issued twice a year, would cost around £80 per issue.

My most successful commission was *The Enyclopaedia of the Community Charge*, better known as the poll tax. The poll tax stemmed from Mrs Thatcher's belief that everyone – not just the householder – should pay for the local government services they received. 'The duke should pay the same as the dustman', was the rubric. Local government finance was then largely derived from the rates, levied according to the value of land and the buildings on it. The last revaluation had taken place in 1973, the longest period between revaluations since the reign of the first Queen Elizabeth. It was increasingly obsolete, mainly because of the decline of prosperity in the North and the increasing affluence of the South-East. Revaluation does not increase the total amount of money collected, but only its incidence: it would clearly increase the burden in the South and diminish it in the North. Those who voted Conservative would suffer most. The government baulked at revaluation: those who gain keep quiet; those who stand to lose make a fuss.

The disparity in valuations became increasingly conspicuous (a situation repeated in the new millennium, since no revaluation has been carried out since 1991 when the poll tax was scrapped and replaced by the council tax: incongruously properties are valued at their theoretical value in 1991 even if they were not built until thirty years later). Accordingly, in the 1987 Conservative manifesto, Mrs Thatcher promised to scrap the rates and replace them with 'the community charge', soon rechristened 'the poll tax' after the levy which sparked the Peasants' Revolt in 1381. This provided for a charge per head at a rate set by the local authority.

In Scotland the new tax was to replace the rates from the start of the 1989/90 financial year and in England and Wales from the start of the 1990-91 financial year. The Scots 'were put in to bat to test the wicket'. North of the border the resulting umbrage marked the virtual eclipse of the Conservative party in Scotland. In England the poll tax caused riots. It increased the bill for larger families and reduced it for those in more valuable houses.

The poll tax quickly hit problems. Though the idea was that every individual would pay the council tax, it was pointed out that in many cases one of the partners in a marriage – most often the wife – had no source of income except that provided by the spouse. So the legislation had to provide that spouses would each be responsible for the other spouse's poll tax. It was quickly realised that not everyone living together is married, so the legislation had to provide that people living together as partners should be responsible for each other's poll tax. The issue then became the definition of 'partner'.

Decisions on these knotty problems were assigned to the valuation courts – far removed from their area of expertise in property values. They decided that sexual relations would be the test of partnership. But that proved difficult too: there was the case of a student flat where two occupants had occasional sex after a party but did not regard each other as partners. So it was decided that the test had to embrace frequency. But what about those aged over 80? Should the criteria be different for the over 80s? The Valuation Courts became deeper and deeper embroiled in such arcane considerations and the system became increasingly discredited. The front page of the *Daily Mirror* featured the headline *Sex and the Poll Tax*. As the Valuation Court decisions were recorded as precedents, the supplements to my Encyclopaedia grew fatter and fatter; the price increased; and so did the yield from my royalties. I imagined that my children and grandchildren would enjoy a happy lifetime source of income. But then, thanks mainly to the poll tax, Mrs Thatcher fell and the poll tax was abolished. That was one of the few occasions when Mrs Thatcher and I had something in common: we both had some element of regret at the disappearance of the poll tax, dreadful tax though it was.

Life after Westminster, Sex and the Poll Tax

At that time, the state of the environment was emerging as a topic of national concern. The Director of the Local Government Training Board, Professor Michael Clarke, asked me to write *The Environmental Role of Local Government* for a fixed fee of £200. There seemed to be nothing to draw on. As a result my publication was almost all original thinking – or, if you prefer, groping for ideas. It appeared shortly after Chris Patten took over as Secretary of State for the Environment and planned legislation (which became the Environmental Protection Act 1990). The Bill was preceded as usual, by a White Paper. Struggling to identify practical proposals, the White Paper quoted extensively from my book. As a result the book sold over 20,000 copies, sadly with no increase in my fee.

One of the joint bodies created by the three national local authority associations was LAMSAC (the Local Authorities Management Services Advisory Board). It was in financial difficulties. The three Associations asked me to review it. LAMSAC had been set up when local authorities were seeking direction in the new world of information technology. It provided useful services at first but the growing speed of IT and the increased sophistication of local authorities overtook its usefulness. I had no hesitation in recommending its closure. The local government associations gave the job of closing down to me. It provided me with a useful lesson in union negotiations. The package I proposed for the redundant staff was as generous as it could reasonably be. The union negotiator came to my office and agreed. 'But', he said, 'let's argue about it for a bit so I can be seen to wrest it from you.' As the soon-to-be-redundant staff waited anxiously outside, he raised his voice from time to time in the middle of our chat about politics, football and world affairs. After a reasonable length of time he left the office and triumphantly announced the terms of the redundancy package to the anxious staff, taking credit for its positive elements.

28. The Future

The press publicity on my departure from Westminster communicated my availability to Sir Bryan Askew, the chairman of the Yorkshire Regional Health Authority and a prominent Conservative. He asked me to take on the Chair of the Bradford Health Authority, which then had a temporary chairman who was, coincidentally, Jim Britton, the former Deputy Public Relations Officer of the West Yorkshire County Council. Those were the days when such appointments were made by grace and favour, without advertisement and without audit by the Public Appointments Commissioner. I took the job, marking the beginning of a long connection with the Health Service.

On the Board of the Health Authority were three Bradford City councillors, which helped to cement relationships with the local authority. At that time Bradford Council was the centre of national attention. Its leader was Eric Pickles, later a Cabinet Minister and peer, a Conservative dedicated to the introduction of neo-Thatcherite policies in Bradford. To win a vote in council, Eric and the Conservative party depended on the casting vote of the Mayor. Every Council meeting was a dramatic cliffhanger and usually finished at 4am. Among other economies, Eric scrapped all the posts designated for liaison with the Health Authority. Unlike the Jackdaw of Rheims, no-one seemed a penny the worse as a result. Eric and I developed a good relationship, which, unexpectedly, was to prove crucial in determining my future.

Later in 1989 the Association of County Councils (the ACC) advertised for a chief executive. I applied. The selection committee was deadlocked between the chief executive of Cheshire County Council, Robin Wendt, and myself. The chief executive adviser to the appointment committee was Robert Adcock, chief executive of Essex County Council, whose father had been Clerk of the Lancashire County Council. He advised the committee that if they were deadlocked, then they should choose 'the county man'. Accordingly Robin got the job. Conservatives on the committee would have come to a different conclusion had they known that, under a nom-de-plume, Robin penned Philippics against the Tory government for *Tribune* magazine.

After that disappointment I joined the accountancy practice, Arthur Young, shortly to merge to form Ernst & Young, and worked with them as a consultant. One of my colleagues there was the immensely able Helen Bailey, later to have a distinguished career as a local government chief executive. She had oversight of the Metropolitan Police when Boris Johnson was Mayor of London. I also took on consultancies on my own behalf. One of them was with Stroud District Council, where five or six different political groups were represented on the council. The problem was that every committee of the council had a different combination of members, so that as issues meandered through the council's committees, decisions were regularly overturned, restored, reversed and reinstated.

In Spring 1990 I was working in Stroud. While I was there I heard that Alun Gronow, the Secretary of the Association of Metropolitan Authorities (AMA), had died unexpectedly. The

The Winding Stair

AMA was the organisation which represented the metropolitan authorities in Greater London, Tyne and Wear, Merseyside, Greater Manchester, West Yorkshire, South Yorkshire and the West Midlands, just as the ACC did the county councils. The job fitted my cv admirably, since I was a former chief executive of a metropolitan county council and had worked throughout my career in urban authorities. The job particulars mentioned that the candidates would be expected to take the Rorschach personality test, where the candidates' emotional and intellectual health would be revealed through their interpretation of inkblots. The candidates would also have to take an IQ test. I had never taken an IQ test.

When I finished for the day in Stroud I took the train to Glasgow, where I was working on another project. On the station platform in Gloucester I bought a book, *Test your IQ*. Anticipating my application to the AMA, I spent the journey doing just that. My first effort was unproductive. The book embarrassingly suggested that my *métier* was not in intelligence. But by my third attempt I had got the hang of what they were looking for. The results of the fourth questionnaire counselled me to buy the advanced version, intended for super intelligent people. The practice stood me in good stead: when I took the AMA test my IQ was put in the top one per cent of the population (no doubt a tribute to the manual rather than my IQ).

The ACC was normally Conservative-controlled, but alienation from Mrs Thatcher had contrived to put the Labour party in power for the first time in the organisation's history. But the AMA was naturally Labour-controlled. Its chairman was an old-style Labour politician, Sir Jack Layden. Jack was the secretary of the Rotherham branch of the National Union of Miners, a job that brought with it the jobs of leader of Rotherham Council and chairman of Rotherham United football club. Jack distinguished himself by addressing Mrs Thatcher as 'Luv', the standard appellation for the opposite sex in South Yorkshire (though that was not the only reason for Mrs Thatcher's antipathy to local government). Jack was, of course, chairman of the Selection Panel, which included Oxbridge graduates like Sir Jeremy (now Lord) Beecham and Clive Betts, now chairman of the back-bench House of Commons local government committee. Sir Peter (now Lord) Bowness was there with the influential Labour member (now Dame) Margaret Hodge and the Liberal leader, (now Sir) David Williams. The second Conservative representative should have been Eric (now Lord) Pickles from Bradford but he couldn't attend. Constitutionally he should have nominated another leading AMA Conservative. Unconstitutionally Eric sent one of his fellow Bradford councillors, never previously seen at the AMA, entrusted with strict instructions from Eric to vote for me.

The main competition came from Timothy Hornsby, who had taken a First at Christ Church, Oxford. I might have emerged from the IQ test in the top one per cent of the population, but Timothy was in the top 0.1 per cent. Coincidentally he was a former escort of my wife, Clare. The Personnel Officer of the AMA was (now Sir) Stephen Bubb, himself a Christ Church alumnus (and later a close friend), who was naturally rooting for Timothy. Stephen and another member of the AMA staff, Matthew Warburton (also an Oxford graduate), were former Lambeth councillors surcharged after their refusal to set a rate.

As in my interview at the ACC, the selection panel was deadlocked. Timothy captured the votes of the Labour intelligentsia on the Panel, whereas I gained the veteran Labour vote, together with the two Tories (Eric Pickles's nominee voting for me as instructed) and the Liberal Democrat. Jack Layden's chairman's casting vote came for me. Interestingly, I did not secure the votes of the leading Labour members, for whom I developed great admiration and with whom I was to work most closely. I hope that by the time I left the AMA they would have voted for me.

The Winding Stair

As soon as she heard of my appointment Shirley Porter visited the AMA building and annulled Westminster Council's membership of the Association. Westminster was thus the only metropolitan authority not to be a member. My own time at the AMA lasted for seven years and ended when the AMA merged with the two other national local government associations to form the Local Government Association (LGA). The natural choice as chairman of the LGA was Sir Jeremy (now Lord) Beecham, then chairman of the AMA. This meant that the Secretary of the new Association clearly could not also come from the AMA: I strongly supported the then chief executive of Hertfordshire County Council, my former West Yorkshire colleague, (now Sir) Brian Briscoe, who was duly appointed. My own consolation prize was the award of a CBE 'for services to local government'.

Once more I was cast adrift on the waters of life. By far the most enjoyable period of my life came immediately after my departure from the AMA, when I took on the job of the weekly gossip columnist for the *Local Government Chronicle*. The best part of the job was being part of the editorial team at the *Chronicle,* where colleagues like Jake Arnold-Forster, Richard Vize, Rhidian Wynn Davies and Nick Golding had a journalistic commitment to exposing the undercover story. Several coups came our way and hit the national press – after the *Chronicle* had published them first. Devising the headlines was a particular art form, a triumph being when Dame Helena Shovelton was ejected by the Government from the chair of the National Audit Office: *Push Comes to Shovelton*. A proud day came when the *Local Government Chronicle* team beat the *Guardian* in the quiz at the local pub (the *Guardian* office was then in Gray's Inn Road, just across from the *Local Government Chronicle* office). And I experienced the exhilaration of an author by seeing on the Tube a reader of my weekly column laughing aloud.

Working with the *Local Government Chronicle* team was a joy but was a by-product of my professional life. After the merger of the local government associations, I became a serial quangocrat, chairing several public sector organisations, including the National Electricity Consumers' Council, the Commission on Accessible Transport in London, the General Social Care Council, the Quality Assurance Agency for Higher Education and the Leeds (formerly West Yorkshire) Playhouse. I was also a member of the boards of the Westminster Primary Care Trust, the Ethics Standards Board for Accountants, the General Medical Council, the Community Development Foundation, the Tavistock Institute, the Internet Watch Foundation, Capacitybuilders, the Royal Association for Deaf People (now Action on Hearing Loss), the Royal College of Pathologists and various National Health authorities. I worked as a consultant for the governments of China, Colombia, the Gambia, Guyana, Hungary, Poland and Russia, usually at the prompting of the UK government. My work on ethics in the public sector was translated into Shqip (the language of Albania). As a result of all this I didn't earn much money but was knighted 'for public service' in 2007.

A new chapter of my life opened up. But that is a different story – one I hope to tell in due course. *Encore un moment M le bourreau.*

Epilogue

My main concern in writing this memoir is that the text should arouse your interest. My professional life coincided with the greatest changes in society since the industrial revolution: the end of the extended family, the decline of the cohesive force of religion, the waning of deference, the dissolution of trust, much greater geographical mobility and the end of the post-War settlement. It was also a period of upward social mobility, when more than 50 per cent of boys (40 per cent of girls) reached a higher social class than their parents (Selina Todd, *Snakes and Ladders*).

The period coincided with the deterioration in the importance of local government. Post-war local government had attempted to tackle the problems of deprivation. Increasingly the emphasis shifted to the problems of affluence. The three post war decades saw rising living standards, falling inequality, greater freedom and expanding welfare provision. The following decades saw the opposite. The belief that problems would be solved by spending more money evaporated. Increasingly public services were financed by charging, not by taxation. Public expectations rose with the decline of faith in post-war remedies, such as urban motorways, multi-storey flats and town centre redevelopments. Ministers introduced innovations before any assessment could be made about the effectiveness of their precursors. Rather than tackle a problem, governments changed the structure of the agency dealing with it. Responsibilities of the state were transferred to the private sector. An underclass of casual workers was created.

My local government career placed me in the middle of these changes. It also put me at the centre of issues of national interest: the miners' strike, the Helen Smith story, the Yorkshire Ripper, the Bradford City fire, the collapse of system built flats, the 15p sale of Westminster cemeteries and the Westminster Homes for Votes scandal. I was present for the last reading of the Riot Act before its repeal. Like Edmund Burke, 'in my course I have known and, in accordance with my measure, have co-operated with great men'. I have filled the text with anecdotes about such men (and women). According to Leslie Stephen, creator of the *DNB*, 'No good story is ever quite true.' I hope that my tales have not gained too much in the telling. I believe the stories to be largely accurate.

The memoir records my journey from humble beginnings to what Joe Lampton (hero of John Braine's 1957 novel, *Room at the Top*) would certainly have regarded as the 'Top'. Indeed his ambitions were modest compared to my achievement. Yet I have climbed only the foothills. Above me loom Himalayas of achievement, heights which I shall never scale. But a light on the winding stair which I trod might illuminate the understanding of others who wish to ascend.

I hope that these memoirs will have contributed to the pleasure of its readers. I do have a second justification: to describe and celebrate local government over the half century in which I have played a part. Sadly, I do this by chronicling its slow decline during that period. Local government reached its zenith in the 1930s. In *Telling Tales*, Alan Bennett, wrote: 'No child brought up in Leeds, or any large provincial city, can help but be aware that his life or her life is under-pinned and overseen by the Corporation. The arms of the City of Leeds are embossed on public library books and on the exercise books we write in at school; they are emblazoned on the side of the trams and on the dustcarts; any public celebration sees medallions with the arms of the city fixed to lampposts and public buildings...over the entrance to the City Markets...the Police Department and the City Library...and found growing in Roundhay Park'. When he became Secretary of State for Health, Sir Keith Joseph, apostle of the market economy, wrote that when he toured an NHS hospital, he would be shown the grubbiest, cobwebbed and most down-at-heel example his hosts could find. But when invited to tour a local authority old persons' home, the Lord Mayor would proudly show him the smartest and most up-to-date specimen. Sir Keith drew the appropriate conclusion, but did not persuade his disciple, Mrs Thatcher.

Even in my time some of the grandeur of local government remained. It is difficult for their successors to envisage the overweening pomp and majesty of the clerks of the county councils in the days before local government reorganisation in 1974. Nor can today's citizens imagine the importance of local government in those days. Though the supply of gas and electricity, public assistance institutions (the former workhouses), hospitals and asylums had been removed from local government by the post-War Labour government, public health remained the responsibility of local authorities, as did public transport, water and sewerage. Local authorities ran the courts of Quarter Sessions and were responsible for the criminal prosecution service. Public services like police, probation and coroners were annexed to local government. In Scotland the responsibilities of local authorities even included the regulation of charities – in Scotland called mortifications. Thus in Aberdeen the chief officer responsible for charities enjoyed the enviable title of Master of Mortifications.

Centralisation has severely eroded civic pride. Employers are no longer based in the vicinity of their operation. They are in London at best but now more likely in Europe, the United States or China. Their commitment to the locality and to civic duty has disappeared. No Sir Thomas Beechams will be inserted by their mayoral fathers into the world of conducting. Local government itself is a pale shadow of its former past. When I started my first professional job in 1962 in Rochdale, most public life in the town was controlled by the council. Leaders of councils like Sir Dick Knowles of Birmingham were public personalities.

Though, unlike Scotland, council responsibilities did not include the regulation of charities, local government was the key agency in the lives of ordinary people. They looked to the council to safeguard their welfare. Rochdale local government in 1962 seems almost as far removed from the twenty-first century as Periclean Athens. Like other public sector workers, local authority employees believed that their labours contributed to the public good, not to private profit. It was a world where everyone – cooks, cleaners, typists – felt part of the team responsible for the welfare of the public. I chronicle that disappearing world of public service. The transfer of local authority functions to the private sector and to a congeries of unelected quangoes precludes the implementation of a collective vision and strategy for the locality. The public service ethic has been replaced by the profit motive.

The Second World War and its aftermath changed Britain from a localised and voluntaristic country to one controlled by central authority. The proportion of public spending controlled from the centre is now twice that of France, Japan and Italy and more than three times that of Germany. The decline in the importance of local government accelerated as a result of Mrs Thatcher's contempt for the intermediate institutions of society, those located between the individual and the state. When the six metropolitan county councils and the Greater London Council adopted policies uncongenial to Mrs Thatcher, they were simply abolished. But, pervasive as was her influence, Mrs Thatcher only accelerated the decline. Societal change and the new media focus attention on the centre. Local newspapers, once a vital part of their community, are now in terminal decay. The concentration of power in London and the resulting constraints on local policy-making and spending seem irreversible. More than 90 per cent of UK public spending is controlled by central government. Central government has imposed a Procrustean bed on local authorities, giving them responsibilities but not the resources to fulfil them. In the current climate of austerity local authorities have faced a loss of government grant of up to 60 per cent. The cuts fall most severely on the poorest areas, those dependent on government grants and with the greatest need for public services. The most deprived 20 per cent of local authorities have had to cut their spending by over 30 per cent, forcing the curtailment of the services most valued by the public. The coronavirus epidemic demonstrated the resulting diminution in resilience. But in coping with the Covid epidemic 'it has been local authorities and their staff who have shown unremitting dedication and ingenuity, while central government has floundered and outsourced its wheezes – £1.7 billion worth – to private companies which have often proved equally clueless.' [Ferdinand Mount, *London Review of Books*, 2 July 2020]. Polly Toynbee contrasts 'No 10's contempt for local government' with the need for central government to recruit local government chief executives to run their programmes' [*The Guardian*, 13 August 2020].

At the same time as power has gravitated to the centre, the capability of ministers and civil servants has diminished, as Ferdinand Mount points out. In my early days in local government I would find in Whitehall civil servants who knew as least as much about a topic as I did. The opposite is now true: Whitehall struggles to retain knowledge and expertise in key policy areas. Gross blunders are made through lack of expertise, magnified because they are national. Gone are the days when an initiative could be tried locally and, if successful, adopted more widely. Initiatives are begun, but abandoned when a new Minister arrives. The Ministers themselves are less competent: the new brood has had no grounding in 'real life'. Before they entered Westminster politics, ministers like Denis Healey, Herbert Morrison, Michael Heseltine and Peter Walker had substantial experience (and success) in the world outside Westminster. Many had discharged major responsibilities in wartime and were leaders of men. Their capability in office stemmed from their previous experience, often in local government. Many of their current successors have had no experience outside the cloistered world of the political parties and Westminster. They may be good at politics, but not at government, as they demonstrated convincingly during the coronavirus epidemic.

The results of centralisation are far-reaching. They encompass not merely a decline of interest in politics but, even more importantly, the contraction of the public realm and the resulting disassociation from government. Those providing services to the public are now often answerable for the profits of their employer, rather than for the welfare of the community. Attainment of a financial target has become the goal. The ethos of competition has replaced the public service ethic. Moreover, privatisation of services has locked public authorities into contracts which are not only punitively expensive but also frustrate their ability to respond to changing needs.

How can we restore that commitment to public good and the shared sense of responsibility for the welfare of communities which has been destroyed by the fragmentation of agencies? The answer is not (as has been seriously canvassed) to distribute doughnuts to those who vote, or to give free entry into a competition for those who put their names on the electoral register. The answer is to have decisions about real life taken by someone who lives in the next street. That brings home the meaning of democracy far more effectively than any other measure. This principle, enunciated by de Tocqueville and John Stuart Mill, seems more important than ever.

The decline of the Roman Empire was marked by a substantial increase in imperial control over local authorities. Municipal civic life became more and more unsatisfying. The citizens grew tired of holding onerous public offices which no longer conferred power. By the beginning of the second century AD local self-government was falling into disorder as the imperial authorities took over. Gradually the imperial civil service assumed the major part of the work of local government. The most able and ambitious of the Empire's citizens had become bored with municipal public life. Far from cementing the Empire together, this centralisation further weakened it and was one of the causes of its collapse.

However – one last word: in 1878 the Town Clerk of Nottingham, Samuel Johnson, wrote and published a letter to the Right Hon. James Stansfield, MP, President of the Local Government Board. It read that under the Public Health Act 1872 'powers have been conferred upon a central authority to an extent unprecedented in this country…In every case the judgment of the central authority would be complete and local self-government annihilated. Men of position and influence would cease to act upon boards where their intelligence and judgment would go for nothing…Provincial authorities deserted by the best local men will become puppets in the hands of central officials. Local government will be dead and the triumph of centralisation complete.'

Plus ça change, plus c'est la même chose.

Acknowledgements

This text has gained greatly from editing by Richard Vize and by my son Magnus. My career in local government relied upon the support I received from outstanding colleagues. Working for me at some stage were the future chief executives of Avon, Basingstoke, Birmingham, Bolton, Cardiff, Cornwall, Kirklees, Gateshead, Hertfordshire, Lancashire, Leeds, Liverpool, Newcastle, York, the Planning Inspectorate, the Local Government Association and the London Boroughs Association (later named *London Councils*). I owe them a great debt of gratitude – and to many others, too numerous to name, whom I remember with great affection. Of course, my main buttress is and has always been my wife, Clare, with my children, Magnus and Antonia.

Some of the affairs in which I was involved have been described in greater detail. Specifically: Paul Foot wrote the history of the Helen Smith affair in *The Helen Smith Story* (Harper Collins, 1983). Andrew Hoskins wrote about Dame Shirley Porter in *Nothing Like a Dame* (Granta, 2006). Paul Dimoldenberg published *The Westminster Whistleblowers* (Politico's, 2006). There have been several books about the Yorkshire Ripper, most authoritatively *Wicked Beyond Belief* by Michael Bilton (Harper Collins, 2003). There are at least 18 books on the miners' strike. My text is drawn entirely from my own records and memory, but these books have provided useful corroboration.

Rodney Brooke, April 2022

Sir Rodney Brooke, The Manor House, Ilkley, April 2022

Index

The Winding Stair

Index

The Winding Stair

Index

Index

Index

Turnbull, James 162
Turner, Dame Eva 249
Turner, John 57–58, 62
twin towns 161, 189–190, 257
Tyne & Wear County Council
  118, 125, 193

United Cattle Products (UCP)
  69
University of Law 58
urban district councils 25, 34,
  119

Valley Parade, Bradford 161–
  162
Vanity Fair (Thackray) 265
Varley, Bill 49–50
Vasary, Tamas 252
Vassall, John 264–265
Vize, Richard 318

wages 29–30, 66, 120, 121–
  122, 123–125, 287
Wakefield 11, 35, 56–57, 104,
  126, 136. see also Queen
  Elizabeth Grammar School,
  Wakefield
Wakefield, Bishop of 136–137
Wakefield City Council 131–
  132, 158–159
Wakefield County Hall 124,
  126, 139–140, 176–177
Wakefield Girls' High School
  14
Wakefield Grammar School.
  see Queen Elizabeth
  Grammar School, Wakefield
Wakefield Mystery Plays 281
Wakefield Town Hall 126
Walker Art Gallery, Liverpool
  218
Walker-Smith, Jonah 234
Wandsworth Council 292
Warburton, Matthew 317
Ward, Clifford 51, 52
Ward, Judith 126
Ware, John 299
WARS (Westminster Against
  Reckless Spending) 240
Warwickshire County
  Council 30
Wasserman, Lord Gordon
  115
waste disposal 150, 199–200,
  233–234, 244–245, 264, 287
Watchdog 235–236
water supply 53–54, 75–76,
  106–108, 109, 225, 247

Waterman, Dame Fanny 4
Weatherill, Bernard 151–152
Weeks, David 239, 240, 244,
  291, 296, 301
Weeks, Wilf 220
Welcome to Yorkshire 191
Welsh, Peter 72
Wendt, Robin 315
Wendy Knitting Wools 128–
  129
Wentworth
  Woodhouse/Wentworth
  Castle 137
West Midlands Metropolitan
  Council 117
West Riding County Council
  28, 31–32, 34, 35, 56, 117,
  123–127, 129, 131–145, 169–
  178, 189, 190
  coat-of-arms 145–146
  coroner 153–159
  education 59, 61
West Riding County Surveyor
  157
West Riding Police Force 104,
  134, 140
West Riding Registry of
  Deeds 157
West Yorkshire Act 149–150
West Yorkshire Combined
  Authority 222
West Yorkshire County
  Council 5, 131–135, 162–
  164, 189, 197–201, 203–204,
  215, 219, 222–223, 225, 226,
  228, 231–232, 247, 259, 314,
  318
West Yorkshire Enterprise
  Board 197–198
West Yorkshire Playhouse. see
  Leeds Playhouse
Westbrook investment
  company 268
Western Synagogue 274
Westminster 252, 257, 289
Westminster, 6th Duke 255,
  269
Westminster Abbey 248, 250
Westminster City Council
  226–236, 237–238, 243–252,
  268, 271, 282, 286–291, 299,
  301, 305, 317
  Dolphin Square 262–268
  gerrymandering 290–299
  spending cuts 273–280
Westminster City Hall 246,
  300
Westminster, Colorado 252

Westminster Primary Care
  Trust 238
Weston, Will 223–224
Whitaker, Rachel 238, 276
White, Martin 56, 62, 65, 82,
  109, 124
White, Merle 65
Whitelaw, Willie 183, 187–188
Widdicombe, David 239
Wigmore Hall 279
Wigoder, Dr 4, 11
Wilkinson, Arthur 'Wilkie' 22
Williams, Sir David 317
Willott, Brian 13, 15, 210
Wilshaw, Sir Michael 119, 271
Wilson, Arthur 120, 121, 123–
  125
Wilson, Harold 24, 102, 117,
  212, 264
Wilson, Keppel and Betty 19
Wilson, Richard 291
Wilson, Trevor 175
wine 127–128, 212
Winter of Discontent 128,
  129, 150–152, 233–234
Winwaed, Battle of 201
Witchell, Leonard 51
Withens Clough reservoir
  53–54
Withnell, Dr Alan 35, 66–67
Witty, David 235
Wood, Arthur 129–130
Woolmer, Ken 144, 166–167,
  171
working class 5, 6–8, 11–13,
  15, 58
Wynn Davies, Rhidian 318

Yorkshire and Humberside
  Industrial Development
  Association 147, 192
Yorkshire Beggars' litany 157
Yorkshire Post 10, 23, 45, 47,
  134, 141
Yorkshire Regional Health
  Authority 314
Yorkshire Ripper case 126,
  182–188
Yorkshire Ski Club 130
Yorkshire Three Peaks 57–58,
  177, 269
Yorkshire Tourist Board 147,
  191–192
Yorkshire Water Authority
  108, 225
Young, Sir George 292–293
Yugoslavia 62–63